COUNSELING
CHILDREN

The Continuum Counseling Series

COUNSELING CHILDREN

Basic Principles for Helping the Troubled and Defiant Child

John B. Mordock

Foreword by William Van Ornum

Continuum | *New York*

1991

The Continuum Publishing Company
370 Lexington Avenue
New York, NY 10017

Copyright © 1991 by John B. Mordock
Foreword Copyright © 1991 by William Van Ornum

Printed in the United States of America

Library of Congress Cataloging-in-Publication Data

Mordock, John B., 1938–
Counseling children : basic principles for helping the
troubled and defiant child / John B. Mordock ; foreword by
William Van Ornum.
   p.   cm. — (The Continuum counseling series)
Includes bibliographical references.
ISBN 0-8264-0487-1
   1. Problem children—Counseling of—Handbooks, manuals,
etc. 2. Child psychotherapy—Handbooks, manuals, etc.
I. Title. II. Series.
HV715.M67 1991
155.45'3—dc20   90–39117
                                     CIP

TO THE FACULTY OF SPRINGFIELD COLLEGE,
WHOSE ENTHUSIASM FOR THE HELPING PROFESSIONS
PROFOUNDLY INFLUENCED MY LIFE

Contents

Foreword

The Continuum Counseling Series—the first of its kind for a wide audience—presents books for everyone interested in counseling, bringing to readers practical counseling handbooks that include real-life approaches from current research. The topics deal with issues that are of concern to each of us, our families, friends, acquaintances, or colleagues at work.

General readers, parents, teachers, social workers, psychologists, school counselors, nurses and doctors, pastors, and others in helping fields too numerous to mention will welcome these guidebooks that combine the best professional learnings and common sense, written by practicing counselors with expertise in their specialty.

Increased understanding of ourselves and others is a primary goal of these books—and greater empathy is the quality that all professionals agree is essential to effective counseling. Each book offers practical suggestions on how to "talk with" others about the theme of the book, be this in an informal and spontaneous conversation or a more formal counseling session.

Professional therapists will value these books also, because each volume in The Continuum Counseling Series develops its subject in a unified way, unlike many other books that may be either too technical or, as edited collections of papers, may come across to readers as being disjointed. In recent years both the American Psychological Association and the American Psychiatric Association have endorsed books that build on the scientific traditions of each profession but are communicated in an interesting way to general readers. We hope that professors and students in fields such as psychology, social work, psychiatry, guidance and counseling, and other helping fields will find these books to be helpful companion readings for undergraduate and graduate courses.

From nonprofessional counselors to professional therapists, from students of psychology to interested lay readers, The Continuum

9

Counseling Series endeavors to provide informative, interesting, and useful tools for everyone who cares about learning and dealing more effectively with these universal, human concerns.

Counseling Children

John Mordock has written a book that will be helpful to parents, relatives, foster and adoptive parents—those who will be in a position to refer a troubled child for counseling, and the many persons ranging from psychologists, school staff, nurses, child care agency workers, and others who as part of their work assist troubled children every day.

Mordock believes that talking with children can be of immense help to them. This simple idea sometimes is lost. If one reads the psychology, social work, and psychiatry journals in recent years, an abundance of articles on changing the environment (behavior modification), altering the family structure (family therapy), or modifying the basic chemical processes themselves (as through psychotropic medications) can be found, and whereas many of these approaches can be very helpful, Mordock brings us back to the basics: that a relationship within individual therapy can be very valuable, even for a child aged six to twelve, the age group that Mordock focuses on in this book.

For over twenty years John Mordock has worked with troubled children and their families, and on a daily basis, through his work in residential treatment, day treatment, child guidance clinics, and the many other programs sponsored by The Astor Home for Children. Through all these pages there are fascinating examples of children as they struggle to become healthier.

The first part of the book (chapters 1–5) can be used by any adult who wants to talk with children who are troubled. Throughout these pages there is a special focus on the aggressive and defiant child. He devotes consideration to the question of whether individual or family therapy is the best route of help for a particular child. He helps everyone understand "the mind of the child," and notes, "I believe that accurate empathy depends upon one's ability to understand how the child's mind works." Six important aims of counseling are listed. In his presentations of principles and cases, Mordock is very encouraging by stressing all that can be done to help a child, yet he reminds that "counselors do not have false hopes." Chapter 3 stresses eight principles of communication, and these will be helpful for everyone who deals with children.

The later chapters of the book (chapters 6–9) offer more specialized material for the counselor, although knowledge about what goes on in therapy can be very helpful to the child's parent or teacher. These chapters contain a discussion on "primitive" versus "more mature" defenses, and provide help for therapists in making interpretations to children. He encourages counselors to learn as much as possible about children, and reminds them that Erik Erikson used to have dinner in the child's home, in order to learn more about the child and the family.

Within the past ten years there has been an increased awareness of how depression affects children. Mordock presents some of the results of his own empirical research with over four-hundred children, reminding counselors that when children are depressed, "giving into it causes a sinking feeling, so most children protest and struggle to keep active." Many ways of understanding the child who is depressed are presented.

Sometimes counselors will work with children who feel cheated by life or who have been cheated by life. Mordock recognizes that "in the long run, these children need help to forgive a world that basically wasn't very good to them."

I think that this book will be especially helpful for anyone who works in a school or with school staff. Often psychological problems first are noticed in school, and this book will be an especially helpful tool for the school psychologist who provides individual counseling to children.

Counseling Children is a guidebook for adults who work with children who are depressed, fearful of school or afraid of other things, defiant or unruly because of underlying problems, timid or preoccupied because their mind is elsewhere, suffering from compulsions, or who experience physical problems that bring along a psychological component. John Mordock realizes that counseling children can even be harder than working with adults, because children many times will act out their problems rather than talk, and he presents both theoretical approaches as well as extremely practical tips for assisting the adult helper enter the mind of the child. Since many adult and teenage problems begin earlier, and are initially expressed during childhood years, application of the principles in this book could help prevent further unhappiness. Based on John Mordock's vast experience, along with his knowledge of the scientific findings of clinical child psychology, the book is wise, readable, humorous, and always sensitive and caring. This is a book that will help many children.

William Van Ornum, Ph.D.
Marist College
Poughkeepsie, New York

General Editor
The Continuum Counseling Series

Preface

Five years before my birth, Jesse Taft wrote the first book on child psychotherapy, followed closely by a much more helpful book by Frederick Allen, the "father" of child psychiatry. Since then, over five dozen books have appeared on the counseling and psychotherapy of children. (A comprehensive list appears at the end of this book.) Why then is another book needed? For several reasons. Foremost, these books were written for those who were or planned to become counselors or psychotherapists of children. They were not intended to instruct people dealing with children in other capacities. In 1983, William Van Ornum and I wrote *Crisis Counseling with Children: A Guide for Nonprofessional Counselors.* This book was designed to expand upon Fritz Redl's notion of the *life space interview,* and to assist teachers, ministers, child-care workers, probation officers, parents, camp counselors, principals, and others to talk in helpful ways with children who were in crisis. Milton Shore, of the National Institute of Mental Health, wrote in his review of this book that the book's subtitle seemed "especially inappropriate, for every professional, regardless of discipline, can profit from this book."

Taking heart from this praise, I decided to write a second book for those helping children and design it in such a way that it would instruct both nonprofessionals and professional counselors. Often I hear teachers, probation officers, priests, and others say, "I'm not trained to counsel children." Even trained counselors will remark, "I'm not trained to counsel that type of child." Often, however, more trained individuals are not available or parents are unwilling to take their child to see such a professional. Very disturbed children will be seen by school guidance counselors, even when these counselors often feel inadequately prepared to counsel them. Probation officers see children for extended periods and do the best they can. Children often seek help from those empathetic individuals who relate to them on a regular basis. Perhaps we have overprofessionalized the helping relationship by implying that considerable training is needed to help troubled children and have thereby created insecurities in those natural helpers that have always existed.

Less than 1 percent of all clinical psychologists are specialists in clinical child psychology, and only 5 percent of psychiatrists are child psychiatrists. Consequently, we have to measure our success with a child against what is possible to accomplish rather than what we wish to accomplish. While we may want to refer a child to a specialist, no such person may be available. The only available helper may be a nonprofessional counselor. One purpose of this book is to help caretakers of children, whether they are trained or untrained counselors, to realize what they can accomplish with each child in their care. Chapters 1–5 will be most helpful to the nonprofessional counselor, while chapters 6–9 are primarily for the trained counselor.

A second reason for writing this book is that my students of counseling have not been happy with the current books in the field. They feel a need for a book with a developmental orientation, as children are children first and troubled children second. They also want a book that gives concrete examples of the principles presented. Many of them have read Axline's wonderful presentation of Dibs, a bright boy who responds wonderfully to Axline's client-centered approach, and wonder why the children they treat don't respond similarly. What do you do when the child won't leave his classroom and come for counseling—or when the child won't leave the counseling room, and when he does, makes such a commotion in the school hallway that the teachers reprimand you for not controlling the child? What do you do when the child continually subjects you to verbal abuse? The book will address such issues.

My supervisees also want a book that defines in understandable terms the theoretical concepts employed by students of child development and child psychopathology. By understandable, they usually mean in terms of their own emotional lives. For example, the term *splitting* is used to denote that a child splits his image of adults in his life—they are viewed as either all good or all bad, and are responded to accordingly. Yet, children are not the only splitters. Romantic love also involves a similar process. Many lovers only see the wonderful parts of each other. If they break up, often they then only see the "bad" parts. Others see each lover more objectively. Relating the concept of splitting to our own "splitting" tendencies helps us to understand this concept better. I will make such an attempt when new concepts are presented.

Last of all, my supervisees want a book that guides them in their efforts to counsel aggressive and defiant children—those whose non-compliance to adult directives has become a way of life. Not only do most of the case examples feature conversations with such children, but two entire chapters, chapters 6 and 8, and special sections of other chapters, are specifically devoted to discussing children who display extreme noncompliant behavior.

Whenever possible, I have used cases cited in the literature rather than my own so that the reader can refer to these sources to increase his understanding of the principles illustrated.

I would like to acknowledge all the staff of the Astor Home and Child Guidance Centers for their untiring efforts on behalf of the children and families served over the twenty-one years I have been associated with the agency. Much of what I have learned came not only from my own clinical work, but from observation of the work of others. The in-service education program, supported by Astor's administrative staff since its inception in 1953, greatly contributed to the views presented in this work. I would like to thank the current executive director of Astor, Sister Marie Burns, as well as those who preceded her—Sister Anne Schneiders, Sister Sheila O'Friel, Sister Mary George, Sister Genevieve, Sister Mary Rose, Sister Ann Marie, and Sister Serena—for their consistent support of professional staff development. All of these Daughters of Charity encouraged and fostered a "results-orientated" administrative philosophy, where sharing what we have learned about helping others was not only our privilege but also our obligation. Astor's policy of dissemination of the findings of the work of its staff serves to subject our views to the scrutiny of others, and results in our own continued growth.

More specific acknowledgment goes to Christine Foreacre and Randall Thomas, clinical psychologists and psychotherapists of the Astor Home and Child Guidance Centers in Dutchess County, New York, for their critical readings of some of the chapters. I have also used case material supplied by Shelly Kitzman, play therapist at the Family Counseling Center in Green Bay, Wisconsin, Anne Marie Jensen and Ina Berg, social work counselors at Dutchess County Board of Cooperative Educational Services Special Education Center, and Chris Brown, senior social worker and psychotherapist at the Astor Day

Treatment Center. In addition, material supplied by Chris Brown contributed to the list in chapter 9 of signs of a child's improvement in counseling.

I would especially like to thank my typist, Eva Kiss, for her untiring efforts in deciphering my handwriting, and Bill Van Ornum, editor of the Continuum Counseling Series, for his suggestion that I write this book. I would also like to thank George Mora, who served as the medical director of Astor between 1961 and 1988, for his commitment to Astor holding an Annual Conference on the Psychiatric Treatment of Children. These conferences served to bring together those of us who had devoted our professional careers to clinical work with children, and bolstered our commitment to the field when it began to wane in the face of national and local priorities being placed elsewhere. It is encouraging to see that many other agencies now sponsor such conferences. I hope that more people will become interested in working with children, and that this book will be helpful to them.

Author's Note

The identities of the people written about in this book have been carefully disguised in accordance with professional standards of confidentiality and in keeping with their rights to privileged communication with the author.

Since the majority of children referred for counseling are males, the author uses "he" or "him" when speaking about the general client. Similarly, since the author is male, he often refers to the counselor as "he" or "him." For both instances, the opposite sex terms could be used instead.

1

Whom Do We Counsel?

The hearts of small children are delicate organs. A cruel beginning
in the world can twist them into curious shapes.

—Carson McCullers

The focus of this book is on counseling the latency-aged
child, with special emphasis on the defiant and aggressive child. The
defiant child presents a challenge to the counselor's patience as well as
to his skill. Sections of this book were written to address specifically
the training needs of those counseling this difficult group.

The book presents basic principles of counseling; it is not a handbook of specific techniques. The reader interested in detailed discussion of the use of puppets, drawings, costumes, telephones, games,
story telling, sand play, bibliotherapy, theraplay, and other specialized
procedures should consult the suggested readings listed at the end of
this book. Nor will the book present a detailed discussion of child
psychopathology. It will include a general discussion of the developmental failures of many of the children referred for counseling, and
it will anchor the discussion within the framework of the normal
period of development we call latency. An entire chapter will be
devoted to normal fantasy play and how it develops.

Almost all children referred for counseling have failed to master
age-appropriate developmental tasks. Basically, their failures result
from employing immature ways to cope with anxiety. The child remains arrested at early stages of development. He makes extensive
use of coping strategies that he should have long outgrown. The
defenses he uses to maintain feelings of well-being prevent his further
development. At the same time that these behaviors are self-enhancing they are self-defeating. For the child, the defenses work. They
keep his anxiety under control. But they also retard his growth.

19

Chapter 6 reviews the defense mechanisms used by children and discusses ways to help the child develop more mature defenses; chapter 7 is devoted to discussing how the child comes to understand himself; and chapter 8 presents ways to help the child to verbalize his anxiety. Chapter 9 illustrates the process by which change takes place. The first half of the book presents counseling practices that any adult could use when talking to children (chapters 1–5). The remaining chapters (6–9) are primarily for those who are engaged in intensive counseling relationships with children.

Who Needs Counseling?

Any child who wants to be rid of symptoms that bother him should be provided counseling. If the child has chronic headache, stomach trouble, sleeping difficulties, excessive worries, or specific and overwhelming fears, he ought to be given help. But this group makes up only a small portion of a counselor's caseload. Many children who experience difficulty in school are referred for counseling. Those placed in special education classes are often provided with counseling, particularly if they are labeled as emotionally disturbed. Unfortunately, assignments to counseling are sometimes arbitrary decisions made by educators who fail to appreciate the essential difference between remedial educational techniques and counseling.

Some children are assigned to individual counseling for training in social skills. The goal is to teach the child how to relate to his peers. Sometimes intellectually limited children are given counseling for this reason, even when their social skills are exactly what would be expected of a child with their *mental age*. Social-skills training is not a reason for counseling. Remedial classroom techniques should include such training, and if the teacher needs assistance, a counselor can join the teacher in the classroom and jointly they can lead a group lesson to achieve this end.

Similarly, children are referred for group counseling to teach social skills. While the use of group counseling for such a purpose is more legitimate, often children who are inappropriate for groups are selected for this counseling modality because they have the poorest social skills. Distrustful children who see other children as rivals for adult attention are not ready for group counseling. One does not simply teach a child to share. The child first learns to share to please an admired and trusted adult. He shares in the absence of that adult because he has come to trust the other child to respect his belongings and to share back. Many aggressive children have not even progressed to the first stage—they do not trust anybody and have no desire to please. Forget groups—these children are not ready.

The chief reason for referring a child for individual counseling in a school setting is his failure to respond to remedial educational techniques. The child has serious *problems with learning* as opposed to learning problems. The child who transfers onto his teachers both his mistrust of his primary caretakers and his ambivalence towards them and who also transfers onto his peers his envy and jealousy of his siblings is a candidate for individual counseling. A child who is a candidate for individual counseling is a child who: cannot really enjoy being alone with one teacher; is constantly on the alert to avoid missing something else; cannot accept an inferior role relationship with the teacher; is extremely self-critical; shows little interest in games and activities, either for the pleasure they give or the praise he receives; fails to be reassured by attention to or interest in him; cannot raise his self-esteem following praise and admiration.

A child who can establish a positive relationship with a teacher in spite of his difficulties is less in need of individual counseling. Some disturbed children manage to circumvent the internalized conflicts that affect their relationships to parents. School becomes their safe place, their haven. They have conflicts in school, but the patience and understanding of the teacher keeps them calm and on the right track. The wish to be loved and admired by teachers makes the child cooperate with their efforts. The child feels bad when he misbehaves and tries to make amends. It is not his misbehavior that is important; it is his attitude about it. All children will try to shift responsibility for their actions onto others and attempt to outwit adults. But if they seek to make amends when they transgress, they are less in need of counseling. What is needed is lavish praise and rewards for achievements other than compliance; stern reprimands for misbehavior; frequent, careful explanation of what is expected and why some behavior is unacceptable; individual help in mastering games and tasks; and efforts to promote pride in appearance. Counseling should be deferred until it is clear that the child is not responding to these caring techniques.

Some Words about Depression

Many children referred for counseling have a depressive core underlying their symptom picture. Depression is a deactivating phenomenon. It causes a move towards conserving, or inward turning, and a lack of energy. Giving into it causes a sinking feeling, so most children protest and struggle to keep active. School work is resisted because the inward looking it requires puts the child in touch with his depressed feelings. When the child gives in to his depressed feelings he can't get to sleep and he cannot get up from sleep, is overwhelmed by minor annoyances, is self-depreciative, is more fearful, and is less motivated.

The cognitive components accompanying depression are: reality distortions; exaggerated responsiveness; restricted risk taking; and a sense of entitlement. The personality characteristics accompanying depression are: despair; a sense that nothing works; manipulativeness; subtle domination; resistance to using resources for problem solving; aversion to influence (responsiveness to others is viewed as coercion); unwillingness to enhance the lives of others (missed out on unconditional love); and recurrent intense anxiety that drains the resources of others. Look carefully behind the masking symptoms of children in trouble and you will find many of them to be depressed.

Richard Carlson and I just completed a study of four-hundred preschool and kindergarten children, primarily those from lower socioeconomic backgrounds. Twenty-five percent of them showed serious signs of childhood depression. These signs included eating problems, aimless activity, lack of enjoyment, lifelessness, mood swings, sleeping difficulties and relationship problems. Studies of children from more well-to-do families showed similar results. Eighty percent of the mothers of the children in our group whom we considered depressed also showed serious signs of depression. Many of these children will be those later referred for counseling.

Individual versus Family Counseling

Several thoughts need to be expressed about individual counseling of the child as opposed to family counseling. With the recent clinic movement of replacing counseling of children with family counseling, some counselors in schools have become disillusioned with their methods. "My husband is a family therapist, he claims I'm wasting my time seeing children without seeing their families on a regular basis." First, it goes without saying that the counselor should involve the parent as much as possible in the counseling process. Often the child controls or manipulates his parents, aggravating his already difficult relationship with them. A child can control adults by making them control him. This can take up the whole day. Children have been known to say, "If I can't be the best, I might as well be the worst!" The parents need help to cope with their child's behavior. Parents of learning disabled children who display immature behavior for neurological reasons need help in relating to their children at the developmental levels they demonstrate, as well as to their age-appropriate needs.

Nevertheless, some children require individual counseling because the parent sees them as the problem. To insist initially that the family redefine the child's problem as a family problem is to confront the family before adequate groundwork has been laid for them to accept this notion. The result will be withdrawal from treatment. Many children referred for counseling live with single parents. Seeing the single parent and child together often results in unproductive sessions because the tension between them cannot be diluted by the counselor asking for opinions of other family members. The child cannot get enough distance between himself and his problem to handle the anxiety that joint discussions with his parent can produce.

A number of children are candidates for individual counseling regardless of parental involvement. These are children who have firmly entrenched intrapsychic conflicts or who have poorly integrated responses to trauma. They display repetitive patterns of maladaptive responses to stress that transcend the specifics of the current family situation.

The learning disabled child with low self-esteem may profit more from individual than from family work. Children with distrustful angry parents who deny their role in their child's problems also need individual help to build trust and to promote growth outside of the family. The child needs to develop trust in his good impulses and the ability to control or mitigate his bad or aggressive impulses. He also has to learn that prohibitions can be protective rather than punitive or humiliating. Some parents are unable to perform this function when continually faced with the child's misbehavior.

Many children need a period of charitable, sensitive, and sophisticated listening that only individualized counseling can provide.

Others need an opportunity to be admired for behaviors other than compliance so that they begin to want to do what adults wish.

A period of individual counseling also helps provide insight into the present situation. Parents who stress only the end product of development and who are unwilling or unable to look at the past reveal little about their child's problems. Observing the child individually provides the clues needed to piece togther his past and to see how his past has influenced his present. The view that those who are ignorant of the past are condemned to repeat it applies both to the child and to the counselor.

While the child may never appreciate how his past shapes his present, the counselor needs such understanding to address the needs of the child. More specifically, he needs to understand how present behaviors were shaped by past happenings. The child's play often contributes to this understanding.

Too Old to Play, Too Young to Talk?

The child in normal latency has left behind the world of make-believe play in the microsphere for playacting in the macrosphere. As a result, when he comes for counseling he does not want to play with the toys the younger child immediately gravitates towards. Yet he cannot sit and actively verbalize his difficulties so he tends to engage the counselor in table games, such as cards or checkers. The counselor can play these games occasionally, but he should make an active effort to get the child to reveal his fantasies. He should encourage drawing, painting, sculpture, and crafts when the child cannot or will not verbalize his concerns. Most children referred for counseling missed the opportunity for mastering play at earlier periods. The counselor's active support for make-believe play with miniature world materials will usually result in the child spending more and more time in such play in spite of his initial reluctance to engage in such "baby" play. In fact, the more disturbed the child, the more he should be encouraged to play in the microsphere. Almost all children will do so when the counselor is persistent. The counselor who constantly builds models or plays table games with the child is not likely to be of much help to the child. Rather than conceiving of the disturbed latency-aged child as "too old to play, too young to talk," he should be viewed as a child who needs to engage in "playful talk."

A child's play provides a handle by which both the child and the counselor can grasp his emotions. Play both encourages delay of action and facilitates remembering. The indirect expression of feelings through play reduces the anxiety and guilt the child would feel if he expressed his feelings directly. When an empathetic adult encourages elaboration and extension of play, the child can reexperience his conflicts and integrate his traumatic experiences in ways that promote growth.

Do Not Parent

The counselor should be forewarned not to engage in parental behaviors. He should not be overly affectionate towards the child nor should he gratify the child's infantile needs, such as giving gifts, endlessly supplying him with models to build or paper to draw on, or rescue him from real-life situations with peers. He should avoid promising rewards ("Do well and you will go back to regular school," "return home," "go to a foster home," "be adopted," etc.), or making threats ("Do poorly and you will go to a more restrictive environment"). Such behavior does not help the child cope with the harsh realities of his life, particularly when counseling can be so easily terminated.

Do Not Have False Hopes

There are many who believe in shortcuts to cure. America is a "quick-fix" culture. This initial optimism can give way to despair and to blaming the client when the shortcuts do not work. The counselor's job is to turn the client's despair into hope, leading to therapeutic optimism. The counselor who believes that he can make an impact on a very troubled child in a brief period will turn despair into apathy. Such magical notions about our impact should be left in our childhood. James Masterson once said, "When we have shortcuts to development, we will have shortcuts to cure."

Helping the child to overcome his resistances to change, to work through his response to therapeutic interventions, to remember and relive repressed and distorted experiences, to shift energy from unconscious conflicts to conscious ones, to strengthen the sense of self, and to transform the conscience takes time and considerable patience. Rome was not built in a day, nor was the Roman Empire!

Confusion Is Inevitable

Because writers of books on counseling, and this one is no exception, cover their material in an organized fashion, they imply that counseling also proceeds similarly. Nothing could be further from the truth. In attempting to reach the child wherever he is—and he may be in many different places at once—the counselor cannot proceed systematically but has to adjust continually to an ever-changing situation. Because the child's development was chaotic, counseling will also appear chaotic. The counselor who is not confused by a child's behavior is deceiving himself. Such counselors are likely to be those who make wild interpretations. When in doubt, silence is best.

I like to think of the initial stages of counseling as similar to two records playing at two different speeds—the counselor plays at his speed and the child plays at his. Eventually, the counselor recognizes the song that the child's record is playing (although the child often switches records) and modifies the speed of his record to accommodate the child's. Eventually, they play parts of the same record and finally they both listen to the same record at a speed where the song is easily recognized. Witness the following verbalizations of one child:

CHILD: Bang it, it still works, beetlejuice (he puts his hand over his mouth) stop it (in clipped speech) damn, damn, damn, bad word today, hope you're not mad at me. Okay, now read a book (he babbles).

While the counselor can speculate that the child has gone from anxiety to anger, that is about all the counselor knows. With time, he may figure out what the contents of this communication mean, but in the meantime he is as confused as the child is anxious. Witness the rapid changes in the next child:

CHILD: (The child writes "doll" on colored paper to make stop signs. He then starts to cut his hair with the scissors and then stops) I don't know what to make, I'm finished. (He then gets a stick, stops, and asks for scissors to cut the hair on the doll)

ADULT: The doll's hair is not for cutting.

CHILD: (He then gets the alligator puppet) This is the alligator that bites kids who do things bad. The alligator is going to attack you.

ADULT: The alligator can attack the dummy and pretend it's me.

CHILD: No, I'll throw sand at you.

ADULT: You sure are sharing all the bad things you feel today.

CHILD: I'll erase the blackboard for you.

ADULT: Thank you.

CHILD: Oh, shut up, or I'll throw this at you.

The counselor speculates that the child feels inner pressure to express an unacceptable impulse. He starts to make a stop sign in an effort to "stop" the impulse's expression. But the thought seems as bad as the action so the child attempts to punish himself by cutting his hair (are there sexual thoughts and corresponding guilt?). But the thought of self-punishment also raises his anxiety. Does he express his punishment symbolically by cutting the doll's hair? When forbidden, he now gets the alligator who "bites bad kids" (another sign of guilt or fear of bodily harm?). This, too, causes anxiety so he regresses to attacking the counselor (children typically hold adults responsible for their troubles), or he attacks the counselor in hopes of getting punished and thereby avoiding self-criticism. He then attempts to undo this attack by doing a good deed—cleaning the blackboard.

While all this was taking place, the counselor was not sure what was happening. Only by examining his memory of the sequence can he reconstruct what might have been going on. He keeps this reconstruction in mind the next time he is confronted with similar behavior. When the child wants to cut the doll's hair he can give the child an acceptable substitute and comment that "For some reason you seem to want to punish yourself for some bad thoughts you may have."

On other occasions the child's fantasy only makes sense when it is related to some recent environmental event. For example, a child reports a daydream of a rich man who has lots of things. A boy takes them and hides them in a tree. The man bumps into the tree and his stolen items fall out at his feet. While this approximates a punishment fantasy that suggests underlying guilt, the story becomes immediately understood when the counselor discovers that the child had taken a toy from the counselor's room following his last session.

While a counselor's comments to a child who is upset expresses a wish to understand him, the child is immersed in his upsetness and struggling to free himself from his discomfort. Like an animal that has been hurt, he is apt to bite the helping hand extended to him.

Beware the Bulldog

Many times a counselor will be led down a blind alley because he failed to respond empathetically to the child. Witness the following interchange:

ADULT: I see that you have scratches on your arms.

CHILD: (Silence)

ADULT: You also have scratches on your face. Have you been fighting a lot? Was this one of the times you got mad? (The counselor should have said nothing or asked if the scratches hurt)

CHILD: Yes—no. I got scratched by a bulldog.

ADULT: You're making that up—you just don't want to tell me.

CHILD: How do you know, you don't even live around my neighborhood.

ADULT: How about an imaginary bulldog—did that scratch your face?

CHILD: Can you see it walking down the road? If it's imaginary, no I mean if it's real (the child is starting to believe his own story).

ADULT: Do you like bulldogs?

CHILD: Most animals like me, except bulldogs. One tried to kill me. I wouldn't get a bulldog.

ADULT: Are you afraid of bulldogs?

CHILD: No. I like animals. One tried to kill me. You know how they rip your leg off.

ADULT: From a bulldog!

CHILD: How do you know?

ADULT: No, I'm asking you.

CHILD: The bulldog is afraid of guns. I brought out a big gun and he went away—you don't believe me.

ADULT: If I lived in your neighborhood I would avoid him (Now the counselor gives advice as if the story is real!).

This response illustrates how a child tries either to fantasize his way out of admitting that he was in a fight or to impress the counselor by fabricating a situation where he is brave and fearless. In either case, the interchange between adult and child is no longer of therapeutic value. With hindsight, the counselor could have played along with the child, but made it clear that the child sometimes wished that he was fearless and perhaps spent time elsewhere engaging in such daydreams. "Sometimes it's fun to pretend that we're not afraid of anything." But chances are the whole sequence was the child's subterfuge to avoid responding to what he perceived to be a blaming statement. Beware the bulldog!

Latency-Age Thinking

Latency-age children tend to jump to conclusions from false premises. They think in response to strong beliefs or what has been called *assumptive realities*. The latency-aged child has developed the ability to reason from assumptions and hypotheses (stage of concrete operations). But in the course of such reasoning, the child often fails to distinguish between his hypotheses and assumptions on the one hand and empirical evidence on the other. The child often treats hypotheses as if they were facts and facts as if they were hypotheses. Ordinarily, we test hypotheses against the evidence, and if the evidence contradicts the hypotheses we reject it and try another. Children, in contrast, often reject or reinterpret facts to fit the hypotheses. They make assumptions about reality on the basis of limited information that they will not alter in the face of new and contradictory evidence. Witness the child and the counselor playing checkers:

CHILD: I go this time; no, it's your move; don't jump me, go to another space.
ADULT: I won't want to play with you if you order me around.
CHILD: If you don't play I'll bite you.
ADULT: How do you play with other children?
CHILD: I only let them play with me if they're nice.
ADULT: And "nice" means they do what you say.
CHILD: Yes.
ADULT: But what if they want you to do what they say?

CHILD: Then they're not nice.

ADULT: But if you won't play with them because you don't like to do what they say, why would they want to do what you say? No two children can play together if both always want to be the boss. Can you take turns?

CHILD: Then they're not nice.

This child is one who storms tearfully down the hallway, crying out that "nobody likes me," but she has got it in her head that "nice" means "doing what I say" and the counselor has not yet found a way to convince her otherwise.

Latency-age children also are quick to both detect flaws in the reasoning of others and errors in their supposed statements of fact. Growing out of their discovery are two complementary assumptive realities that pervade the latency period. One of these is the belief that adults are not very bright. If the adult is wrong in one thing, he must be wrong in nearly everything. When the child discovers that he knows something his parents do not, he assumes that he knows lots of things his parents do not know.

"You mean you've never heard of Pelican West, The Culture Club, King Kurt, Pigbag, The Prisoners, Masson Ruffner, Howard Jones, The Psychedelic Furs, UB40," etc. Any ten- or eleven-year-old girl could create a test that most adults would fail. All she has to do is name the stars of a situation comedy, soap opera, rock music, etc., and ask us who they are and what they do and we will fail. We are instantly stupid: "Anybody who's anybody knows who's in the group UB40."

Because the child is right in one or more things, he assumes he must be correct in most things. This assumption is abetted by the child's belief that he acquires his knowledge by himself. David Elkind has called this complex of assumptive realities, invoking the conception that the adult is not too bright and the child is clever, *cognitive conceit*. This attitude is not overt, but is an underlying orientation that can easily be brought to the fore. In many children's stories, such as "Jack and the Beanstalk," *Tom Sawyer, Alice in Wonderland,* and *Peter Pan,* adults are outwitted and made to look like fools by children. Winnie the Pooh (the bear of little brain) is the essence of adult bumbling and the superbly cool and clever Christopher Robin is the child. Wolfensten, in his marvelous book on children's humor, points out how children's jokes show the child as clever and the adult as foolish.

A mother loses her child named "Heine." She asks a policeman, "Have you seen my Heine?" to which the policeman replies, "No, but I sure would like to!"

A woman owns a dog named "Free Show." While the woman is taking a bath, the dog gets out of the house. The woman discovers this and runs out of the house naked, shouting "Free Show, Free Show!"

The jokes depend upon the stupidity of the adult, that the adults would not know the meaning of "Heine" or be so stupid as to run in the street naked shouting "Free Show."

A good deal of juvenile sophistry also reflects cognitive conceit. The child purposely takes directions from adults literally instead of abstractly. A boy comes to the dinner table with dripping wet hands. When his mother asks why, he says, "You told me not to wipe my hands on the clean towels."

Perhaps the most frustrating consequence (for adults) of cognitive conceit can be observed in children's moral behavior. While children know right from wrong, they still do what is wrong throughout much of latency. While the child has respect for adult authority (fear of punishment), he has less respect for adult intelligence. He, therefore, sees no reason to obey adult imposed rules, except to avoid punishment. He takes the rules as a challenge to his own cleverness and attempts to break them without getting caught. Breaking rules, then, is not a moral matter but more a matter of outwitting adults.

Another assumptive reality related to cognitive conceit is the belief that adults are benevolent and well-intentioned. The child has some evidence to support this assumption, but he also denies and distorts evidence to the contrary (later this phenomena will be referred to as *splitting*). This conviction of the benevolence of parents and adults provides a healthy balance to cognitive conceit. This conviction tempers and mellows the child's eagerness to outwit adults and make them appear foolish. If it were not for this conviction, the latency aged child would be very difficult to live with.

Even when children are aware of this misbehavior, they often make assumptions that excuse or exonerate their act so that they feel completely innocent. When an adult accuses a child of lying, he fails to appreciate that the child believes his assumptive reality to be true.

Assumptive realities emerge in the play of children when they cling to assumptions about reality despite the arguments and evidence offered by adults to dissuade them. Children will spend hours or even days digging in the yard for buried treasure, convinced that the articles they do find are fragments of ancient pottery that have great value.

The latency-age child loves mystery, adventure, and magic. Assumptive realities presuppose a world where facts can be made to do your bidding and hence are controllable. New and unexpected events occur in adventure stories, but they are always mastered by the characters with whom the children identify. Nancy Drew and the Hardy Boys have enjoyed success for years.

At the same time as assumptive realities are believed in, the normal child also operates on a more practical level. Like the Indian who performs rain dances but who still irrigates his fields, the child operates on two planes. On the cognitive level, the child denies his parents' wisdom, but on the practical level, he accepts it. A child knows, on the practical level, that his father is mean and that he had better keep out of his way, but on the cognitive plane, he maintains the assumption of parental benevolence. The nine-year-old boy who has spent an afternoon as a general vanquishing his enemies needs his mother to accompany him upstairs to allay his fears of what might be lurking in his room.

It is only in adolescence, with the advent of formal operations, that these two planes of action and thought are brought into coordination. The adolescent discovers the arbitrariness of his hypotheses, learns how to test hypotheses against facts, recognizes that many of his hypotheses are wrong, and cognitive conceit gives way to auto-criticality. But remember, we never completely give up assumptive realities. Adults can adopt a hypothesis and cling to it regardless of factual evidence to the contrary. The romantic image of love and marriage is clung to by many people despite everyday evidence to the contrary. Scholars attack a major figure, such as Freud, on some minor point, and then dismiss the whole body of the master's work. Having found the real or imagined error, the young scholar is convinced of his intellectual superiority. Many of our beliefs, attitudes, and prejudices are clung to in spite of evidence that fails to support them. Many adults, like children, deny reality and reinterpret facts to support their beliefs.

The Aggressive Child

Many children lock horns with society. They seem unable to appreciate the limitations society puts upon their behavior. They disregard hazards, fail to differentiate reality from fantasy, and respond to dangers no one else sees. Minor frustrations cause panic. Most of these children are undersocialized because of limited opportunity to identify with the controls of nurturing and protective adults. The struggles faced by these children become clearer when they are conceptualized within Erik Erikson's notions of the stages in development.

Trust versus Mistrust

Children rejected from birth have never mastered Erik Erikson's first nuclear conflict of *trust versus mistrust*. Those who move forward with a basic sense of trust in others do so with "a sense of identity which will later combine with a sense of being 'all right,' of being oneself, and of becoming what other people trust one will become." Erikson goes on to say:

> Parents must not only have certain ways of guiding by prohibition and permission; they must also be able to represent to the child a deep, almost somatic conviction that there is meaning to what they are doing. Ultimately children become neurotic not from frustrations, but from the lack or loss of societal meaning in these frustrations.

Alfred Adler, the great individual psychologist, put it similarly. The child whose parents meet his basic needs for affection will develop a bond with society. The child will actualize his potential in ways that will promote society. In contrast, those whose parents reject them will strive for superiority over others at the expense of society. Those well-parented will develop mutual interdependence with society; those poorly parented see society as their enemy and act accordingly.

The child arrested at this early stage of development is a child with almost no internal controls; a child quick to anger at the slightest provocation. This child shows primitive identifications, such as behaving like an animal or a supervillain. He shows no concern for others nor does he expect concern when he is hurt. He has an omnipotent need for control and makes unreasonable demands of others. Often, the child shows minimal overt fantasy expression, and when he does, the content of such fantasy is predominantly aggressive.

These children have not been nurtured or protected. They lack prideful experiences of pleasing and being pleased. They are full of rage. Since they have been intimidated, they become intimidating. They become aggressive to cope with a sense of unsafety, pseudoautonomy, and aloneness. As a result, moral standards are never internalized.

Autonomy versus Shame and Doubt

Already weakened by distrustfulness, the child is then denied the gradual and well-guided experience of making choices. As a child learns to "stand on his own two feet," he must be protected from experiences of shame and self-doubt. If not, then he never resolves Erikson's second major conflict of *autonomy versus shame and doubt.* As a result, the child gains power by stubborn control over minute portions of his life. The shamed child is one who wants to go unnoticed: "Don't notice my exposure." As Erikson states, "He would like to destroy the eyes of the world. Instead, he must wish for his own invisibility." Too much shaming leads, at best, to a determination to get away with things, or, at worst, to defiant shamelessness. Doubt is the brother of shame. Doubt comes from the pervasive feeling that one can never accomplish anything: "I can never do anything right," or "I can't do that."

During the stage of autonomy versus shame and doubt, the child unconsciously decides how much to cooperate and to resist, and how much to express or repress. The child who feels in control of his life develops feelings of goodwill and pride. The child who feels controlled develops a propensity for doubt and shame.

Some children receive relatively adequately parenting up until this stage. Then, either because of an inability to tolerate the child's developing autonomy or the parent's own temporary incapacity, the child is not supported in developing his autonomy. Such a child displays variable controls. He displays strong identifications with aggressive personalities, and shows marked changes in attachments to caretakers, both loving and hating the same person depending upon whether the person satisfies or frustrates his needs. He engages in global self-condemnation, having internalized both marked parental rejection and the externalization of those bad parts the parent rejects about himself.

Because the child has experienced an abrupt, sustained loss of closeness to and ability to please adults at an early age (twenty-four to thirty-six months), he also shows: ambivalence about the need for close contact; violent alienations from the baby-self and a mimicry of adult talk; lightning-swift, unpredictable changes in behavior; and a struggle to be good that is often a fear of the consequences if bad, but with some desire to please adults.

Initiative versus Guilt

When a child moves into the stage of *initiative versus guilt* without having mastered the earlier two stages, he cannot forget his failures quickly. True initiative will not develop. He will be unable to attack problems playfully with zest and enthusiasm.

The child arrested at this stage of development feels he needs considerable aggressive powers to cope with his sense of unsafety, pseudoautonomy and sense of aloneness. The child's longing for a reunion with caretakers is now blunted by a more basic need to save face. This leads to overt defiance of external directions and control, and, even worse, to revenge. Because of repeated humiliations in a dependency relationship, he becomes entrenched in a state of pseudoindependency, which includes an image of himself as a bad child. In reaction, he will resort to self-willed protests of independence and defiance. Because his wishes are still those of a younger child, he now develops a primitive sense of guilt over his wishes. Erikson states:

> One of the deepest conflicts in life is the hate for a parent who served as the model and the executor of the superego, but who (in some form) was found trying to get away with the very transgressions which the child can no longer tolerate in himself.

Industry versus Inferiority

In the stage of *industry versus inferiority*, the child now begins to "handle the utensils, the tools, and the weapons used by big people."

The child's danger, at this stage, lies in his feeling inadequate and inferior. "If he despairs of his tools and skills or of his status among his tool partners, he may be discouraged from identification with them and with a section of the tool world." If the child loses hope of participating in the "industrial" world he will remain fixed in earlier worlds, feeling doomed to mediocrity or inadequacy. "What's the use, no matter what I do it's never right."

Some Dynamics of the Aggressive Child

The child who has failed to master these early developmental stages struggles with three basic issues: *helplessness, shame,* and *hunger.*

The rejected child has learned that he is weak, small, and unable to control what happens to him. When parents communicate destructive feelings toward the child, he creates a sense of safety from the very people he relies on by both identifying with their power and displacing his omnipresent fear of them into an imaginary world. If the parents are extremely hostile, the child's imaginary world will be full of "creatures bent on destroying children." When the parents' hostilities are less intense, these creatures become the allies of the child (like his parents who love him when he meets their needs and hates him when he does not). The child also depersonalizes himself and endows objects with his feelings (e.g., one toy car is consistently used to smash other toys or objects) or he creates the illusion that he is all powerful himself—he is superboy.

At the same time, in order to persuade himself that his parents really love him, the child convinces himself that it is he who makes them hate him because he is so imperfect. The child represses his knowledge of his parents' angry feelings and searches for defects within himself. He is a "monster." But such self-perception creates feelings of shame. To counteract these feelings, the child develops an exaggerated posture of perfection. "There is nothing wrong with me!" Consequently, he develops inordinate sensitivity to criticism. He develops a protective pattern of anticipating blame, accusation, or punishment. He forestalls such events by projecting threats to adults and acting as if he were threatened by others.

The result is a child who is a master at self-deception and repression of feelings. If he acknowledges any fault within him, it not only reveals his shame, but more importantly, it threatens to expose his inadmissible anger at his parents. With acknowledgment of this anger comes awareness of its cause: his parent's rejection. A child with so much retaliatory anger towards his parents needs to conceal this hate from both himself and his parents in order to survive ("Without my parents, I have nobody—I will be all alone—I will die.")

His disappointment in his parents, his shame at his ignorance, and his hateful envy of his siblings are all intolerable feelings that his harsh primitive conscience will not allow him to acknowledge, so he seeks punishment from others whenever those feelings become conscious. His provocative behavior typically results in the punishment he needs to silence his conscience.

Such a child feels that he never gets enough love. He feels empty. Consequently, he can become obsessed with acquiring symbolic equivalents. For some, it is food, for others it is things. The child often steals and hoards possessions. I cannot depend upon others to meet my needs—self-reliance is the only safe course. He also fills his emptiness with fruitless efforts at self-love. His cockiness, selfishness, and inability to admit fault are all efforts at self-love. Inwardly, however, the question of who shall love him becomes intolerably compelling.

The Aggressive Child's Conscience

There is a general misunderstanding of the aggressive child's conscience development. It is often said that the child has no conscience; that he does not feel guilty. From the preceding section we can see that this statement is only partially true. Like all children, the aggressive child's morality begins with internal self-criticism. But it stops there. Because this self-criticism is not softened by self-praise, the child suffers from intensive self-criticism that threatens his sense of well-being. Consequently, he protects himself from this criticism by both externalizing the "bad" parts of himself and by projecting his punishable impulses onto others. (Externalization and projection are defined in chapter 6 and discussed in depth in chapter 7.) As a result, he becomes extremely intolerant of others, and when guilt is aroused, his indignation increases.

There exists in normal development a period when all children have a harsh primitive conscience. Piaget refers to this stage as one where the child believes in *retributive justice* and particularly in *expiatory punishment*, a misbehavior is punished to set things right. The punishment is arbitrary and no relationship exists between the content of the misbehavior and the nature of the punishment. The child is spanked, hit, or sent to bed early for a misbehavior. Painful coercion is used to produce guilt. Later, as the child matures, he begins to realize that adults and peers punish by *reciprocity*. They use natural consequences, such as excluding the child from those he disrupts; depriving him of the object he misused; doing to him what he did to them; or asking for restitution.

Aggressive children rarely develop beyond the notion of expiatory justice. While the normal child will give back two punches for the two he received, the aggressive child will seek revenge well beyond "an eye for an eye, a tooth for a tooth." He will want to kill the other kid. In addition, the child will believe in the superiority of punishment over equality of treatment long after other children's moral development has moved from concepts of retributive justice to those of *distributive* or *egalitarian justice*. The child continues to believe that his disobedience is a breach of normal relations between parent and child and that some reparation is necessary. To accept punishment is the most natural form of reparation, and he will seek it until he gets it.

In contrast, other children come to realize that forgiveness is necessary. They do not seek revenge because there is no end to revenge. They learn to understand the psychology of situations and to make judgments according to norms of a new moral type. For example, if told a story about a boy who is given a roll and then loses it overboard while playing around, most normal children will say that the boy should be given another one because little children are clumsy and not very clever. They will say that while he should have known better, he did not do it on purpose and he should not have to go hungry simply because he was not careful. In contrast, the aggressive child never advances to this stage. He thinks the child should be punished and go hungry. "He was naughty—his mother isn't pleased—he must not get any more." The aggressive child is unable to take into consideration the circumstances of the individual, that the child was small or clumsy. Egalitarian ideals of justice are learned from caring adults and grow out of the child's movement from unilateral respect for adults to mutual respect and cooperation. The child with arrested moral development is one who has responded to the punishing adult with either an inner submission or a sustained revolt.

Because the child's moral development is arrested at the concepts of retributive justice, and because he avows his own behavior and distrusts others, he never develops an attitude of disgust and repulsion towards the destruction of people and their belongings, an attitude necessary for the preservation of human values. Aggressive children need counseling designed to enhance their attachment to and identification with adults who hold altruistic values. Such attachments take considerable time to develop. In addition, the attachments need to be maintained throughout the child's renewed efforts to move through the developmental stages he failed to master.

Efforts to Master and to Move through Erikson's Early Stages

The distrustful child maintains a pseudoautonomy because he has no other choice. He has to fend for himself to survive. The energy he expends to maintain this pseudoautonomy prevents the development of true initiative. With a counselor's help, his injured sense of trust begins to be repaired and he gradually gives up his pseudoindependence, but not without considerable conflict. When he allows himself to become dependent, the vulnerability he feels in this position causes periodic flights into independence, followed by anxiety relief but also by depression resulting from loss of the attachment to the counselor or to others.

This oscillating behavior occurs for a long period. When the child finally allows himself to be dependent and to please preferred adults, he moves towards true autonomy. But such progress occurs along with regular setbacks. Sometimes he will want help on a task, and other times, he will want to do the same task by himself, a typically normal behavior, but his resistance to help will be strong and his response to failure, when on his own, even stronger.

Depression will again follow failure to achieve age-appropriate autonomous actions. And when he takes the initiative, he often will judge his achievements unfavorably in comparison to others, and with competition, will be anxiety-ridden. Again, each time he judges his products unfavorably he will feel depressed and anxious and he will retreat to the safety of his earlier behavior. He will reassert his pseudoautonomy.

Considerable patience is required by all those working with aggressive children. Their "one step forward, two steps back" behavior produces much frustration and despair among those trying to help them. The counselor's role is to serve "humbly" as the un-acknowledged captain of the "team" working with the child and to support and encourage their work. I will talk more about this role in later chapters.

2

Aims of Counseling: Counseling Is What Counselors Do

Time does not heal all wounds—new positive experiences replace them.

What is counseling? Sounds like a naive question. Everyone knows what counseling is! Ask any teacher or parent, and you will be told it is a situation where a troubled individual comes to talk with a trained professional about those things that worry him and that result in self-defeating behavior. Ask the average person if he has ever been to see a counselor. While some will say yes, most will emphatically say no, "I can handle my problems myself." Our society was founded on rugged individualism. To seek help is to reveal weakness. Yet those same rugged individuals refer countless numbers of children to counselors when they are unable to handle or change the child's behavior. Ask an adult if she would make good use of counseling if you forced her to go, and she will reply in the negative. Yet teachers, parents, probation officers, and other adults hope that counseling will work its magic and the troubled child will become less troubling. The "talking cure" will work its miracles. Sometimes, more often than not, these same adults secretly want counseling to fail or, at least, to succeed only marginally. They have tried their best to change the troubled child and failed. If the counselor succeeds, it only reinforces their failure. It will behoove the effective counselor to give others the credit for a child's behavior changes, or at least to show puzzlement about the child's progress.

So often children are referred for counseling because they do not talk about their problems to teachers or other adults. "Maybe you can find out what's troubling him, goodness knows I've tried." Adults often wrongly assume that the child consciously withholds information from them. "Now you tell the counselor what's on your mind," failing to appreciate that children rarely observe their own behavior, moreover, the happenings in their own minds. The child's natural inquisitiveness is directed away from his inner world to the outer world. Only at puberty does self-examination and introspection become possible, and then it is often carried to the absurd.

The prepubertal child is not voluntarily willing to experience any conflict as coming from within himself. The child tends to externalize internal conflicts. For example, he escapes from guilt feelings by provoking others to punish him. Hostile feelings towards parents and siblings are displaced and externalized or projected onto others in the external world. These others then become the persecutors or seducers with whom the child must forever do battle.

This tendency to externalize internal conflicts influences the child's expectations of counseling. He hopes the counselor, through his superior powers, will change his environment for the better. The child who hates and fears his teacher expects help by a change in class. He does not expect or want the counselor to help him realize that he wants a change of teacher to obtain relief from his guilt feelings. The child who expects the counselor to remove him from bullying classmates does not expect to receive help to realize his own passive self-punitive inclinations. Nor does the child who expects separation from bad companions in order to end his temptations expect the counselor to help him to understand his own delinquent impulses and sexual aggressive fantasies. In short, the child expects the counselor to approve of and to aid him in the gratification of his infantile demands. When the counselor refuses to accept this role, he very soon becomes, in the child's view, an adversary rather than a helper. Often parents, too, prefer environmental to intrapsychic changes.

The lack of introspection that characterizes childhood is employed as a protection against mental pain. Only when the child can identify with an adult he trusts and is therefore in alliance with him, can the denial of conflict be given up and replaced by a more honest view of internal discomforts. When children do speak, they speak primarily of the present. They do not expect to speak of the past nor of present thoughts that have been kept secret for a long time. The latency-aged child regards his personal history as desirable to relate to others only when it serves to mitigate his current errors or fears. The child has no interest in accepting insight into his cumulative pattern of behavior or into its precursors. In the counselor's favor, however, is unconscious pressure to reveal preoccupations through play, playful acts, or actions.

So what is counseling? Is it trying to get a reluctant talker to talk? In a way, yes—but in a way, no. A child who is impulse-ridden, whose inner and outer realities are confused, and who is seriously disorganized by his own strong feelings, needs counseling designed to help him gain control over himself and his environment. The child's talking may be a large part of his gaining control, but counselor behaviors can be more helpful than mere talk. Before discussing the aims of counseling in detail, the concept of the therapeutic alliance needs to be presented.

The Therapeutic Alliance

A chief task of counseling is to help the child form an alliance with the counselor. When an alliance has been formed, the child can engage in what others view as counseling. He can think and talk about his problems. The term *alliance* designates a state of functioning where one part of the child's self is able to look at, listen to, feel, and even analyze another part of the self. The counselor allies himself with the child's observing split-off self. The child's observing part is the more autonomous adaptive part of the self; whereas, the observed portion contains the painful, conflicted parts.

To achieve this alliance, the counselor must first help the child to handle the strong feelings he experiences, to synthesize data received from within and from outside the child's self, and to perceive the counselor as a helper. This is no easy task, primarily because of the child's propensity for action rather than reflection. But it can and must be done and it cannot be hurried. While this book contains numerous examples of counselor's putting a child's worries into words (defined later as interpretations) such actions by themselves do not produce change. In fact, in the zeal for helping a child, a counselor may put the child's worries into words before the child is able to handle such awareness. If this happens, he will lose the child from counseling.

The alliance forms as the counselor accepts whatever material is brought by the child into each counseling session. Tactfully, the counselor interprets the defenses the child displays when he is anxious and verbalizes the affects contained in the child's words and behavior. The often obvious wishes and needs of the child revealed through his play, dreams, or actions are left untouched until an alliance is securely formed. For example, a thirteen-year old told his counselor the following dream:

CHILD: Last night—you know the star of *Ghostbusters*, Bill Murray—in my dream my mother was mad at Murray and he challenged her to a race in his car, except he is a tricky guy and he drove his car along a road that led to a cliff, except that Murray knew that his car was on the side of the road where, when he went over, he would land in the water. My mother's car was on the side that would land on the rocks. When I went down to the rocks, my mother's head was missing and it was weird. Her body was like it had been zipped down the middle but there was no blood or guts, only veins, like in a biology book.

ADULT: That was a scary dream but remember it was only a dream.

The boy was described as a buffoon. He displayed clowning, clumsy, passive-aggressive behavior. The counselor felt the boy was not yet ready to accept his identification with Bill Murray, who plays inept characters in his movie roles, nor with his thinly veiled hostility towards his mother. If the boy interprets his own dream along this line with no apparent anxiety, then that is fine, but beneath his hostility is an even deeper concern. From other material, the counselor is aware that the boy is cut off from his feelings. He thinks (is "heady") rather than feels and has denied sexual interests. In the dream, his mother is headless and her dead body is without substance, without sexual parts. But he is perhaps not ready to deal with his sexual feelings until a solid alliance has been formed.

Signs of a Developing Alliance

The first sign that an alliance is forming may simply be a slight pause for silent reflection, or a question: "Why do you think that?" A child may offer an interpretation of his own behavior:

CHILD: I know why I keep coming to see you when I'm always angry at you. It's so I can be angry at you and not at my family.

An eight-year-old spent the early months of counseling attacking the counselor and complaining that she would rather be somewhere else. The counselor kept commenting that she attacked the counselor because others attacked her (identification with the aggressor) and that these attacks kept herself and her counselor from working together on her real worries. The angry defense gradually subsided. One day she paused in surprise and commented, "I just had a thought about my anger but I can't remember it now, maybe I can later."

Oftentimes an alliance is formed when the child gives a name to the unacceptable part of himself. "Tough Joe made me do that." The counselor and the child can attempt to figure out, understand, and tame this "Tough Joe." Other children will project the unacceptable parts of themselves onto an imaginary character or an object in the therapy room. The counselor can then talk to this "other person." Still others will make the therapist a partner in their dramatic play and direct the partner to play various roles while they play others.

Children who most easily form an alliance with the counselor are those whose conflicts cause suffering, such as those with headaches, sleep disturbances, skin eruptions, digestive upsets, phobias and obsessions or rituals. All these problems either restrict the child from doing what other children do or place him at the mercy of unknown and compelling forces.

Often the child's feelings about his problems are openly verbalized. The compulsive child may express his helplessness when his counselor witnesses his ritualistic behavior. "Now you can see what my worries force me to do." Children with school phobias often relate that, "I want to go to school. Each night I say tomorrow I am going. And then in the morning I feel so nauseous I could faint." Some conduct disordered children will express, "Why am I so bad?" revealing the gulf between their ideal self and their real self and their frustration at being able to change either.

Difficult Alliances: The Aggressive Child

Children with severe behavior disorders stemming from marked parental-child conflict—a conflict that has existed from the child's first "no"—are the most difficult children with whom to form an alliance. The disruptive behavior of these children is a vital extension of their self. Their lying, stealing, extreme noncompliance, and other antisocial acts is their way of handling both their anxiety and their emerging impulses. These children have faced overwhelming stress and their way of mastering this stress is to do to others what has been done to them (identification with the perceived power and the tactics of the aggressor). Their antisocial behaviors are those they have adopted to combat overwhelming feelings of helplessness and rejection.

These antisocial behavior patterns prevent the split in the self necessary for self-observation. To observe one's helplessness and despair, to become painfully self-aware, is avoided at all costs. Such children use action and motoric outlets for their feelings. They are rarely in touch with their positive feelings for others. They may like you when you meet their needs but this quickly turns to hate when you frustrate their needs. For a child to remain in touch with affectionate feelings for another, even when that other frustrates him, requires a bond with a loving adult or with the memory that such a bond was once experienced with an adult. Many of these children never had such a bond, or if they did it is long forgotten.

These children constantly bombard the counselor with their hostile, attacking defenses, often eliciting urges to retaliate. The child initially ignores comments that he must be attacking the counselor because he himself has been repeatedly attacked or that underneath his rough exterior he craves love and attention. But the observing split in the therapist's self and his failure to counterattack presents a consistent model for the child to observe and with which to identify. When he wants to be like the counselor, he will then be able to form an alliance and examine his own self-defeating behavior.

> ADULT: Every time I see you, you order me about, try and break toys and hope to get me angry. When I tell you you can draw or play out your angry feelings with the dolls, you laugh and run around the room. You are here for me to help you figure out your worries and to either talk or playout what bothers you. If you continue to want to be boss and break the rules here, then I will have to prevent you from behaving this way until you can talk or playout your angry feelings.

Some children want the counselor to restrain them physically as restraint fulfills a wish to be hurt and attacked. With such children, the counselor may need to terminate particular sessions.

ADULT: I will not become a policeman and hold you when you misbehave because this would fulfill your old wish to be hurt and attacked. We will have to stop counseling today and your wish to attack me can be worked on in our next session when you are able to talk or play it out.

Counselors in school systems will experience considerable difficulty terminating such sessions early because the child will refuse to leave the room, often yelling, "You can't make me!" If you try and escort the child back to class, he will either run away or require that you carry or drag him. This feeds his need to be attacked and disrupts the class when he returns. Often these same children will refuse to leave counseling even when the session is terminated at the usual time. If the counselor leaves the room instead of trying to escort the child, the child will attempt to destroy the room or disrupt others by running through the hallways. This makes the counselor feel and look helpless and ineffective to others; the child has done to the counselor what has been done to him. It also makes the counselor late for his next counseling appointment, angering both the waiting child, who tries to wait patiently, and the child's teacher who has to deal with her student's anxious anticipation.

No counselor can handle such children without supports, even when the counselor is big enough to restrain the child.

ADULT: See, you win. You got me to physically restrain you. You left me no choice. Now you can yell and scream that all adults are mean and rotten. But who's the loser? Not me. You're the one who secretly wants an adult to care about you and play with you, but your anger at us is so strong it gets in your way! You want us to feel as helpless as you have felt.

The counselor will need a place to take the child, and often help getting him there, so that the child can be controlled and return to class without venting his anger at the teacher. If the child is bigger than the counselor, as is often the case, then the program in which the child is enrolled will need a crisis counselor to assist in the child's removal. After the children get used to the crisis counselor's presence, often they will leave on their own.

ADULT: Bill, you have a choice, either you leave on your own or I'll
get Mr. Brown to escort you out. I'm not going to get into a
scuffle with you. That's how you handle all your dif-
ferences with people.

BILL: You can't make me, so you get someone else. Big deal! I
don't care!

ADULT: You're right, I can't physically make you leave. In fact, I
can't make you do anything you don't want to do, and you
can go through life challenging all adults who could care
about you, and I can't do anything about that. Now please
leave on your own or Mr. Brown will come and escort you.

The counselor's firm stance with children like Bill often serves as
the turning point in the child's counseling. Considerable work with
aggressive children involves preparing them for what others would
call counseling. It takes a long time for such children even to become
aware of their problems, moreover to talk to someone about them.

I will now discuss the aims of counseling and talk about the techniques employed to reach these goals. Then counseling can be defined by what counselors do and not by what others think they do. The
six chief aims of counseling are:

1. Strengthen relationships with caretakers
2. Increase the capacity for sound judgment making (improved
reality testing)
3. Reduce excessive and unrealistic self-preoccupations and increase understanding and acceptance of self
4. Increase understanding of the feeling world
5. Increase understanding of choices and consequences
6. Fortify defenses that are weak and ease others that are rigid.

Aim 1: Strengthen Relations with Caretakers

Because the child has a counselor who attempts to understand him
and convey this understanding to others, the child is helped to maintain and to strengthen his relationships with important adults in his
life. The counselor serves as the child's advocate. No matter how hard
the child tries to hide his vulnerability in group situations, where he
would be at the mercy of others, he reveals them in counseling. It is
much easier to like a child and to see his strengths and vulnerabilities

when with him one-on-one than when he is disrupting a group or family activity. Caretakers almost always define a child's problems as misbehavior. Anxiety attacks are defined as manipulations, not eating is viewed as not minding, etc. The counselor's efforts to get others to think about the child's behaviors differently, even though it may often appear that these efforts fall on deaf ears, helps the child to stay attached to these significant others. They need the counselor's support to continue to reach out to the child.

Supporting teachers. Teachers can be of help in many ways. For example, helping a teacher realize that calling home to a parent to report on the child's misbehavior is counterproductive and that encouraging her to send home notes when the child has been productive can reap dividends. Such notes improve parent-child relations and interrupt the cycle of the parent's being embarrassed by the child's misbehavior, responding with inappropriate and often severe punishments, the child's increased anger at the parent, and the child's displacing the anger back onto the classroom teacher.

A retarded teenager had developed a strong attachment to a teacher aide in her special education class. Whenever the aide was absent or assigned to another setting, the girl would experience considerable separation anxiety and become disruptive. She had taken to "stealing" small items from the aide. It was suggested to the aide that the child needed some belonging of hers to hold onto whenever she was assigned to another setting. Could the teacher give the child such an object whenever the aide was out? All agreed that this was a good idea. Several weeks later I asked if this suggestion was working. The teacher said it had not, because the child had thrown the object on the floor yelling, "I don't want this!" What had worked was a lecture from the teacher that she was not going to tolerate any of this nonsense from her each time the aide left. Of course, the teacher neglected to mention that such lectures had never worked before and that the child always retrieved the object from the floor after her verbal tirade.

On numerous occasions, I have observed children upon the request of a teacher who has told others that the child needs a more restrictive setting. Following the observation, I have been genuinely impressed with the child's progress under the teacher's instruction. When I communicated this to a teacher, her response was often, "Yes, I agree he has come a long way." Teachers need constant feedback about the progress a child is making, progress they do not see because they are too close to the situation. If ninety-five light bulbs are turned on in a room and I turn on five more, most people will not notice the difference. Children's progress often occurs in barely perceptible steps. Someone, and often it is the child's counselor, needs to notice that the lights are brighter.

Stopping Counterattacks. The counselor's willingness to listen to frustrations with and complaints about the child help draw off some of the counteraggression that it is natural to feel towards noncompliant children. All adults are influenced by the child as much as the child is influenced by them. They will be friendly towards friendly children, angry towards hostile children, and irritated by irritating children. The opportunity for caretakers to discuss the child with an empathetic adult can serve to rekindle their interest in the child. But since the counselor represents the child in their eyes during such interchanges, she should not be surprised if anger felt towards the child is expressed towards her. Just remember, better the feelings be expressed towards you (the counselor) than towards the child.

A follow-up study of a large group of emotionally disturbed children treated in the residential center with which I am affiliated reveals that many of the children who lived with their natural families following discharge were no longer enrolled in school. In contrast, those who, at the time of the follow-up study, were discharged to foster or group home were still in school. We believe that the foster and group home children remained in school because they had a social worker assigned to them who went to the school to advocate for the child each time he was threatened with suspension.

Supporting Parents. Problem children awaken parents' own childhood conflicts and render parents less objective when disciplining their children. Problem children threatened the parents' hopes and their trust in the future. Problem children are symbols of their failure as parents. When their child is referred for counseling, some parents' fantasies of how much their child will change prevent them from noticing the actual changes made. Others fear that the child's progress will make them look bad as parents; the counselor will discover some major mistakes the parents made earlier in the child's life. The counselor's awareness of these fears and his empathy for the parents and their difficulties, in addition to his efforts to help parents understand their child's needs, can reap great dividends. Support for the overwhelmed parents can result in their renewed support for their child.

A mother, who saw nothing positive about her son and misused behavior modification suggestions made by the counselor, was reported to the Child Protection Services by the counselor for not fixing the child meals and for parading around the house nude in an alcoholic stupor. After allowing the mother to ventilate her anger, the counselor insisted that the child have a neurological examination (he had not had a physical examination in eight years). Because of his disjointed talk and his inability to follow his thoughts through to conclusions, the counselor thought he might be neurologically impaired. Unless such an exam was given, the child would be referred to a residential school.

Following the examination, which did reveal minimal neurological problems, the child was placed on Dexedrine. The mother then admitted in relief that for years she had avoided taking her son to a doctor for fear that he would be found "crazy" like his father. The medication and the relief of the mother's long-standing fear resulted in an improvement in the child's impulse control. The mother, for the first time, began to see some positives in her son. She remembered that he had once taken care of a stray dog, so she bought him a pet. Later, she actually thanked the counselor for forcing her to deal with her problems by reporting her to CPS and by insisting on a neurological evaluation for her son.

A follow-up performed by this writer of a small number of families (fifty) seen in an outpatient child-guidance clinic revealed that close to 80 percent of the families were satisfied with the services provided. Yet, in at least 60 percent of the satisfied cases, parents' descriptions of their child's functioning would suggest that their child was still experiencing considerable problems. Our feeling is that many parents come to understand, to accept, and to tolerate their child's difficulties. Such attitudes help their child to maintain a positive relationship with them.

Aim 2: Increase the Capacity for Sound Judgment Making (Improved Reality Perception)

The counselor's task is to stir the child to think about how he is responding to the environment he lives in. The counselor demonstrates concretely and empathetically how the child unwittingly holds distorted views of others, misperceives his own emotions, intentions, and capacities, and misconstrues those of others. The counselor provides a model by which the child can make new judgments about his inner reality and particularly about his own contributions to the difficulties that have beset him.

The counselor also helps the child to move from displaying massive anxiety of unknown dangers to articulating specific fears. With developmental advancement in cognitive growth, the child's anxiety forms change. As the child grows from an undifferentiated to a differentiated being, anxiety changes from: (1) a global conception of one's destruction, disappearance, and helplessness to more limited possibilities of injury, pain, or loss; (2) an implicit, diffusely experienced dread to a more delineated experience of signal anxiety; (3) a relative absence of temporal and spatial causality, where anything is possible, to reality testing and distinction between probable and improbable.

Some seriously disturbed children fail to show this progression, while others regress to earlier forms when under stress. The counselor helps the child to differentiate his anxiety from global to specific fears.

An important principle to remember when attempting to help a child perceive reality as it really is rather than as he has constructed it to be is the following: *What the counselor asks about or comments on helps to determine how children construct their experiences and therefore what they report and how they report on it.* Distortion is an inevitable consequence of conflict. Remember that the child comes about his beliefs honestly. What he believes is what he thinks is true. Helping the child to examine his conflicts and related beliefs helps him to clarify what is real from what is not real. Unlike adults, who remember by thinking, children think by remembering. Getting the child to think is akin to getting him to remember. But, of course, to remember painful events is to reexperience painful affects. Consequently, the child will resist this effort.

I will discuss more fully in chapter 5 how the child comes to terms with his compulsion to recall painful experiences by distortion of memory through the use of masking symbols. Uncomfortable affect is masked, modified, encapsulated, and even isolated. Such efforts protect the child from being overwhelmed by anxiety and make possible extended periods of calm, but they also distort reality. The counselor's job is to help the child remember in manageable doses, and in so doing, the distortions can be examined and corrected.

A seven-year-old boy, admittedly hated by his mother because he looked like his real father, was left with a number of sitters for the first four years of his life. His mother was now considering divorce from his stepfather, and in response to this conflict, the boy had begun soiling again. He had a long history of impacted bowels and of taking enemas. In the waiting room of the counselor's office, he was very anxious, tense, teary-eyed, and in a hurry to get to the playroom. Upon entering the playroom, he immediately drew a picture of the "Six-Million Dollar Dummy."

TAD: Plastic face—it's a stupid she. She-dummy has a dumb peanut on her shirt. She-dummy has a plastic face, plastic shirt, dumb pants, dumb colored teeth, pointed head, dumb hair, girl's hair. She-dummy has a she-dummy heart. She-dummy has green pants and black boots. She's a real "Six-Million Dollar Dummy."

ADULT: (Silence)

TAD: (Discovers clay—starts to roll it around and pound it— looks nervously at counselor)

ADULT: Here, you can play with clay and get messy without getting scolded.

TAD: What you need is a good slap in the face. How would you like a good slap in the face—you need that. (He starts to throw the clay at the counselor who restrains him)

ADULT: I can't let you throw things at me, but you can draw me and do what you want to the drawing.

Tad starts to draw a picture of the counselor and then "messes her up" with "cow-pies" before he is done drawing it. He covered the eyes and then the mouth. He liked the "sticky splat" it made. He then liked slapping the clayed-drawing against the floor, peeling the clay off and then slapping it again. With lots of nervous laughter, he told the counselor that "She'd better 'watch it' or she'll get a slap in the face." He continued to mix the clay with water, rub it, and stick his fingers in the mound he made, remarking how sticky and neat it was. He then washed up and decided he wanted to paint more on the large paper provided.

He said that he had to paint a ship. First he painted the ship's base. Then he made lots of churning water and said that the ship was bouncing all around.

TAD: My mother's afraid of water. She can't swim. Once she had to be carried like a baby from the dock to a boat because she was so scared.

ADULT: (Silence)

Once he had smashed a ship model that his mother liked a great deal. He continued to paint with great zeal.

TAD: The ship needs to be tied up to a dock. It is still choppy. I'll draw an anchor. The anchor would help keep it docked.

Tad then made dark waves rising higher and moving faster. He drew a sailor and said the sailor was dumb. He tried to catch a fish but the fish swam right past him. "I should throw clay at the dumb sailor." He began throwing clay with the intent of covering the whole ship. He said that he just had to cut the line, to keep throwing clay until he wiped out the whole ship.

Tad is typical of impulse-ridden children. But he had some controls. He agreed to display his anger in make-believe, although he was never far from expressing it directly, and he often halted his own regressed behavior by switching activities when he got too anxious. Tad's behavior illustrates how confused such children are. His anger at his mother and stepfather is confused with his own self-hate. His desire to slap the counselor is a reflection of his own experience of being slapped. But he does not know what compels him to want to slap and mess up the counselor, nor does he know why he holds back his stools and then soils. The counselor refrains from responding because Tad's communications, while revealing, are not fully understood. Who is the sailor fisherman? His stepfather? Himself? Is the ship he draws and destroys the one prized by his cold, indifferent mother (plastic-faced)? But then, why does he try to anchor the ship against the waves he created? To save the ship from his own destructive urges? There are too many unanswered questions to respond appropriately to Tad's productions, productions made rapidly, as if he was compelled to draw them. And remember, Tad's play is not just his compulsion to master his rejecting home life but also his fear and anticipation that the woman counselor will treat him similarly.

Because the counselor will let Tad play with minimal interruption and in an accepting yet limiting manner, his play will become less diffuse and more organized. When Tad's play becomes less driven and more organized, the counselor can comment on and attempt to clarify the child's confusions. Tad can then begin to understand his behavior and its role in reinforcing his mother's view that he is like his father, further solidifying her rejection of him.

A less extreme example is Troy, an intelligent, articulate and pleasant eleven-year-old who was troubled by extreme restlessness that resulted in school failure. He could only sit still when drawing spaceships and space platforms. He had no explanations for his hyperactivity except that he had been to a neurologist who had put him on a medication that had not helped. He then spent numerous sessions drawing and describing his fictional ideas about traveling and living in space. At the beginning of each session, he would state that everything was fine in his life (all reports continued to emphasize his hyperactivity). He would draw and relate his fantasies while he moved nervously around the counseling room. All efforts to get him to examine why he might prefer to spend so much time and energy in an unreal space than in the world of peers, family, and school, met with resistance. He would simply reply that his space world was more fun.

The counselor knew that much conflict existed between Troy's divorced parents and that Troy may fear getting mixed up in their battles. By staying in his space world he could avoid problems in the real world. With continual reassuring comments from the counselor that most boys would worry about the family problems he knew Troy was experiencing, Troy moved tentatively from discussing space to discussing his family.

ADULT: Troy, staying in a space world is like the ostrich with his head in the sand, who, because of his position, is more vulnerable to a surprise kick in the rear than he would be if his head was up and looking around. While you are out in space things are happening over which you now have no control.

Troy began to look at his frozen views of his parents. Neither were seen realistically. He began to look at both parents independently from one parent's view of the other. The counselor gave him "homework" assignments to find out what other adults thought about his dad. He learned to refuse to pass along messages to Dad from Mother about visiting arrangements. And he tolerated the notion that part of him accepted the divorce because he had Mother all to himself—a thought that also caused him great anxiety but that was normalized by the counselor's comments. Troy's flights into space also represented a retreat from sexual feelings toward his mother, as well as banishment for replacing his father. His restlessness was not only a motoric discharge of his anxiety but also was connected with sexual fantasies.

When Mother started to date again, Troy's hostility towards her dates was interpreted as rivalrous jealousy. At the same time, the counselor stressed that Troy would no longer have to be so disturbed by his fantasies about his mother because she now had a boyfriend. Troy began to concentrate on his schoolwork, and teacher feedback indicated less hyperactive behavior.

Aim 3: Reduce Excessive and Unrealistic Self-preoccupation and Increase Understanding of Self

Because many disturbed children feel rejected and unloved, they have not developed genuine self-love. They only like themselves when they have gotten others to meet their needs. Their whole life becomes centered around having their needs met. Their self-love is injured by excessive worries that they cannot manage their life. Troy's preoccupation with his space world kept him from achieving in the real world, and part of him knew that and felt guilty about it.

When we show children like Troy that they have been inwardly and unconsciously compelled to act and feel in certain ways, that their disturbance is understandable, we offer some healing to their injured self-love. Our explanations provide relief from painful self-accusations that have been keeping self-esteem low. When we show children that the behavior of others has reasonable meanings and can be responded to reasonably, we indirectly contribute to decreasing unhealthy self-absorption. The child is helped to see that some of his wishes are worth gratifying and that appropriate ways exist to gratify them. This knowledge increases the child's feelings of authenticity.

With children who are rejected and who never develop self-love but instead become self-preoccupied and absorbed in compensation fantasies of self-importance, the task of replacing self-preoccupation with true self-love is extremely difficult. Such children have unrealistically high ideals because of their compensation fantasies. Consequently, any praise they receive or accomplishments they achieve are never enough. "To love myself I must be a world champion—anything less is failure." "I won't do that baby stuff."

The counselor must spend hours listening to their fantasized exploits at the same time that he makes special gestures toward them (e.g., helping with schoolwork, advising how to handle specific situations, showing interest in their achievements, negotiating for them with others). Their fantasized exploits are attended to, but the counselors try to ascertain what the children might be able to do, encourages adults in their child's life to expose them to these activities (bowling, pool, table games), and then concentrates his questions on the children's real, rather than their fantasized, achievements.

When a child experiences that he can be liked and attended to, and sometimes can give pleasure to an adult, he begins to like himself better. At that time his achievement will become meaningful. Many of us want to believe that if children learn and master concrete tasks that their problems will disappear. Yet many bright and creative people fail to appreciate their own self-worth. It is difficult to love ourselves (and appreciate our own accomplishments—which are extensions of ourselves) without having been loved by another. While acceptance and understanding are not love, they are the best substitute. Out of such acceptance, self-love may grow. When children gain an awareness and tolerance for their inner emotional needs, they feel better about themselves.

Aim 4: Increase Understanding of the Feeling World

During counseling the child comes to learn that there are many different feelings that people can experience, and that people can have different feelings about the same situation. He learns that people can have similar feelings, but that they may differ in strength. Perhaps the most important thing about feelings that he learns is that feelings are not "right or wrong." He will often hear people say that he has no "right" to feel that way—that he "should" feel differently. He will learn to disregard these beliefs, safe in the knowledge that feelings are not subject to rational analyses; that when he is hurt, he is hurt. People will be angry at him for having his feelings, but he should not try to inhibit his feelings simply because others do not like how he feels. He will learn that it is his behavior and not his feelings that get him into trouble, and that he can behave differently if he wants to.

He will learn different ways to handle disappointment and frustration, he will learn to differentiate real fear from imaginary fear, and he will learn different things to do when he is angry or upset.

Aim 5: Increase Understanding of Choices and Consequences

The aim is to help the child to think about his action in light of his motives. "Why did he do that?" He will be able to respond with options to questions such as "Hitting is one thing you can do. Is that a good idea?" He will come to appreciate how another will feel if he engages in a particular behavior. He will be able to try alternative solutions and to anticipate alternative consequences to various behaviors he displays following feelings he experiences. In short, he will develop the ability to plan his response to frustrations in contrast to his typical pattern of being overwhelmed by them.

Aim 6: Fortify Weak Defenses and Ease Rigid Defenses

Chapter 6 is devoted to achieving the aim of fortifying and building defenses. Chapter 7, on the interpretive process, focuses on helping the child to understand the defenses he uses and how they are both self-reinforcing and self-defeating. He is encouraged to give up these rigid defenses and to utilize those that will enable him to receive the love and attention he so desperately craves. At the same time he will be helped to master age-appropriate developmental challenges.

3

Principles of Communication

I have this great unbelievable fear of people not liking me. How can that ever be proven false unless I go out there and talk to people?

—A patient of Hilda Baruch

While it goes without saying that professional counselors need to understand the basic principles of communicating with children, teachers, principals, pastors, and other natural helpers would do well to study these principles, for their understanding could help prevent the need for professional counseling of some children. Eight basic principles of communication underlie counseling. These eight principles are:

1. Paying attention to affect verbalization increases affect verbalization.

2. Expressing feelings to someone who can be trusted is a means of gaining control over feelings.

3. Children can reveal themselves in defending a challenge.

4. When children talk about the feelings of others or attribute feelings to other people, they often are talking about themselves, their own wants, wishes, and fears.

5. Feelings communicated in counseling are most often feelings held toward the counselor or elicited by the counseling situation.

6. Fantasies revealed are less frightening than those bottled up.

7. Related remembrances of our past are stories because they are created from our present.

8. Guided discussions where the child is drawn to explain himself and then to reflect upon what he is saying is the "seed crystal" to learning.

Counselors trained in active listening and client-centered approaches to counseling are taught to concentrate on communicating

59

the feelings behind a child's verbalizations; to reflect back to the child the feelings expressed. Such reflection helps the child to clarify how he feels so that future communications come closer to the feelings actually confusing or troubling the child. The assumption behind this approach is presented as the first basic principle of communication.

Principle 1: Paying attention to affect verbalization increases affect verbalization. Witness the following interchange between adult and child:

CHILD: It wasn't my fault, Jimmy hit me; you always blame me and never the others. He hit me first.

ADULT: When you stop shouting at me, I'll be glad to talk to you more about it.

CHILD: I'm not shouting, and besides, how come you don't talk to Jimmy? He started it.

ADULT: I'll talk to Jimmy later. Right now I want to hear your side of the story.

CHILD: You just want to blame me for the trouble; you always blame me—talk to Jimmy first.

ADULT: I don't always blame you; you're exaggerating.

CHILD: No, I'm not. Yesterday you shouted at me for talking during the movie when I was just trying to get Kathy to shut up so I could hear.

ADULT: I didn't shout, I simply told you to be quiet.

This interchange proceeded smoothly until the child accused the adult of being unfair and the adult defended her actions. The child then counterattacked. As a result, the adult lost an opportunity to both explore the child's feelings about blame and to help the child feel understood. Remembering to focus on feelings, the adult now responds differently to the child's accusations of unfairness:

ADULT: No wonder you feel so angry if I'm always blaming you for things.

CHILD: You do! You do! I'm always the one in trouble. The other kids love to poke me and watch how you scold me when I poke them back. They giggle and laugh.

ADULT: It's upsetting to always be getting into trouble with grownups.

CHILD: Yeah! Why do you just pick on me?
ADULT: You feel that I single you out for scolding.
CHILD: You do! You do! Why do you single me out?
ADULT: You must think I don't like you at all to be picking on you so.
CHILD: You don't like me, you don't. No one likes me!
ADULT: How awful to feel no one likes you.
CHILD: They don't!

The adult now has to cope with the child's feeling unloved or unappreciated, feelings often underlying expressions of persecution. Many adults would have ended this interchange before these feelings were revealed. Others, feeling helpless when despair is expressed, might end the communication by attempting to rescue the child from these feelings by again becoming defensive. "Yes, I do like you; lots of people like you." The child will not feel reassured; in fact, he will not feel understood. Despair and hopelessness are experienced by many children with disturbed behavior.

Principle 2: Expressing feelings to someone who can be trusted is a means of gaining control over the feelings. Children are easily overwhelmed by strong feelings. They lack the automatic coping skills to help them through stressful periods. Adults in crisis manage strong feelings by falling back on long-established routines to get them through the day. They "go through the motions." In contrast, the child is continually bombarded with new challenges. Consequently, the child may refuse to face these challenges when faced with feelings that confuse him.

SCOTT: I've done all the problems I can. I can't do anymore.
ADULT: Scott, you've only done two; come on, you can do lots more. I'll help you.
SCOTT: I don't need your help, and I'm not doing anymore. They're too hard!
ADULT: They are no harder than those I gave you yesterday.
SCOTT: (Silence and passive noncompliance)

Once again, the adult is defensive. He tells Scott that the problems are no harder than those given the day before. Furthermore, he denies Scott's feelings of helplessness when he encourages him to tackle problems when he feels incapable. Scott refuses help because he does not feel understood nor does he want to admit to helpless feelings. More meaningful communication results in the following:

ADULT: Yesterday you did some hard problems. It seems like you just don't have the energy today to do these.

SCOTT: Yes, I do. I just don't want to do them now.

ADULT: Perhaps you have a worry on your mind today that keeps you from concentrating.

SCOTT: I do not—I just don't feel like it.

ADULT: Sometimes we don't feel like doing something because our mind is on a worry and not on our work.

SCOTT: (Silent glare)

ADULT: You didn't need my help yesterday because you had energy, but I'll be glad to help you today; maybe you just need some help to get started. Here, let's do the first two together.

SCOTT: Sometimes I get discouraged.

A word of caution: Simply because you are attuned to a child's feelings does not mean he will actually verbalize their cause. Often children do not connect their feelings with troubling events. Rarely will the child turn to the adult and state, "I don't have the energy today because my mother and father got into a big fight last night and I heard Dad say he was going to leave." Even when children do make connections, they are quite superstitious, often believing that verbalization of a fear will cause the feared event to happen. Don't speak the unspeakable—it makes it real! Scott may put his fears aside and do several problems simply because the adult acknowledged their possible presence. The adult did not press the point, but he did communicate that he understood that Scott was going through some unpleasant experience, and he offered to help without implying that Scott was helpless.

When children do openly express their feelings, they usually are in better control of them. The child who angrily strikes another child or disrupts others in his class has lost control over his feelings. His anger has taken over, and his judgment has been clouded by the strong emotions he feels. But the anger is typically a response following another feeling, a feeling of being wronged, hurt, or made anxious.

One child calls another child a name, "Fatso." The child reacts with anger, but it was the attack on his self-esteem that he first felt. The counselor needs to direct his interventions towards the *basic hurt*, not just the anger. Upsets—distressing disturbances—are composed of three chief elements: thwarted intentions, unfulfilled expectations, and undeliverable communications. The child had planned to do something and the plan had not worked out, the child expected something due him and it was not forthcoming, or the child wanted to say something and didn't or couldn't. The counselor must direct his communications at those three elements.

John, an eight-year-old in a special education class for the emotionally disturbed, is working on an art project at a table with a group of classmates. Suddenly, he swipes his arm across the table, knocking over his paint cans and spilling paint across the length of the table. "What did you do that for?" demands another child, ready to square off at John. John responds with, "Screw you." And the class is instantly in a state of chaos, with all the kids, drenched in paint, ready to pounce on John and avenge themselves of his actions.

John is escorted out of the room. When his screaming subsides, the teacher attempts to talk with him. Obviously, something has upset him. John has now stopped cursing and become sullen.

ADULT: John, for the last three days you have lost control in the classroom. Something is bothering you and these troublesome feelings overwhelm you and you lash out at those around you.

JOHN: (Sullen)

ADULT: Sometimes when we get upset it's because we want something to happen and it doesn't or we want to do something that we can't. What did you want to happen during your art project?

JOHN: Nothing. Can I go back to class? I'm calm now.

ADULT: You think my talking with you is a scolding?

JOHN: No, I just don't want to talk about it. Everyone here always tries to get you to talk when you don't want to.

ADULT: Sometimes talking about your troubles brings back the pain that you're trying to forget.

JOHN: Yeah, everyone here says we shouldn't get upset, we should stay calm and then when I get upset and calm down they want to talk to me and I get upset all over again.

ADULT: We'd be helping you best if we just let you alone after you calmed down?

JOHN: Yeah!

The counselor now must switch from reflecting feelings to confronting the child gently with the reality that his calming efforts, his conscious efforts to suppress his strong feelings, only work when he can be alone and isolated from others. John needs to learn how to handle strong emotions when faced with them in interpersonal and social situations. He must learn to express his feelings in small doses so that they do not build up to the point where they spill over into behavior.

ADULT: I'll tell you what, John. I can't let you go back to class just now because the other kids are hopping mad at you.

JOHN: I don't care.

ADULT: Well, I do. I don't want anyone to get hurt, and some of them are angry at you because of the paint you spilled on them and your seeming not to care that you ruined their projects.

JOHN: I can handle them.

ADULT: But they're not ready to handle you. I'm going to tell you why I think you got upset and you don't have to talk if you don't want to.

JOHN: Well, I'm not going to listen, either. (Puts his hands over his ears.)

ADULT: I know you'd like to try and forget what troubles you so you'll calm down, but I think you're grown up enough to listen to me without losing control.

JOHN: I ain't listening!

ADULT: Well, I guess I'll just be talking to myself, then. But here goes. I think you got upset because you were unhappy with your painting. You wanted it to look one way while it was turning out to look another.

JOHN: I stink, I'm no good at drawing.

ADULT: It must feel awful to think you're bad at some things, but I'll also bet you were making that drawing for someone special and wanted it to look a certain way.

JOHN: My mom, I'm visiting my mom this weekend.

ADULT: And you wanted to give her something special.

JOHN: I'm no good at making anything.

ADULT: I can imagine how awful you must feel. But maybe your mother would be just as proud of you for something else you've done this week.

JOHN: I've done nothing well this week.

ADULT: Have you completed any school assignments that you could show her?

JOHN: No.

ADULT: Did you try hard in school or gym this week?

JOHN: Ask the teachers.

Talking with John's teachers revealed that he not only had a bad week but a bad several months as well. Writing a note to his mother acknowledging him for his effort was, therefore, out of the question. John wants to win his mother's love by giving her an art picture. He needs to verbalize this need and perhaps ask for help from others. The counselor had lots of options to help John handle his frustrated desire to give his mother a picture. He attempted to assist John by searching for other ways for John to impress his mother. Another way would be to help John to examine his (or perhaps his mother's) unreasonably high standards for his performance. Why was the drawing not acceptable? What made it unacceptable? While we know that depressed individuals underestimate the quality of their performances, even in the face of concrete evidence to the contrary, we can help them to examine this more realistically.

ADULT: While I didn't see what you were painting, your teacher tells me that you always think your drawings are bad.

JOHN: I told you I stink at drawing.

ADULT: And yet, knowing this, you still try to draw and then paint a picture for your mother?

JOHN: I thought I'd do better this time.

ADULT: John, I'm fairly certain that you could tell me what you didn't like about your painting. Maybe you made a leg too long on a person. But with painting you can't erase. You need to work with colored pencils, where you can erase. But I'll bet after several erasures you'd crumple up the paper. I'll bet you're never satisfied with what you do. So making a drawing for your mother is doomed for failure. Maybe you don't really want to give something to your mother.

This challenge "maybe you don't really want to give something to your mother" can lead counseling along an entirely different path. John's response to this challenge illustrates *Principle 3: Children can reveal themselves in defending a challenge.*

JOHN: I do so.

ADULT: Then why do you pick giving her a painting when you admit to feeling like a lousy painter and know that you'll never paint one good enough for her?

JOHN: Well, she never gives me anything I really want!

Principle 4: When children talk about the feelings of others or attribute feelings to other people, animals, or things, they often are talking about themselves, their own wants, wishes, and fears. Such talk can take many forms. The child can tell you a fantasized story about monsters or animals or a story about another child simply to size up your reaction to this "child" so he can anticipate how you might react to him.

CHILD: Billy used to be my friend, but last week he borrowed my toy truck and he never gave it back. He said I had lots more and that I didn't need it.

ADULT: Friends aren't supposed to take another's toys.

CHILD: Yeah, but he said I didn't need so many, that he didn't have any and I had lots.

ADULT: Did you tell Bill that all your toy cars are special to you and that he can borrow any of them but not if he doesn't give them back? It's upsetting to have even one car taken. Special people gave each one to you.

CHILD: He should be punished?

ADULT: Perhaps not. If he gave it back, would you forgive him for wanting something so bad that he would risk your friendship to get it? He must have felt real bad about not having any toy cars.

Children often communicate about themselves through imaginary play, or through drawings.

SALLY: This is Sherry. She lives all alone on the moon. She has no one to take care of her.

This story drawing can be the communication of a wish (perhaps a wish to escape frustration—to live alone on the moon and take care of herself), a fear (my mom could abandon me and I would be all alone) or a reflection of actual feelings of rejection (I feel all alone). The rejection could be felt (overly sensitive child), actual (rejected child), or a combination of the two (child extremely sensitive to times of parental indifference).

By knowing something about the child's history and present life circumstances, the counselor can respond accordingly. When you have no idea about the meaning of the child's communication you have to elicit more information. But always ask your questions within the metaphor of the drawing.

ADULT: What did Sherry take with her to the moon? Can you draw that?

SALLY: I can't draw those things so well.

ADULT: Would you like me to draw them for you? You tell me what they are and I'll add them to your drawing.

SALLY: Yes. She took her puppy, her hamster, and all her story-books.

ADULT: Won't Sherry's parents miss her while she's on the moon?

SALLY: No.

ADULT: That must make Sherry sad.

SALLY: They're glad she's gone.

The counselor must be careful because Sally may be "punishing" her parents for a perceived transgression on their part. Children can feel so revengeful towards parents that they will deprive themselves of a need in order to get back at a parent. Because Sally has a puppy, a hamster, and storybooks, the counselor theorizes that the child's parents have given her things that instill a sense of responsibility and, therefore, are not completely rejecting adults. (Of course, the child may not actually have any of these things.) Counseling without some knowledge of a child's family life is a difficult task.

ADULT: Did Sherry do something to make her parents so angry with her that they would send her to the moon? I wonder if Sherry isn't also mad at them and ran away to the moon.

SALLY: (Silence, draws stars around the moon)

ADULT: I once knew a little girl who got so mad at her parents that she ran away so her parents would miss her so much that they would be sorry for the things they did that made her mad.

SALLY: Who?

ADULT: My cousin (Children are more impressed with such statements than they are with, "Another child I had in counseling").

SALLY: She did that? Did they miss her a lot?

ADULT: Yes, but they also worried that something would happen to her. My cousin was so mad that she risked getting hurt when she ran away, so she decided that running away wasn't such a good idea. The next time she got real angry at her parents she decided to draw her angry feelings.

A corollary to principle 4 is that *children will often ask you questions that reveal something about their lives.* "Do you hit your kids?" "Do you drink?" Such questions often tell you about the lives they live. "Do you hit your kids?" may also be an effort to find out how you will react to them when you get angry.

Principle 5: Feelings communicated in counseling are most often feelings held toward the counselor or elicited by the counseling situation. Let's return to Sally's drawing of "Sherry on the moon with no one to take care of her." While the counselor related to feelings he suspected Sally had towards her parents, his initial comments could, and in most cases should have, been guided by adherence to principle 5. To a child new to counseling the response might have been:

ADULT: When Sherry is in a new situation with a strange adult, she would like to get as far away as possible and take care of herself.

OR

ADULT: Sherry hopes her new friend will help her not to feel so all alone.

To a child who has been in counseling for some time:

ADULT: Maybe Sherry expected that her new friend would take better care of her and now she feels let down.
CHILD: What friend?
ADULT: Maybe Sherry has a friend like you have me for a friend.
CHILD: Yeah.
ADULT: Perhaps sometimes you feel a bit like Sherry.
CHILD: Yeah
ADULT: Sometimes kids in counseling want things from their counselors that they don't get and it makes them feel alone and unloved. I wonder if you feel like I don't care about you sometimes.

To a child who is terminating counseling:

ADULT: Now that Sherry will be leaving her "friend" maybe she wonders if she'll feel all alone and uncared for.

All recommendations to a child about the possible meanings of his productions need to be put tentatively. Get in the habit quickly of always prefacing comments with "Maybe," "I wonder if," "Perhaps," "Is is possible that," or "I may be wrong but maybe."

A child may choose a topic to draw, play, or discuss because of the feelings generated in the child's relationship to the counselor. This relationship may be real of fantasized. The female child may draw or play out sexual themes because she has sexual feelings about her male counselor. The female child may play more maternal themes in the presence of an older female counselor. While the themes may reveal the child's concerns, the counselor must remember that the concerns are present ones, concerns about the counseling relationship; concerns about the similarity of the counselor to other meaningful adults in the child's life. Too often, counselors try to connect the child's feelings to other caretakers when the actual "feelings" are those between the child and the counselor.

ADULT: I wonder if banging the toys together is your way of expressing your anger at me for something I've done that hurt your feelings.

· · ·

ADULT: I wonder if the drawings you make of tanks and guns is your way of feeling more powerful and less afraid of me.

ADULT: I wonder if the drawings you always make of smiling, neat little girls is your way of telling me that you want me to think of you as a nice girl who never gets into trouble.

When you make comments that attempt to reflect possible feelings held but not directly expressed by the child, do not expect acknowledgment. It will take many such communications to the child before he will feel comfortable enough to express more directly feelings held toward you.

The child will wax and wane in becoming more directive and his indirect expressions will vary in style. He may show his anger toward the counselor by a violent drawing, knocking over blocks, punching a doll, hiding in a corner, displaying mock anger, or playing catch and throwing the ball poorly to the counselor. When his feelings change to positive ones he will do things for the counselor, make the counselor things, or brag about the counselor to others. He will rarely say, "I like you!"

Principle 6: Fantasies revealed are less frightening than are those bottled up. Children rarely express their fears directly. Many of their fears are only partially remembered. They are *screen memories.* Screen memories are bits and pieces of traumatic experiences that have been repressed but that enter consciousness in disguised forms, when the mind lets down its guard, most often at night just prior to sleep, in dreams, or in response to reminders in the environment. For example, a child who has repressed the memory, and along with it the connected pain, of being sexually molested by an alcoholic father may be extremely bothered by a screen memory (or flashback) when an adult with alcoholic breath leans over to pat her head. By quickly leaving the area she avoids such an event from happening again. Often, however, the child does not connect her anxiety and partial memory of a dreaded event to her past experience. As one six-year-old boy from a violent family described it to Louise Silvern and Lynn Kaersvang after a year's counseling, "I used to think memories exploded you. It turns out that they do only when you don't really know what they were memories of."

The complete memory of the past experience can be so overwhelming that all experiences are avoided that could result in the memory being revived. The girl's leaving the friendly but odorous adult is an example of *acting out.* When an emotion becomes unduly intense, and therefore in need of repression, remembering immediately gives way to action. The girl flees without knowing exactly why she does so; to know why is to remember, and to remember is to be overwhelmed.

Many children distance themselves from parental rememberances of abuse and rejection by displacing the danger felt into an imaginary world. The fantasy of "creatures bent on destroying children" is much less agonizing than fear of a parent.

But it is these fears that continually cause the child difficulty, often disrupting the child's development long after the reality of his situation has changed. The parent may no longer be abusive or the child may be living in a foster home. Yet, fantasies of destructive creatures still preoccupy the mind and prevent mastery of age-appropriate tasks.

The child can be encouraged to concretize these fears through play or drawings.

Betty, a nine-year-old, told the following story to her drawing of a pumpkin, a witch, and a girl, a drawing she made in a counseling session several weeks before Halloween:

> A girl and a cat pumpkin with a black light inside. She's got whiskey hands like cats do. The figure on the right is Grandma from the TV program "The Addams Family." She's got pointy fingers. The pumpkin is their cousin and they don't like her 'cause she's mean. The blood dripping is from her loose tooth that came out when she yelled. No, I'll make this red orange juice. She was sitting on a chair in the kitchen and the pumpkin came in and scares her and she yelled and forgot about the glass of orange juice she had there and it spilled. The pumpkin has points on his hands.

Over the course of several months each of the girl's stories contained threatening figures with "pointy fingers." Early drawings and stories to the drawings were quite chaotic but seemed more organized and recognizable as the counselor continued to reflect the feelings he thought lay behind each verbal and written expression. A later story to a drawing of a one-eyed monster is more revealing than earlier stories:

> She has all red hair, her chin is blue, and she has one eye. Her hands are like witches' hands. They're no good either. And one

day she was dripping blood out of them because she killed Wednesday. She scratched Wednesday and then killed her. (Why?) Because Wednesday was her daughter, but she didn't like Wednesday 'cause she played with the little boy in "The Addam's Family" and she was supposed to play with Mama and not with anybody else. But she never did play with Mama 'cause Mama told her not to.

After a year in counseling, the girl realized that her initial preoccupation with pointy fingers, and later with long fingernails, was a screen memory of part of a sequence of abusive interactions with her mother when she was a toddler. Her mother, a prostitute who kept her fingernails long and polished red, scratched her when angered. She also would bend over the crib at night and threaten to scratch her if she bothered her during the night.

Jennifer, an eight-year-old suspected of being sexually abused as a preschooler, told the following story to her drawings:

> Mrs. Jones says "my poor little Sara. She's been dead, but I can't help her 'cause she's dead." Mr. Jones came and said, "You killed Sara." Mrs. Jones laughed, "Ha, Ha, I killed her with my own bare hands because she lied." (What did she lie about?) She lied in bed. And I put my bare hands on her and she is dead. I touched her and she died. And Mama came and said, "You witch, you killed Sara." But Sara was not really dead, she was in the attic playing with her yo-yo. And she called Sara three times, and Sara reappeared and was walking toward her mother and said, "Yes, Mother." Sara was a bat. She didn't have no hands. She said "Yes, Mama." Sara has a big knife. She's going to kill her mother. (Sara wasn't really dead?) Nope. She put a dummy in her bed that looked like her and then went up into the attic. She killed her mother and is now the queen of the house. (Sara is glad her mother is dead?) Yes, because her mother was wicked. And the husband is mad. He stays up in the attic all day long. And then Sara got married to Mr. Jones.

The girl takes another sheet of paper and continues:

> Here's the wedding. (Sara married her father?) Yup. Even though her father didn't want to get married, he married her. (How come he did what he didn't want to do?) She forced him.

He told nobody about it. Here's Sara's long black hair and some flowers, and here's Mr. Jones. He has long hair. (What color?) Orange. (Who do you know that has orange hair?) I don't know. Here's the alligator that Mama plays with. She wrestles with an alligator and the alligator is in the wedding. He's holding the ring for them. He puts the diamond ring on her finger. Then you know what happened? (What?) When he put his hand around her the alligator came over and opened his mouth wide, took his teeth and bit her and she died. Now Sara's dead and Mr. Jones killed her and now he has her crown. (I thought the alligator killed Sara?) But Mr. Jones sent the alligator to kill her.

Both Betty and Jennifer's stories revealed the tremendous confusion each child experienced. Both try and make sense out of their experiences but they cannot because the experiences made no sense to them when they happened. The stories also reveal confusion about what each child did to get abused. The mother did not like Wednesday because she played with a boy rather than with her, but mother also told her not to play with her either. Most likely Betty was abused at the mother's whim rather than for her actual misbehaviors. Children try to make sense out of parental behavior and would much rather be a "bad" child than have a bad mother.

Jennifer's stories reveal the anger that sexually abused children often feel toward their mother as well as their developing concepts of sexuality. Jennifer related sex with marriage, the abused must marry the abuser. She also reversed roles. She made the abuser marry her and "he told nobody about it." Also notice that when the counselor asked the question, "Who do you know that has orange hair?" she stopped communicating within the metaphor. He should have asked her, "Who does Sara know who has orange hair?" Jennifer's answer of "I don't know" followed by the introduction of the orally aggressive alligator suggests that the direct question raised her anxiety and her fantasy productions regressed in response. Children's fantasy stories and play behaviors are an effort to keep distance between themselves and the feared experiences. When they lose this distance anxiety is aroused.

Both Betty's and Jennifer's stories also illustrate *Principle 7: Related remembrances of our past are stories because they are created from our present.* Jennifer's stories are quite different from those she might have told to drawings made at an earlier age. At each stage in Jennifer's development, she attempted to integrate into her personality the unintegratable experience of being sexually abused. With increasing knowledge about sexuality, she will attempt to reinterpret her earlier experience. Since this experience is partially repressed, her efforts are directed at handling the screen memories of this experience rather than the repressed experience itself. In some sense, Jennifer's personality is organized around a traumatic experience. But these organizational efforts are directed at only part of the experience, and often these parts are kept separate. For this reason, the term *deviant mental organization* has been used to label the functioning of abused clients. As Jennifer's thoughts become less disturbing in response to the counselor's interventions, she may actually reinterpret her experience in light of her developing relationship with the counselor. She may see traits in her past abuser that she didn't see formerly. She may remember him differently.

A less complex example of principle 7 is the child who experiences his positive feelings for a foster parent as a loyalty conflict and who tells the counselor how wonderful his parents treat him at home. He is only in this awful foster home because his parents are not well and cannot take care of him. This fabrication is not a lie, it is what the child needs to believe in order to keep a positive image of his parents alive. This is his sustaining function. To admit that his parents are neglectful is to affirm that he is worthy of neglect.

As the child is allowed to express his positive feelings about his real parents, and they are not challenged (his fabrications, his sustaining functions, are accepted as real), he will begin to express more mature feelings and the counselor can help him to interpret both the positive and negative feelings he has about his parents.

Principle 8: Guided discussions where the child is drawn to explain himself and then reflect upon what he is saying is the "seed crystal" to learning. Child-development specialists suggest that prior to adolescence children are not able to reflect upon their actions. Since counseling is a process that requires self-reflection, some experts believe that one cannot counsel children. (Rarely are these experts counselors themselves.) But why is it that children are not self-reflective? Is it because they are not developmentally ready? Or is it because other factors get in their way? The latency-age child often jumps to conclusions from false premises, is blind to inconsistencies, and avoids dealing with emotionally charged themes. Asking appropriate indirect questions can help the child get past these tendencies and reflect upon his behavior.

ADULT: Billy, Jimmy doesn't like to be pushed like that.

CHILD: (Continues to push Billy)

ADULT: (Intervenes, preventing Billy from pushing Jimmy)

CHILD: Let me go, Jimmy started it!

ADULT: (Takes Billy aside and asks:) Did Jimmy "start it" for a reason?

CHILD: No.

ADULT: Was Jimmy upset over something?

CHILD: I don't know.

ADULT: Should we ask him?

CHILD: No, he had no reason to bother me so I pushed him.

ADULT: So when you're bothered you want to push somebody.

CHILD: Sometimes.

ADULT: Can you remember another time when you were mad enough to push somebody?

CHILD: If they called me a name, but I didn't call Jimmy anything.

ADULT: Have you ever wanted to push somebody because you didn't like how they were looking at you? You were struggling with a hard problem and yelled, "Don't look at me or I'll punch you"?

CHILD: Yes.

ADULT: Suppose you hadn't been working on the hard problem. Suppose they looked at you—say when you hit a double to center field. Would you get mad at them?

CHILD: I don't know, I guess not.

ADULT: So how you feel inside sometimes determines how you react to things outside?

CHILD: What do you mean?

ADULT: If you're having a good day, you feel good inside, you feel happy, or proud. What other kids do bothers you less than when you're having a bad day, when you feel sad inside, maybe sad, hurt, or discouraged.

CHILD: Okay.

ADULT: So is this a good day or a bad day for you?

CHILD: A bad day.

ADULT: Do you want to tell me why today is a bad day and the feelings you have that make it a bad day?

CHILD: No. Can I go back to my desk now?

ADULT: Yes, but I want you to tell me in private when you feel like you're having a bad day, when things seem harder to do than usual. These are the times you are most likely to get into trouble with another child. This is when your feelings are most likely to get hurt. I also want you to think about all the things others do, including grown-ups, that bother you and what you do to try and stop the bothering.

A corollary to principle 8 is that: *Expression of thoughts results in reflection upon the thoughts expressed and what they mean to the self.*

The counselor who keeps these eight principles of communication in mind when interviewing children, as well as the nine interview goals to be presented in the chapter to follow, is more likely to achieve the basic aims of counseling reviewed in the last chapter.

4

Interview Goals in Counseling

The time of true listening must be devoted solely to the child; it must be the child's time. If you are not willing to put aside everything . . . then you are not willing to truly listen . . . truly listening to a child of this age is a real labor of love.

—M. Scott Peck

Much counseling takes place in settings other than a child-guidance clinic where the child is brought by an anxious parent who may or may not have provided the child with a proper orientation. Structuring the initial interview in such a setting is quite different from one where the child has been placed in a special education class and assigned a counselor to help him with school-adjustment problems. Still different is counseling where the child reveals himself spontaneously to a teacher, guidance counselor, or probation officer, or where the child is in crisis and needs what has been called a life-space interview. Assistant principals in public schools do a great deal of crisis counseling, talking with children brought to them for violation of school rules or troubles with peers. Nearly every adult counsels children at some time.

For this chapter, general goals of interviewing that cut across all settings will be presented. Everyone interviewing children will relate to them more effectively if they keep these goals in mind. These goals are:

1. Establish that the interview has relevance to the child's problems and that the interview can help him to meet his needs.

2. Start off showing concern about external events and people in the child's life.

3. Encourage the child to talk about anything.

4. Encourage the child to tell what is on his mind in his own way.

5. Detect unacknowledged aspects of the child's communication.

6. Be alert to the possibility that the child may be reexperiencing some vital moment from his recent or distant past.

7. Keep the reality of the counseling situation alive and relatively unclouded by fantasies.

8. Avoid assuming that you know what the child means; hear with an ear like a child's.

9. Give the child hope, but always share his despair or your hope will be experienced as insensitive.

Now, many will say that everyone knows the value of these goals. Who would not keep these goals in mind when interviewing children? Only a fool would do otherwise. Well, we are all fools, then, because many counselors, including this writer, have interviewed children in ways that kept them from reaching these goals. All the counseling statements in this book, both good and bad, come from process recordings of actual counseling sessions of trained counselors. Witness the following:

ADULT: Did your mother tell you why she brought you to see me today?

DANIEL: It's about my behavior.

ADULT: Your behavior?

DANIEL: I get into fights and don't listen.

ADULT: Okay. But how did Mom explain why coming to see me would keep you out of fights or help you to listen?

DANIEL: I don't know.

ADULT: Ms. Smith, would you tell Daniel again why you both came to see me today?

MOM: I told him that you were someone who understood children's worries and troubles and you would help him to understand why he did the things he did.

ADULT: You mean like why he gets into fights and doesn't listen?

MOM: Yes.

ADULT: And what did you say to Mom when she told you that?

DANIEL: (Silence)

MOM: He said that he didn't have any worries. That he gets into fights to defend himself and he didn't listen to teachers 'cause they were stupid.

ADULT: And what did he say when you asked him why he didn't listen to you?

MOM: He doesn't answer—he never does. It takes me physically threatening him to get him to do what I ask and I'm afraid that when he gets older he'll never do anything to help out the family.

So far the interview with Daniel and his mother has nothing to do with Daniel's problems. It has concentrated on the problems Daniel's behavior has created for others. We do not know if Daniel's behavior is a problem for him. Obviously, it gets him into trouble, but he may not conceive of this trouble as his problem. So far Daniel may only see the counselor as the dutiful servant of his teachers and parents, someone to lecture him, scold him, or wheedle information out of him. So the counselor now turns to the child and remarks:

ADULT: While I could ask your mom to give me some examples of how you don't listen to her, suppose you tell me some of the things Mom does that you don't like.

This remark violates our first goal. The counselor's job is not to make things equal, to give Daniel a chance to have his day in court. Such a remark also will alienate all but the most sophisticated of mothers. To reach *Goal 1, to establish that the interview has relevance to the child,* the adult should proceed as follows:

ADULT: Daniel, it would seem that adults you care about are upset with you so much of the time that you can't enjoy them and they can't enjoy you.
DANIEL: I don't care about my teachers.
ADULT: You care about your mom.
DANIEL: (Silence)
ADULT: And there was a time when you cared about some teachers. Am I right, Mom?
MOM: Yes. He liked his first-grade teacher very much.
DANIEL: I did not!
MOM: Daniel, don't lie.
ADULT: Daniel may get so mad at his teachers sometimes that he doesn't remember that he liked one some time ago. Okay, Daniel. But other kids in your school like your teachers very much and because they do they enjoy school more. I would not like school very much if I didn't like my teachers and they didn't like me.
DANIEL: I don't—I hate school.

Now, the interview has begun to establish that counseling may relate to the child's problems and not just to others' problems with the child. Following up on Daniel's relationship with Mom, the counselor remarks:

ADULT: Daniel, I'll bet that both you and your mom want to enjoy each other more. All kids I know want to be happy with their mom and want their mom to be happy with them. For some reason you and your mom kind of stopped enjoying one another some time ago. Would you like to get along better with your mom?

DANIEL: Yes. (mumbles)

ADULT: Tell me some of the times that you and your mom get along.

DANIEL: What do you mean?

ADULT: Like, do you play games with Mom that are fun?

MOM: I don't play well. My parents never played with me as a child.

ADULT: Daniel, are there any games you could teach Mom? What are some games that you like to play by yourself or with your friends?

The counselor has now reached *Goal 2: Start off showing concern about external events and people in the child's life.* He has shown a concrete interest in what the child enjoys, and implies that Daniel can offer his mother something—he can teach her something he knows. Let's take another situation?

ADULT: Jim, you had counseling last year with Mrs. Brown and this year you have a new teacher and I am your new counselor. Can you tell me what counseling is all about?

JIM: You know—I'm supposed to talk about my problems in school—my behavior.

ADULT: And what is supposed to happen when you talk about your behavior?

JIM: I don't know.

ADULT: Some people believe that talking about those things that get you into trouble with adults will help you to learn how to stay out of trouble. Do you believe that?

JIM: I don't know.

ADULT: But I'll bet you wonder how talking can help you get along better with grown-ups. You're not even sure you want to get along with adults. Most adults don't seem happy with you and want you to change and part of you likes you just as you are.

JIM: (Silence)

ADULT: Well, I don't think anyone can talk about their worries or troubles with someone they don't know. I know that I would only tell my real worries to someone I trusted and someone who knew me. For a while I'd like to learn more about you. What do you like to do best?

JIM: I have a baseball card collection.

ADULT: Could you bring some of it in to show me? Who are your favorite ball players?

Getting a child to talk about his interests is reaching *Goal 3: Encourage the child to talk about anything.* This goal is not just to encourage talk—a child's interests tell you something about him, they help you get to know him. Who he is is what interests him.

Goal 4: Encourage the child to talk about what is on his mind in his own way. This goal is one to reach when the child actually has something on his mind that he wants to communicate.

Children do not want to be upset and typically get upset simply remembering a troubling event. Often they come to scheduled counseling sessions perfectly content with their day and unwilling to look back in time to review a troubling situation. Goal 4 is most often implemented when the child is being interviewed following or during some upsetting situation. Below is an example of a counseling session in which the adult has "forgotten" goal 4. The child had been removed from assembly because he became angry when he did not receive an award for achievement in baseball.

RAYMOND: Let me go. Damn you!

ADULT: I'll let you go when you're calm.

RAYMOND: I'm calm!

ADULT: When you stop struggling so much I'll let you go.

RAYMOND: (Now calm)

ADULT: Raymond, you didn't get an award because you missed

three games. Remember that the rule was you couldn't miss more than one game.

RAYMOND: But I played well in the games I made.

ADULT: Remember the rule, if we violate the rule we need to pay the consequences.

RAYMOND: Screw you!

Raymond never expressed anything more than what angered him superficially. He never really got to say what was on his mind. The adult, possibly annoyed with Raymond's need to receive an award without putting in the effort required, felt the need to remind him of reality. Adults working with disturbed children often feel their "job" is to confront the children with their attempts to modify reality to suit their needs. Nevertheless, reality itself is an all-too-frequent reminder that the child has not lived up to expectations or followed rules. They usually do not need reminding following their outbursts. They need help in becoming calm. Children also view the world as unfair since it is unfair to them. Disappointments should be responded to as disappointments even when they seem unreasonable. *There is no such thing as an unreasonable feeling.* When a child is disappointed, he is disappointed. Your choice at these times is to counsel him or leave him alone to sulk. Since this is a book about counseling, let's continue to interview "sulking, angry" Raymond:

RAYMOND: But I played well in the games I played.

ADULT: You did make some great plays, Ray, so I'm sure your disappointed that the award wasn't given for them.

RAYMOND: I deserved an award.

ADULT: It was really disappointing not to get an award.

Raymond cannot feel disappointment and damage to his self-esteem when he blames others for his problems and gets angry at their behavior (not giving him the award) instead of at himself (for not following the rules). What the counselor is trying to accomplish is to help Raymond deal with disappointment with a more appropriate defense than blaming. But merely making the child aware that he goes from disappointment, to despair, to anxiety, to anger, and to blaming will not change the pattern—it is all the child knows how to do. Making him aware is the first step. Helping him find another way to express his disappointment is the second step.

When you make the child aware of this cycle of response to disappointment you put him in touch with his disappointment and the cycle will repeat itself before your very eyes. Be prepared for escalation of defensive behavior when you counsel children. It is the chief reason many children do not get counseling when they are upset since it takes a skilled interviewer and the proper environmental supports (space and isolation from others) to carry it off. Ray's response below is typical:

ADULT: It was really disappointing, Ray, not to get the award.
RAYMOND: (Getting agitated). Yea, that bitch, screw her, she can take that award and shove it.
ADULT: Raymond, it's really hard for you to stay in touch with your disappointed feelings. Here you wanted to show the award to your family and all you're left with are yucky feelings.
RAYMOND: (Gets up and tries to leave the room; the room is empty of everything he could destroy) That f——ing bitch. I deserved that award.
ADULT: It's better to be angry at your coach than at yourself for missing three games. If you got as angry at yourself as you are with your coach you'd probably hurt yourself in some way.
RAYMOND: (Sullen silence)
ADULT: How did you get to be so hard on yourself? Why did you want the award so badly?
RAYMOND: My dad used to be a baseball player, but what business is it of yours?

Now Raymond is beginning to tell you about what underlies his upset. He was telling you before—his own way is to begin with a blaming communication. And when it is accepted, and often the situation is such that it cannot be (no environmental supports), the child will reveal more of the feelings that contribute to his reactions. But it is not enough simply to learn about Raymond's thwarted intentions. Many a disappointed child can get to the bottom of his feelings in the right interview situation. I have led many of them into the depths of despair and then out of it, and many come to rely on me each time they go through a crisis. Nevertheless, unless I teach them better ways to handle their feelings, they are doomed to repeat them. Reeducational techniques will be discussed in later chapters.

Goal 5: Detect unacknowledged aspects of the child's communication. Remember the old saying, "Actions speak louder than words." Counselor attention to nonverbal cues is extremely important. But achieving goal 5 is not simply paying attention to nonverbal communications, it is anticipating what might be in the child's mind and deciding how to respond to these thoughts. Unlike classical client-centered counselors, I believe that accurate empathy depends upon the counselor's ability to understand how the child's mind works. This requires knowledge of child development, particularly cognitive development. It also requires some knowledge about how a child is liable to conceive of counseling. Children bring to counseling their ideas about what counseling is all about. Whether they are initially seen alone or with their family, these ideas need to be addressed. Almost all children brought to counseling for the first time view it as part of the discipline their parents or another adult have been trying to impose. They get sent to the principal when they misbehave. Now they are being sent to another type of principal. Many are given false information about counseling from their parents or redefine parent information in terms of their own conceptions. Many parents do not want their child in counseling and communicate this to the child. They also communicate that they want the child to change. But the child's maladaptive behavior is his best adaptive effort. He knows how to behave, and knows he behaves on many occasions, but he does not know why he cannot do it all the time. He does not realize what motivates him to misbehave. He experiences pressure to change as a threat to his already-shaky identity. This unspoken fear must be addressed in the initial sessions. For example:

ADULT: I'd like to acknowledge both you, Jim, and your parents for having come to see me today, because I know that you're very nervous. Neither you nor your family want to be here today. In fact, Jim, when you heard you had to come here I'll bet you tried very hard to behave so your parents would change their mind and not bring you here. And, I'll bet that you folks almost didn't come because Jim seemed to be doing better this week. Could someone start by telling me how you think this service can be of help to you?

MOM: I'd like to see Jim show respect for adults. He doesn't listen to me or the teachers at school.

ADULT: Whose idea was it to come—the family's or the school's?

MOM: The school psychologist evaluated Jim and suggested we come here, but I also know that something was wrong because he never listens to me.

ADULT: How about you, Dad—did you also feel that the family needed help with Jim?

DAD: He listens to me—my wife is too easy on him. If she'd toughen up he'd be okay. He's a boy, all boys misbehave from time to time—I wasn't such a good student either.

ADULT: So part of you thinks it's "much ado about nothing"?

DAD: Yeah.

ADULT: But there's another part that would like more family harmony. It's tough coming home from work and being the disciplinarian?

DAD: Yes.

ADULT: And it's no fun hearing from his teacher that if Jim's behaviors don't improve he might be put in a special class?

DAD: What do you mean, special class?

ADULT: The schools refer many children like Jim to us because they hope we can prevent their having to remove the child from the regular classroom. Because he's not profiting from instruction they may place him in a smaller class where he can get more attention.

DAD: Well, Jim's not going to any special class.

ADULT: Then we all need to see how we can help Jim to pay more attention to adults, particularly your wife, so both of you can share with teachers what works. Dad, what luck have you had trying to teach your wife how to discipline Jim?

MOM: Jim's afraid of his dad, I can't use fear!

This initial counseling session has addressed several unspoken issues: the family's reluctance to come, Jim's effort to behave, and fear about special class placement. In past years, I would emphasize to Dad that his view of "no problem" puts his son in a bind. To mind Mom and his teacher is to be "unlike" Dad. He hears from Dad that "boys will be boys" and sees no reason to change. He also hears that Dad was like him as a boy and turned out all right. To change, he would be disloyal to Dad! I also might have reflected that perhaps there was a part of Dad that wanted more for his son than he had for himself, and that working to help Jim behave in school would help him realize this goal for his son. Over the years, however, I have come to appreciate two facts. First, communicating to a couple about how their differing feelings can create a conflict for one family member does not *necessarily* mean that they can do anything about it. Family members often feel blamed by such comments—an unspoken fear that all parents and other family members have when one of their members is in trouble. Second, there is a difference between the process of empathy and the counselor's response of being empathetic. The intrapsychic feeling, the intuition, that the father wanted more for his son, was the process of empathy. If I had communicated my understanding of Dad's inner experience in a way that allowed him to feel understood and soothed him, I would have been empathetic. Unless I am sure that being empathetic is going to be helpful, I now refrain from communicating my empathy. Some clients sense emphathetic comments as the counselor's seeing through them, as if the counselor is reading their mind. Such feelings reinforce the often unspoken fear that "head shrinkers" can read your thoughts.

In the interview with Jim's parents, the counselor responded to five unacknowledged aspects of the family's communications addressing goal 5. These were:

- The family's reluctance to come;
- Jim's "flight into health";
- Fear about special class placement;
- Fear of being blamed;
- Fears of the "power" of the counselor.

Now let's look at an initial interview with a child:

AULT: Bill, it took some courage to come into my office. Most kids I see are really nervous and somewhat scared the first time they see me, for they don't know what to expect. What did your folks tell you about coming here?

BILL: That you help kids who get into trouble—who have bad behavior.

ADULT: Who thinks you have had behavior?

BILL: Everybody.

ADULT: Who is "everybody"?

BILL: My mom, my teachers, my dad.

ADULT: You mentioned your dad last. Does he feel as strongly as the others?

BILL: I get along good with my dad.

ADULT: So your dad's not so sure that your behavior is so bad.

BILL: He tells me to mind my mother and to listen to my teachers.

ADULT: But you don't?

BILL: I guess not.

ADULT: Did you ever hear your dad tell your mother that he was like you as a kid and he turned out all right?

BILL: Yes, when they argue.

ADULT: And did you ever hear Mom say that Dad could have made more of himself if he had stayed in school—that the family could have more money?

BILL: Yes.

ADULT: I'll bet it's tough to hear your parents argue and to feel like you're caught in the middle—that maybe you have to take sides. But Mom won out because you're here to see me today.

BILL: Dad said she could bring me here if she wanted to.

ADULT: But he wanted no part of it.

BILL: He thinks I should listen to my mother and teachers.

ADULT: And what do you think?

BILL: I guess so.

ADULT: Most kids who come to see me try hard to behave better when they learn they might come for counseling. How about you?

BILL: I was good all week.

ADULT: And I'll bet that you've tried hard to behave many times before, and it worked for a while, and then you were in trouble again.

BILL: I don't like my teachers, they're dumb.

ADULT: And your mom?

BILL: She nags, just like some of the teachers. If they left me alone I'd be okay. Don't bother me and I won't bother you.

ADULT: And coming to counseling is adding another adult, namely me, to nag you to behave.

BILL: (Silence)

ADULT: Most kids who come to see me expect another lecture or scolding for their misbehavior. If these things worked, I'd do that, but they don't. You've had many scoldings, and yet you're still in trouble a lot or you wouldn't have to come here.

BILL: (Silence)

ADULT: So if you're not going to get a scolding you're wondering what this "counseling" is all about. All kids wonder about that. Some even think the wrong kid in the family had to come, that their sister or brother should be here instead.

BILL: My sister makes me sick. Mom never yells at her. She's a "goody-two-shoes." But behind Mom's back she does things that get me into trouble.

ADULT: It doesn't seem fair that you should be labeled the "bad" kid in the family. But since you're not here to be scolded or punished, even though it may seem like it 'cause you had to come, let's talk more about what can happen here.

BILL: (Silence)

ADULT: We know what's troubling others—what they want—I'm sure your mother and teachers could make a long list of things you do that bother them, and you've said a little about what you want—to be left alone. Counseling is trying to get adult's wants and your wants to be the same. I also know that most kids have a part of them that wants to behave and another part that doesn't. It's my job to get these two parts to work together better. Most kids want to get along better with adults but something keeps them from doing so. Counseling is to help find out what this something is.

BILL: But why do I have to come—why isn't my mom in counseling?

ADULT: It's not fair that only you have to come.

BILL: (Silence)

ADULT: What are some things you like to do when you're not in school?

In this sequence of communications, the counselor has acknowledged how:

- The child might feel about coming;
- His fear that the referring adults and the counselor are aligned;
- His possible feeings of being scapegoated;
- His anxiety about what counseling is all about.

The counselor has not yet acknowledged several other fears, but he will do so in later sessions. There are the child's fears about how he will be handled for displaying misbehavior during counseling sessions and his fears about what will be communicated to his parents. Most kids expect the counselor to communicate to their parents how they behave in counseling sessions. For this reason, some try hard to behave in their initial sessions so that good behavior will be communicated. Talking to children about confidentiality is relatively meaningless—actions speak louder than words. What needs to be communicated is the pattern of behavior expected from the child and why it is expected. For example:

ADULT: Since most kids who come here come because of misbehavior, they try to behave well each time they visit me. But they still misbehave in other places. If this happens, then we need to look at why you can behave here and not elsewhere.

Most older children never ask the question, "What if I misbehave here?" They do not expect to misbehave. The counselor can communicate his expectations that the child will misbehave and that this misbehavior will remain between the counselor and the child, but the child will not believe it until it happens. In fact, most children will test the counselor by doing or saying something relatively innocuous and then wait to see if it gets back to the parents or teachers. It is very important that the child not hear others' interviews, see others' folders around, or hear you talking about him to other staff. Otherwise, when confidentiality does become an issue, your words will be meaningless. The child should know what you will tell parents and teachers, for he knows you talk to these adults about him. While it is important to address this issue during initial interviews, what the child actually experiences following your feedback to others is what he will learn about confidentiality. For example:

> ADULT: Bill, I'll be talking with your parents and teachers throughout counseling. While I can ask you how you're doing outside of counseling, most grown-ups have a need to tell me how children they have referred (or sent to) counselors are doing in school or at home. They also want to know how the kid is doing in counseling. I simply tell them that you're doing as I expected. Usually they ask if there is anything I learn about your concerns that they can use to help you. I answer such questions only with your permission.

Goal 6: Be alert to the possibility that the child may be reexperiencing some vital moment in his recent or distant past. Children may view coming to counselors as they have viewed earlier visits to other professionals. The child may equate the visit with going to a doctor. Children who have been threatened with removal from home may think they are coming to counseling as a first step in their removal. This is often the experience of children who have been in foster care. They expect that when the session is over they will not be going home. These fears should be explored.

The child's play or aspects of his relationship to the counselor can bring to mind earlier experiences. I recall an initial session with a young girl who played out a scene of a girl being scolded by her mother for wetting her bed. I let this play go on too long, and the girl became quite anxious. She refused to come back to the playroom but did agree to see me in my office where there were no play materials. Children who show strong emotions during counseling which appear unrelated to ongoing events most likely are reexperiencing earlier traumas.

Goal 7: Keep the reality of the counseling situation alive and relatively unclouded by fantasies. As counseling progresses, the child may develop fantasies about the counselor. The young girl can easily form a crush on a gentle, empathetic male counselor. She may then become anxious by her emerging sexual feelings towards the counselor. Similarly, the young male can develop a crush on the female counselor. These feelings can lead to a flight from counseling and a refusal to return.

Other children, those not overwhelmed by their fantasies, continue to come but because of their preoccupations make less use of the counseling hour. Counselors can address these possible feelings as follows:

ADULT: I get the feeling that you don't want to come to counseling now because you've developed some feelings for me that make you uncomfortable.

CHILD: I just don't want to come—it's stupid. I don't like coming here.

ADULT: I wonder if you also think I might have the same feelings towards you. Girls I have in counseling sometimes get a crush on me or think of me as a boyfriend. And they think I feel the same way.

CHILD: That's disgusting!

ADULT: While I like you, I don't think of you in that way.

Children rarely ask you questions about your personal life. When they do, they suggest more than professional interest. Are you married? Do you kiss your wife? How old are you? Do you have children? Pay attention to your own feelings if you are uncomfortable; chances are, so is the child. Children who are openly seductive, suggestive of past or present sexual abuse or a sexualized household, need to be confronted directly, as illustrated below:

ADULT: You don't sit very ladylike in here and the way you dance around and parade your body suggests that you think of me as a potential boyfriend and not as a counselor.

CHILD: You're disgusting.

ADULT: Now, stop dancing around and sit properly with your knees closed and your dress pulled down and we can get on with counseling.

The counselor both defines acceptable behavior and gives the message that his feelings differ from the child's. These actions help the child to keep impulses under control. Some children construe these actions as rejection. They are so used to relating to others in a sexualized manner that rejection of their behavior is experienced as rejection of them. Bill Van Ornum and I talk more about counseling sexually abused children in our book on crisis counseling.

Adoption fantasies occur in all children when they are angry at their parents or when they become disillusioned by them. Children from rejecting homes or those living away from home frequently fantasize that the counselor will adopt them or become their foster parent. These fantasies need to be addressed:

ADULT: Sometimes I think that you'd like to come and live with me.

CHILD: Yeah, could I?

ADULT: It's only natural that you'd want to live with someone who you trust and feel kindly towards. I like you very much, too. But if I took all the kids home to live with me who come to me for counseling I wouldn't be able to care very well for any of them—there would be too many.

CHILD: But you could just take me.

ADULT: It would be wonderful if I liked you best of all the kids I counseled and made an exception for you.

CHILD: Yeah, could you?

ADULT: I know it's very painful not to feel special when you're not always sure who loves you. My taking you home would help with that pain. But I can't help you that way. I can only help you to work at how your pain sometimes keeps you from getting affection from other adults in your life.

CHILD: (Sulks for a while, and just prior to the ending of counseling asks for something on the counselor's desk) Can I have this pen?

ADULT: You'd like to have something of mine to keep me with you even though I can't take you home to live with me.

CHILD: (Silence)

ADULT: You can't have my pen, but next time you come I will make you something that you can keep.

CHILD: (Storms out of the room).

While this child requested the counselor's pen for solace, others try to take things from the counselor's office for other reasons. Defiant children will repeatedly request objects. These children, while often deprived, typically ask for these objects or take them, not because they want the object (they are usually quite good at stealing from stores when they want something) but because they want control over the counselor. (Later, they may take them to feel attached to the counselor.) Acquiring things from others feeds fantasies of power and omnipotence, fantasies that function to compensate for feelings of helplessness and despair. Other children ask for things because they know you will say no; they can turn you into a rejecting adult, and thereby justify their own aggressive actions towards you.

CHILD: Can I have this car?
ADULT: The toys are all for use only in the playroom.
CHILD: But it's only one car. There are lots more here.
ADULT: All the toys stay in the playroom for use here.

While it is very tempting to explain to the child why toys cannot be removed, "If every child took a car, all the cars would be gone in a day and there would be no cars left for anyone to play with," or, "Next time you'd want another car," the chid would vehemently deny the "facts" you present. "I only want this one." It is important to limit clearly the child's actions with no perceived avenue of getting around the rule. If the child can manipulate the counselor, no good will come of counseling. "The toys are not for taking" is the clearest message. The child's disappointment, his anger, and his manipulative efforts, can be responded to later.

ADULT: Jim, you've asked me for everything in my office, and now you're asking me for a paper clip you found on the floor that you know I don't really need. You sure are trying hard to make me look like a meany because I'm going to say no to this request also.
CHILD: But it's only a paper clip and you don't even need it.
ADULT: I know, Jim. It's like you're saying, "You don't even like me enough to give me one lousy paper clip!"
CHILD: Yeah, give it to me!
ADULT: Whenever you feel real bad about yourself you want something, it doesn't matter what it is, and if you don't get it then you can replace your bad feelings with anger at the stingy world, and stingy me.

Goal 8: Avoid assuming that you know what the child means; hear with ears like a child's. I'm often asked about this goal. How can I hear with ears like a child when I'm not a child? Counselors who are more in touch with their childhood have less difficulty achieving this goal. They remember the hurts and joys of their youth. Those of us who have lost touch will need to ask more questions of the child. We adults tend to be more abstract and analytical than the child, causing us to jump to conclusions about the child's feelings. We have understood the general while the child wants us to understand the specific. A young girl goes into detail about how her sister got a new dress. The counselor responds with how the girl must feel bad because Mommy seems to like Sister best. Yet all the child was communicating was her desire for the same dress. In our book on crisis counseling, Bill Van Ornum and I talk about asking children comparison questions. Asking children to describe how two people in two situations are alike or different will help you to elicit answers from the child, which will enable you to listen like a child.

Listening like a child also requires that you understand children's interviewing techniques. When the child asks, "Who broke this toy?" he is usually asking, "What happened to the boy who broke this toy?" But listening like a child requires the counselor to understand the mind of the child. The world that the child constructs between the ages of four and eight (and many emotionally disturbed and developmentally delayed children well past age eight continue to construct such worlds) is dynamic, magical, menacing, animistic, and governed by irrational causality. Inanimate things are not only alive and conscious, but are motivated and able to punish. Moral laws are exacting, severe, and often arbitrary. Thoughts and dreams are poorly differentiated. Matters of mind, like dreams, are given concrete existence—the monsters of the dream become the monsters in the bedroom. The child places himself at the hub of the universe and much of his speech reflects his egocentric thought, serving more of an expressive function than a communicative one. The child's soliloquies reveal jumbled and juxtaposed thoughts; non sequitur is a normal part of his speech. The child's syncretism can lead to confused understanding from the adult counselor. Being aware that you will be confused makes the confusion more palatable!

Goal 9: Give the child hope, but always share his despair or your hope will be experienced as insensitive. The hopeful attitude of a counselor is easily picked up by the child. No matter how much a child blames others for his problems, he is not free from worries. He may be well defended against their expression, but they are there just the same. The child who fears abandonment but who keeps the fear repressed still worries over events symbolic of abandonment. The counselor's hopeful attitude that he can help the child handle these worries is a basic requirement of counseling. Unfortunately, many counselors are not always so hopeful. "What I can do when the child has so many other real problems in his life." "Counseling was never designed to help a child handle the real stress he's feeling." "His family doesn't love him. He's forced to grow up too soon." "My husband's a family therapist. He thinks I'm wasting my time seeing the child and not the parents, but the parents won't see me."

When any or all of these attitudes prevail, seek consultation from a colleague who does not feel this way, someone outside of your system. How often does the child you are seeing get the undivided attention of an adult for even an hour a week? And how often is this adult's attention directed towards the child's feelings? And remember to set reasonable goals; a remedial teacher does not expect a child to catch up to grade level in a short period. Often her goal is to keep the child from falling further behind. A physical therapist does not always expect a cerebral palsied child to walk; she requires the child to do stretching exercises to keep up his muscle tone and to prevent muscle atrophy from disuse. Hope is also conveyed in small doses. Hope is holding out for the child that he is not helpless, that he can master feelings that occur within him.

ADULT: You're angry at me because I took you away from your mother who is waiting for you in the playroom.
CHILD: (Angrily crying)
ADULT: You don't want to be here. You want to be with Mommy. But I know you can stay with me in spite of your feelings.
CHILD: I can't. I want to go now.
ADULT: I know that you can stay with me for a while. Mom is still waiting for you in the waiting room.
CHILD: I want to see her.
ADULT: I know she's still there. I asked her to wait for you.

I remember a time when I was an experienced counselor but not a very wise one. When it was recommended that June, a severely schizophrenic girl whom I was seeing, be referred from a residential program to a foster home, I proclaimed the foolishness of this plan. A Daughter of Charity turned to me and remarked that I underestimated the power of hope. She was right—the girl did just as well in the foster home as she had done in the more restrictive setting. Bill Van Ornum and I end our book on crisis counseling with a short chapter entitled, "Love, and Do What You Will." Never underestimate the power of a hopeful attitude. As you read the remaining chapters, keep June's "success" in mind and "a child shall lead the way."

5

From Anxious Action
to Symbolic Play

And you look at the other person only to find her always in a hurtful context . . . Maybe when I was little I didn't think about what I was seeing—I carried it on through life and made it the only thing I ever saw.

—A patient of Hilda Baruch

For many, the term *acting out* is synonymous with disruptive, antisocial behavior. The term actually means something else. A child bitten by a dog, who then pretends to be a dog, is a child who is acting out. A child who witnesses the brutal murder of his siblings from under a table and who later hides under tables or in closets is acting out. A child who has been thrown against the wall and who then throws himself and other objects at walls or out of windows is acting out. A child who manages to escape from a kidnapper by climbing out a window and for months afterwards plays escape games and climbs out of windows at school is acting out. The child who is trapped in a can and who later gets into trouble at school for playing around garbage cans, and who is called "stinky" by his peers, is acting out.

None of these children could tell you why they "played" these games. None connected their "play behaviors" with their earlier traumas. Many get into trouble for playing their "games."

Acting-out behavior results from the child's reproducing forgotten memories, attitudes, and conflicts in action, rather than in verbal descriptions, without conscious awareness of why he engages in these actions. In chapter 3, I discussed screen memories as unconscious motivators and described the girl who fled from the friendly but odorous adult without knowing why. This behavior, too, was acting out.

The acting-out child has been characterized as an actor, a playwright, or a novelist whose greatest artistic creation is his behavior pattern. James Masterson remarks: "His behavior is like a drama which constantly reproduces his past in the present in symbolic form in order to avoid the painful feelings associated with the conflicts of the past." The child acts instead of remembering fully with the appropriate attending emotions. While acting out is a substitute for recall, it does not have the therapeutic effect of the latter.

Some children, like those just presented, act out in the larger world, or macrosphere. Others act out in the world of fantasy play, or microsphere. Instead of playing at being a dog, they play with toy dogs, causing them to bite toy people. Instead of hiding themselves in closets, they hide miniature figures in dollhouses or boxes. Still others act out in the "autosphere," or the body. Instead of throwing dolls against the wall, they throw themselves. Instead of cutting a doll, they cut themselves.

In his play, the child becomes master of the threatening experiences rather than the mastered. Visits to the doctor are followed by playing doctor, the funeral for a loved one is followed by play burials, the kindergartner plays school upon his return home during the early weeks of school. When parents remark that their child "loves school because he plays it all the time," it's a sure sign that the child is quite anxious in school.

There is a strong tendency to repeat in play traumatic experiences in an effort to master them. This desire to master at times compels the child to reexperience the cause of his anxiety. During World War II, many children who stayed in air-raid shelters spent large portions of their playtime creating imaginary air-raid shelters, accompanied by much shooting and shouting. Children who have been exposed to the same traumatic experience play so similarly that their play is considered part of a post-traumatic syndrome that Lenore Terr has called "post-traumatic play." Post-traumatic play has been observed in children as young as fifteen months. (An infant repeatedly sat on the head of her seven-month-old sister who did not protest; both had been involved in satanic rituals where babies' heads were sat on.)

The child's ability to handle stress symbolically in fantasy scenes helps him to maintain a psychological distance from terror and rage, emotions that might otherwise be expressed directly in behavior and overwhelm the child. To maintain this distance, the play also involves some distortion. Children who have been traumatized play their "game" repetitively until they reach an emotional understanding of the connection between their play and the original psychic trauma, which many achieve only with the assistance of professional help. The play is usually a simple repetition of the experience or a simple defensive elaboration, such as identification with the aggressor, undoing, or turning the passive into the active. The child who bit her parent's legs and the child who threw objects out the bus window are examples of these whose play reveals identification with the aggressor. The play of such children is far less elaborate than the imaginative play of nontraumatized children.

In normal play that decreases anxiety, each play episode carries with it a "cure," an opportunity to identify fully with a well-meaning aggressor (parent, doctor, teacher) or an opportunity to turn the tables and spank the doll or give it shots. No one is hurt, catharsis occurs and anxiety diminishes after a few play episodes.

The repetitive play, or acting out, of the post-traumatic child, as opposed to ordinary play, does not allay the anxiety generated by the traumatic event. Terr reports that the child who barked and bit like a dog did so for more than four years. She continued her frantic play in the face of ever-increasing fears. She first feared going outdoors, then she feared her own room, believing that a dog would enter her house through the "dog door" and bite her in her sleep. At age twelve, after having played at being a dog for years, she reported terrifying dreams of being killed by a dog. In normal play, normal increments of anxiety are dissipated with each play experience. This does not occur when the child has experienced overwhelming stress.

Post-traumatic play is stimulated by a stressful, external event rather than an internal anticipated occurrence. Play, while successful in diminishing anxiety associated with minor stresses or fantasized ills (e.g., Mother will abandon me), is ineffectual in dealing with overwhelming events and their consequences. Post-traumatic play actually creates anxiety because the concrete and stereotypical nature of the play serves to re-create the traumatic event. The fact that the link between the play and the trauma remains unconscious is not surprising because this phenomenon is true in normal play. The child does not realize he plays school because he fears school or plays doctor because he fears medical procedures. It is for this reason that the counselor first comments on the doll's feelings and not on the child's feelings. Only later, when the feelings attributed to the doll have been fully discussed, can the child discuss her own feelings.

A counselor directly asks the child if he ever had an experience similar to the one he repeatedly plays. Sometimes, the child will remember. For example, the counselor can ask:

ADULT: Children can become frightened being forced to do something they didn't want to do. Have you ever been forced to do something you didn't want to do?

While such questions may prove fruitful with children who experience an isolated trauma, those who experience repeated and severe trauma require intensive and long-term counseling involving re-education and affective repair.

We have seen that children play to master anxiety. Some play in the macrosphere (jumping out windows) while others play in the microsphere (confine their fantasized activities to relatively controlled fantasy play). To understand why children differ in their response to anxiety, we need to examine the development of impulse mastery.

As a child matures, he gradually builds up and consolidates delaying and inhibiting structures. His direct actions are modified into trial actions. At the same time, he gradually shifts from expression in action to communication with words.

Stages of Impulse Mastery

The infant's mode of functioning is instant need gratification. The first most primitive problem solving of the human mind is instant impulse discharge. The first step in impulse delay is hallucinatory gratification by means of vivid fantasies of the need fulfiller. Hallucinations delay the panic reaction that accompanies need frustration. Following breast feeding, the infant plays with his mother's nipple. This play is a reenactment, a trial thinking by which a baby tries to recall the past; since he cannot recall in thoughts, he recalls in actions.

The child's first playful acts are created by mild threats to his sense of well-being. The infant hallucinates his mother's face in her absence and he repeats the touches and the sounds she makes. As he grows older, he plays games of recognition, especially games involving "blindfolds." He plays games that his first loved object, his mother, is not lost and will not abandon him. He throws and retrieves objects, plays bye-bye, peekaboo, and hide-and-seek, and pulls along pull toys. The child's self-representations in fantasy free him from depending on the actual presence of his parent. When younger, he got his refueling by periodic attention from her. Now he can delay these periods by getting symbolic refueling in his play.

Play action, the first major achievement of impulse delay, is an unstable behavior and frequently cannot be maintained. If too much stress burdens the child, play action is unsuccessful in counteracting this stress, and he returns to solutions extending to panic reactions, the first action he used to summon a rescuer.

As the child's mental and language development continues, he replaces some elements of play action with expressed fantasy and higher modes of thought. Action-fantasy, the second major step, is an initial identification with a fantasized figure in order to play at mastering the future. Fantasy is the highest form of "play action" because the action component is given up. These stages of mental development, discussed in more detail by Rudolph Ekstein, action without play, hallucination of need fulfillment, play action, pure fantasy, action-fantasy (play acting), and reality-oriented thought—are not distinctly separate from each other. One may dominate the others at any given time.

Understanding the developmental progression from acting out to thoughtful planning helps the counselor to make some sense of the presenting behavior children display during counseling sessions. Most disturbed children are unable to play freely because the play becomes interrupted by anxiety occurring in response to vague memories associated with the play. When the play is interrupted, often it is not replaced with silence or a change of topic, but by acting out. Play action may become so stimulating that it can lead to impulsive action. The unconscious conflict is not reenacted in play but is reenacted in actuality (The child climbs out the window instead of having toy people climb out the dollhouse window.) This turn of events creates technical problems for the counselor since communication via action tends to destroy the counseling situation.

The counselor can conceive of an impulsive behavior (acting out) as a *thoughtless act* and fantasy as an *actless thought*. The *thoughtful act* is one in which a child can act upon a thought in a planful manner—a major goal of counseling.

Purpose of Play

We have already seen how play helps the child to master anxiety created by threats to well-being. I have classified the other purposes of play and make-believe into six categories. These are:

1. To assimilate what goes on around the child into his present scheme of knowledge.
2. To master both himself and his environment.
3. To transcend situations.
4. To increase relatedness.
5. To express feelings.
6. To master threats to self-esteem and anxiety created by unconscious conflicts.

To Assimilate Experience

The child's play enables him to relate himself to his accumulating past by continually reorienting himself to the present. The child rehearses his past experiences, assimilating them into new perceptions, and creates new patterns of relating himself to his environment. By this ongoing process, the child advances into the future.

The child develops imagery by employing symbols to represent what he has witnessed. The development of symbolic skills depends, in part, upon a child's exposure to certain experiences. For example, when a young child plays that he is "telling an elephant to sleep," he must speak words, reconstruct from memory how an elephant behaves, or how he thinks it behaves, and experience some of the kinesthetic sensations relative to sleep. Make-believe play helps create novel environments, environments that, because they are actively created rather than passively experienced, further the development of complex memory. But because of his cognitive limitations the child's play often results in distortions of reality. For example, a child playing ice-cream truck man says, "I'm playing college," because he has overheard his father say that he worked as an ice-cream truck driver while in college.

Attempts as Mastery

Play helps the child to master himself, to achieve control over his body and its functions. Witness the games of "staring without winking," whoever winks first loses, or "whoever winks when a hand is waved over his eyes loses." The actual contest is against the reflex. The real antagonist is part of the self, mastery over one's own person, and only secondarily over another. "Who can hold their breath longer" or "who can spit farther" are other examples.

Mastery play gives the child an illusion of control. The symbolism the child makes in play, such as a stick standing for a horse, gives him unlimited possibilities for apparent mastery. Block building, climbing, running, and chasing are all mastery games. Play provides an opportunity for many more victories than could occur in real life. And victory is a victory and defeat is not a defeat because, "After all, it's only a game." Play helps a child to master his feelings of helplessness. He can be the master of his comings and goings instead of the passive victim. Cultural anthropologists have traced all modern games, whether they be simple skipping games, foot racing, or more complex games played with a bat and ball, gambling, or card playing, to an intimate association with religious or primitive rites designed to minimize tribal and personal helplessness. Children's games are no exception.

To Transcend Situations

Successful play in the microsphere can be expanded into the macrosphere. The child's rearrangements in small dimensions can be tried out on big objects and on big people. The child's play elaborates on his experience—an actual incident can be given a different arrangement and a different outcome. Playing out his past experiences and present problems puts them outside himself, enabling him to see them more clearly.

To Increase Relatedness

The child's imitation of what goes on around him reassures him that there is purpose and meaning in the adult world. His repetition of need satisfactions keep him in constant touch with those who satisfy his needs. The young child plays feeding baby, clothing baby, reading stories to baby, and so on. He makes same and different comparisons and develops the capacity for self-observation. The older child plays Daddy and what he thinks Daddy does. In addition, the child's representation of others in his play helps him to differentiate himself from these others and molds his ideal self.

To Express Feelings

Children express aggressive or erotic feelings and repeat pleasurable experiences in their play. They also display forbidden behavior in play (e.g., talking back, hitting grown-ups, messing). They dissipate guilt through play by punishing themselves symbolically (e.g., "bad girl, go to your room, you're going to get a spanking").

Games allow for the expression of sibling rivalry. The rules of the game temper the aggression. Children make a game of assaults. Bob chases Bill, growling like an animal. Often the withdrawn child pretends to be the fierce lion. Competitive games provide an opportunity for children to learn control over aggression and mitigates against their fear of losing self-control. The fusion of aggression and erotic feelings is seen in the playful wrestling that occurs among boys, the hair pulling and chasing of girls by boys, and the taunting of boys by girls.

The boy who cannot directly dispute his father's authority plays being Superman who controls and suppresses those who oppose authority. The illusion of power replaces his helplessness. The child has attained passive mastery of the helplessness inherent in being a child.

Erotic feelings are revealed in doctor play; the erotic fantasy of being the victim of a powerful man. The child fears the doctor will discover his sexual activities, playing the doctor removes this helpless feeling.

Children are easily stimulated to primitive wishes, wishes that are forbidden or impossible to fulfill. In play, they can adopt the role of the antisocial character, the seducer, or the aggressor without feeling guilty.

A child who smacks and beats her doll unmercifully may be expressing guilt feelings for having been bad and has projected these feelings onto her doll. The child also gets the feeling of power when acting as a punishing adult.

To Master Threats to Self-Esteem and
Anxiety Created by Unconscious Conflicts

In addition to mastering the anxiety associated with threats to well-being, the child also plays to master threats to self-esteem. He "becomes the other instead." Play can help to vitiate a humiliation and free the child to attend to alternative paths to solutions. (The game Monopoly was created by an unemployed salesman during the Depression.)

Similar to post-traumatic play, play created by unconscious conflicts is repetitive and does not appreciably reduce anxiety. Because expression of feelings is tension relieving, the play produces a transient discharge of anxiety, and with it an illusion of mastery. The play is reinforced and, therefore, repeated. But real maturation occurs only with mastery of the real conflicting situation.

To summarize, make-believe play and games develops out of a need to manage and control feelings and to widen the tolerable range of impacts from without, without disrupting the child's feelings of well-being, safety, or security. Play is an effort both to alter intolerable limitations and frustrations imposed from without and to defend against disruption from within. Play is also a means by which the child masters developmental challenges, assimilates his culture, and prepares for the future. If a child's play is not disrupted from within or interrupted from without, it has the effect on the child of a few good hours of sleep. After he is through, he is ready to take new chances.

Developmental Progression in Play

The counselor of the disturbed latency-aged child is often confronted with regressed play. The child hides in cupboards, buries toys in the sand, wraps up in a blanket, or feeds dolls. The child is communicating through this play. He is struggling to master earlier development challenges or to relive earlier conflicts. In order to understand these communications, the counselor needs some knowledge of the thematic play of children at different ages.

The original preplay of the infant is play around the mother and her body. Later on, play will involve fantasies about a loved one lost, a past loved one or a loved one regained, utilizing external objects, called transitional objects. The child holds onto his special blanket, a teddy bear, a doll, or a milk bottle. Holding this object helps the child to tolerate the absence of the beloved parent. Later, the child will move from the transitional object to playing with ordinary objects, but his play is rarely devoid of an object; it may be the original object, the mother, or the transitional object, the teddy bear. The object's presence is often unconscious since the child uses symbolism to represent it. Children who engage early in fantasy play are those who have had positive, nurturing experiences and who have extracted from these for fantasy expression the pleasurable aspects of basic routines with caretakers. The child incorporates good and bad images of his primary caretaker. The image of the good mother helps the child through times of stress. The ground is prepared for the child to develop a tie with the mother that lasts beyond the gratification of a need. (Psychoanalysts use the term *object-relationship* to label such ties. When they say a child has a poor object-relationship, they mean that the child's attachment wanes when his needs are not immediately satisfied.) The child has established a basic sense of trust, but his need for the transitional object can last for a long time. Some children will not part with this object until as late as seven or eight years of age.

The toddler's play is both a "self-imitative" reflection of his own behaviors and an imitation of selective attributes of his caretakers. Separation and individuation games predominate (hide-and-seek, etc.) and the child moves towards mastering feelings of autonomy.

The child next tries to be like the admired parent. Domestic scenes engross the child. The characters are fluid, with the continuity of the play in the action rather than in the nature of the characters. Hurts and misfortune predominate. Body parts are broken or damaged. The two-year-old is a mobile, into-everything child, who often falls and hurts himself, and his play depicts this behavior. When the two-year-old's early experiences include significant but not overwhelming adult aggression, the child will show identification with those aspects of the parent by hitting its own hand or hitting the "naughty doll."

The child's affection for his parents prevents his direct expression of aggression against family members. He develops a wish to please and guilt when he fails to do so.

The three-year-old imagines himself as the cause of many events and attributes to himself omnipotent powers. The boundaries between fantasy and reality are weak. The child's fantasy actions suddenly become real actions. The child who makes mud pies that he pretends to eat suddenly wants the adult to eat his productions, "Taste it, taste it!" Some children will actually attempt to eat the clay food they make during play. The term *fluctuating certainty* is used to describe such play. The child displays an inability to distinguish firmly between a pretend and a real act. A child who plays a witch suddenly becomes frightened by his own dramatizations and stops his play.

Fluctuating certainty generally disappears after age four but it can recur with the arousal of strong emotions. Witness your own behavior when you are home alone and watching a horror show on television. You are apt to check the locks on your windows and doors, a chore you did not do the evening before. Disturbed children often display fluctuating certainty—believing boogeymen to be hiding behind every tree when they go into the woods. They use direct "I" representations in their primitive play. They play "I'm a witch" rather than taking distance from the feared object and playing "she's a witch." The child who cannot distinguish between real and pretend dangers is less able to engage in fantasy play and will act out his conflicts.

The Use of Symbolism

At about age four, children discover that "things can stand for things." The child makes an analogy between two different objects or situations. One thing can take the place of another. Young children see many objects as alike. Similar sounds or movements from different objects make them "alike." A quality common to two objects that elicit the same emotion can make the two objects alike.

Almost any object with an enclosing space can, on occasion, serve as a symbol of birth curiosity. Houses, cupboards, hollow tree trunks, hiding in corners, hiding small objects, or as one child said, "a little box inside a big box," can all stand for the birth process. Concepts can become symbolized by a chance association. For example, a china doll symbolized death for one child because a playmate of his died, whose parents likened her to a "china doll."

As the child develops, he supplements and corrects his subjective ideas, moving from his personal, subjective, egocentric attitude, and corresponding fantasies, to a more socialized, objective, and realized attitude.

At around four or five, children, wanting to enjoy what grown-ups enjoy, develop compensatory fantasies of being big and doing what big people do. Their play themes become more elaborate. They play house, work, etc. In addition, they defend against the helplessness felt in needing their parents by fantasizing that their parents are not their real parents. In their search for their real parents, they must go far and wide. These fantasies kindle their interest in far-off places. They become rebellious and self-assertive. "I can get along by myself—me Tarzan!" Twin fantasies occur, and such alteregos decrease the child's reliance on his parents.

The young boy realizes that he is weak in comparison to his father's strength. But he sees that his father's power is used on his behalf. How can he obtain this same power for himself without losing the protection and security he enjoys under it? He solves the problem by identifying with Father so that Father's demands become his desires. And he thereby shares his father's power. "My dad can lick anybody!" The child's play reveals the extent of his identification.

At around age six, the capacity to experience guilt appears. Prior fantasies of taking over the roles of parents are now associated with guilty discomfort. Anxiety aroused by sexual wishes is followed by imprisonment fantasies or ones where a poor child kills the king in a faraway place. When the child becomes more independent from his parents, at age seven or eight, he begins to feel more alone in a big world. Monster fears develop, masked representations of the child's defensively mobilized aggression. The boy who dresses in an army suit and helmet, who builds a fort, and leads his soldiers to war, is the same boy who fears going up to his room alone, talks incessantly to his mother downstairs when alone in the upstairs bathroom, and sleeps on the floor by his mother's bed at night.

At around age nine or ten, the child is now ready to break free of parental control. He objects to the passive role he plays in relation to the decision-making parent. Thoughts about becoming a movie star or a professional athlete, owning a motorbike, skateboard, and other action-oriented objects occupy his mind. "I don't have to study. I am going to be a race-car driver, get rich, and buy a Porsche." Those children in conflict with their parents deflect their feelings into fantasies of defiance. They fantasize about theft and crime, which at times are acted out. Others accompany fantasies of defiance with doubt and guilt that blocks their ability to manifest the fantasy in play, thought, or action. These children are likely to develop symptoms to resolve their conflicts.

In late latency, the child's active struggle for independence causes him to fabricate a harsh, limiting or condemning parent. This fantasy of the hostile parent results in the child's placing limits on his own activities, which in turn evokes most hostility. The real parent is even more distorted and becomes a "wicked witch." These feelings can be transferred onto other adults who control the child's life.

A thirteen-year-old girl came to counseling and spent the better part of her hour telling the counselor how mean and awful her principal was. He didn't like her, never took her side, hated kids, should be in some other business, etc. This went on for months, but gradually gave way to discussing problems in her home. Some months later, the counselor met this principal and was impressed with his warmth and genuine concern for children.

The later phase of latency is characterized by a softening of the conscience. Fantasies contain figures that represent people: monsters and ghosts are replaced by robbers. The child can accept his urges more, and so he can represent his parents with symbols that are less disguised. The child becomes more aware of the world and his place in it.

By the time the child reaches twelve, he no longer makes much use of fantasy for drive discharge. His fantasy now involves thinking about present and future roles. Drives, once handled by repression and fantasy production, gradually reassert themselves. Latency wavers, puberty appears, and adolescence begins.

The Structure of Latency

Fantasy and the stage of development called *latency* are intertwined. The term latency was applied to that period of development when the drive urgency of earlier periods seemed to vanish. The child became calm, interested in learning, and more easily socialized. Freud declared that latency occurred when "the sexual drives diminish in strength." When analyzing adults, Freud noted that they could recall sexual feelings and fantasies both prior and subsequent to this period, but not during it.

Observations of children who were in latency revealed that they arrived at this state as a result of an active process of self-organization in the face of social demands. The child in normal latency has developed a host of defenses to mitigate against regressed functioning.

Sublimation, obsessive-compulsive activities, doing and undoing, reaction formation, and repression are defenses the child employs to produce the latency state. These defenses will be discussed more fully in chapter 6.

The previously messy child now keeps his possessions neatly arranged, his dresser drawers in order, collects stamps, wants clean clothes for school, plays repetitive and relatively meaningless games, constructs elaborate forts, and organizes Barbie dolls. Yet, if the child's drives are strongly stimulated by seductive adults, the child's "latency" can quickly vanish. If environmental seduction is not extreme, the child handles this stimulation by organizing a "structure of latency." The child quells drive stimulation by dismantling the memories of stimulating events, and the fears they arouse, by reorganizing and synthesizing them into *highly symbolized and displaced stories*. By living through these stories in his latency play, the child finds a safety valve for his heightened drives.

This ability to employ fantasy to mitigate drive expression depends heavily on the capacity to form masking symbols, which in turn requires abstract thinking, delay, and repression. The child who can use masking symbols can handle conflicts or feelings that cannot be experienced consciously because of the strong fears or intense feelings they arouse. The child who, angry at a parent, develops a fantasy of "consuming flames that burn down a house and kill a mean mother," is one who is able to transform anger into a symbolic story.

Children who have not achieved these developmental advancements, either because of intellectual limitations or exposure to continual traumatic stress, are unable to develop the structure of latency. These are the children referred for counseling. They also are children who may not be able to play.

Why Some Children Don't Play

Some children enter a counselor's office or an equipped playroom and never really play with the materials provided them. They want to ride in the toy trucks, play catch with the counselor, throw the sand in the sandbox or pour water in it, make a mess of the finger paints, climb on the furniture, and shortly thereafter want to leave the room because it is too confining. Efforts to get them to play make-believe with the miniature-world toys fail dismally. They do not know how to play in the microsphere and their macrosphere play is primitive and undeveloped. Often they simply mimic the behavior of a superhero or supervillain who runs around stabbing and shooting everybody. Upon close examination, these children are still playing in the autosphere with the supervillains merely extensions of their own small selves. Why did their play never progress beyond this point?

What if the environment that surrounds a child is a confused jumble of stress-producing images that bombard his immature nervous system? Only when the child interacts with novel stimuli that are within his capacity for mastery will he continue to show interest, alertness, and positive emotional responses to them. When material is presented too rapidly or in too chaotic a fashion, without an opportunity for the child to assimilate it effectively, he will startle and become frightened. If confronted for an excessive period of time with a high rate of unassimilable material, the child will both act out and shut down.

If a child's past experiences were stressful and disorganizing, he will resist reorganizing them. They are too painful or too difficult to manage and to recall. Consequently, the emotional concomitants of these experiences persist as increasingly incongruous parts of the self and compromise the child's ability to play and also to mature. The child who finds it difficult to play out his past cannot put these experiences outside himself to see them more clearly. He cannot transcend the actual situation in which he finds himself. He will not use play to imitate what goes on around him and therefore he cannot reassure himself as to the purpose and meaning of the adult world. He cannot use play to express feelings because the initiation of playful behavior is associated with painful affects. There are no pleasurable experiences to repeat, only unpleasurable ones, and these tend to get repeated in action rather than in play because play development is disrupted by high anxiety levels. Play produces anxiety rather than masters it.

In his mother's absence, a baby hallucinates his mother's reassuring and loving face in order to mitigate the anxiety that accompanies her short absences. But what if the mother's face produces anxiety? What if the mother is an angry, disturbed woman whose baby is a source of frustration to her or a reminder of her mistakes, and who is angry at the child every time she has to feed him? What if she angrily props the baby in a chair and shoves the bottle in its mouth? What if she never soothes or comforts the baby, and her only contact with him is to feed him when he is hungry and change him when he is wet, tasks that she actively resents? The answer to these questions is the following: the baby will experience extremely ambivalent feelings about his mother. Hallucinating her image will produce anxiety and rage. A baby who is left unattended not only cries when he is in need but also angrily protests when his needs go unmet for long periods. Eventually, if all remains the same, these protests turn to despair and then to apathy. Such a child will not hallucinate an image that is not need satisfying. The child's very first play behavior, the prototype for later play, never fully develops. If the infant does hallucinate his mother's face, the image will quickly fade, establishing early the prototype for play interrupted by anxiety.

Action is an attempt to master reality immediately, to make it subservient to the needs of the individual. In contrast, play action delays action in reality. The "play" of traumatized children is sometimes closer to action than to play action. Since post-traumatic play is observed in children who are capable of ordinary play in other situations, no wonder we see an absence of symbolic play altogether in the severely and repeatedly traumatized child.

Does Play Reflect Reality?

Many adults assume a direct correspondence between a child's play and his experience. If the child plays out a scene with a "mean, cruel mommy doll" beating a baby doll, these adults assume that the child has experienced similar beatings. These adults fail to appreciate the nature of children's moral development. As discussed in chapter 2, during one phase of development, children are harsh punishers who punish more for the consequences of an action than for the intentions of the actor. If a child breaks teacups, he should be punished more than the child who breaks only one cup, even when the ten were broken accidentally and the one purposefully. The child at this stage has internalized the harsh and judgmental aspects of his parents' personalities as separate from their protective-loving aspects, and only later, with increasing maturity, will the child fuse these disparate images. Terence Moore, after observing the play of normal four- to six-year-olds, made this remark: "Parents are commonly made far more punitive than any real parent would be, and many children take obvious pleasure in portraying them thus." For example:

CHILD: She's got to stay in the bath all night and sleep there.

CHILD: (Child makes father doll smack child doll hard) She won't have a bath, and no jelly, and she's got to go to bed. Then mother comes and smacks her. (Batters and squeezes child doll with mother doll in a violent assault)

CHILD: The father—he's going to fight with mother—and then with the children. He kills them and eats them up, and they are all dead.

Young children think of the characters in their play at any given moment as either good or bad. And without comment, the child's play will reveal a sudden change of heart. "Now he's good," "Now he's naughty." Such children have difficulty answering the question, "Is Daddy mostly good or mostly bad?" Only the very mature preschooler can answer with, "A little bit bad and a little big good." This leads us into a discussion of the child's use of play materials.

Identification with Dolls

When a child draws parallels between the dolls in a counselor's office or playroom and his own family, some measure of identification has taken place. Some children will even express complete identification with one of the dolls by giving it his name. Typically, however, identification of the dolls with the self and family members is less explicit and develops as play proceeds. Children can reveal total identification, where one doll represents a total person (self or other), but more often they reveal partial identification. Different aspects of the person are projected onto different dolls. Thus, one doll may represent the good self (or other) and another doll the bad self (or other). One doll can become the independent self while the other the dependent self.

Identification with the parent-dolls is also of the partial kind. The child uses them to represent particular aspects of his images of a parent, and he often distorts and caricatures these images in order to express accumulated affect. Consequently, the actions of parents in the child's play do not necessarily resemble the behavior of the child's real parents. Often, the aggression expressed towards them in play can also be intended for the persecutors within.

Dolls can also represent an idealized image of the perfect parent as a wish fulfillment. Consequently, the child whose domestic play is exclusively nurturing may be simply incapable of imagining anything outside her own protected environment, or she may be defending against any thoughts of badness, reflecting a wish fulfillment, or in a phase where a nurturing environment is extremely important to her.

To conclude, no consistent relationship exists between play content and real life. A child's fantasy play fulfills different needs at different times. The diagnostic value of play lies not ferreting out what happens at home, but in detecting both the child's conflicts, and how he is handling them, and his dominant concerns.

The Oscillating Nature of Normal Play

The normal child's play typically reveals clear alternation of positive with negative feelings. A child initiates play by spanking a doll in a mild and playful fashion, slightly later the play becomes more aggressive; the play then meets with parental retaliation, which becomes increasingly more violent. But the sequence of play is interrupted again and again by harmonious family life where children are fed, clothed, and put to bed. Parallel with this oscillation of affect, the play swings back and forth between realistic and unrealistic fantasy as a result of fluctuating certainty. As fantasy becomes freer, aggression is released; this aggression produces anxiety that some children moderate by momentarily turning back toward reality. When made anxious by their play, they can: (1) make it more realistic and derive reassurance from the knowledge that reality has limits that fantasy lacks; (2) make explicit references to real life; or (3) step back and view the play as nothing but play (e.g., "These are just toys"). Another option is to distance themselves from frightening fantasies by making the play not more but less realistic. The healthy child uses distance to make the play so obviously impossible that it looks ridiculous. It becomes a slapstick farce. Because this play is so unreal, it enables the player to laugh at his fears. The pleasure in such humor lies in the child's realization that he is strong enough to master dangers, that the clown will survive his outrageous misfortunes. But for the truly traumatized child, there is no such knowledge. He cannot use distance in this fashion, but instead uses it to create a never-never land where, deadly serious, he spends as much of his time as possible.

Pathological Use of Distancing

Many children, particularly those who have been severely and repeatedly traumatized, and these labeled psychotic, display very little make-believe play. But when they do, it's often make-believe about faraway battles, space monster, evil emperors, and brave warriors. They seem to have stayed in those faraway places they sought when first disillusioned by their parents. The child uses the monsters as the personification and receptacle of all his bad impulses, which enables him to establish distance from them and deny them as his own. The child also puts the monster out in some distant space, far away from him. The undesirable, unconscious, forbidden, and repressed are sent far away. Anxiety is defended against by distance.

CHILD: Here's a witch killing people, cowboys eating people up! (Child becomes anxious, loses distance, remarks:) It's just a story.

CHILD: (Very anxious child asked to tell a story introduces her task by immediately distancing) I don't know any stories, but I'll tell one that isn't true.

Dragons and monsters have always been the basis of early conscience development; the small child experiences the parent as both threatening and punitive, and as magically omnipotent and giving. Normally the child's early images become modified and synthesized into developing moral structures. As the internalization of values and identification with parents proceed, the archaic, distorted features recede. In contrast, the disturbed child is unable to synthesize the good and bad parental images and, thus, remains with only the primitive precursors of a conscience, derived from a period in development where loving and hating are fused rather than synthesized. His fantasies reflect this integrative failure.

Such children suffer from certain integrative deficits. Their personalities are composed of disconnected and fragmented parts (split-off parts of themselves). Some children distance from their problems by maintaining a strong, though not total, commitment to a self-centered, illusory world of pleasure. Yet even these fantasies, upon close inspection, actually reflect terrors being denied.

Martha, a nine-year-old girl, spent most of her waking life daydreaming about life on another planet where a cyclops and his wolf were her guardians. There was an abundance of food, beautiful scenery, and a temperate climate. In art class, Martha would draw aspects of this world and each drawing would be accompanied by gleeful laughter and much pleasure—the only times she showed pleasurable emotions. She involved another girl in this fantasy, with both of them planning to live in such a place when they got older.

One of the major functions of her fantasies was to fully separate pleasure from nonpleasure and to keep the pleasure world intact. Martha's fantasy life filled each session and tolerated little interference. Any references to her daily life experiences were viewed as irrelevant intrusions. In fact, if her life became more troubling, her fantasies would intensify. Denial was used extensively to split off the intrusive reality. Unlike less disturbed children who can allow painful themes to be elaborated upon and dealt with in therapy, Martha resurrected and intensified these stereotypical fantasies in the presence of even mild anxiety. On one occasion when I (as Martha's counselor) became frustrated with both her insistence that she was as powerful as any Planet X person and her denial of fearful feelings, I challenged her to arm wrestle (a rather untherapeutic procedure). She of course lost, but explained that her right hand was her weakest. When she again lost using her left hand, she responded that her left hand was more tired than usual and that she would win on another day; she then became agitated and left the session. Needless to say, confrontation only bolstered her defense.

I had the opportunity to follow Martha's development over a ten-year period. While distance remained her primary defense against anxiety, its use became more adaptive. She developed an interest in the occult and in ancient Egyptian artworks. She went on to a local junior college to study archaeology.

Materials to Use in Counseling

Before leaving the topic of play, I would like to mention the materials a counselor should have available to promote verbalization through fantasy. In general, most of the materials a counselor needs can be stored in a suitcase. Most children tend to play with a limited number of materials. Play materials should include: a supply of hand puppets (among them should be a wizard, to make interpretations; a snake, for phallic aggression; and an alligator, for oral aggression), a lion or tiger, a hen and rooster, a cow, a timid animal such as a rabbit, several superheroes, a witch, and people to represent a family; a dollhouse with small family figures; a doctor kit; baby bottles; some large dolls; a cape; a small blanket; small plastic animals, including dinosaurs; clay (plasticene); Magic Markers and paper; glue; cardboard (for making figures); string and tape; scissors; a toy telephone; a bounce-back punching bag with good-guy/bad-guy on each side. In the initial sessions with aggressive children, a pegboard and hammer set, little tanks and trucks, little soldiers, a Nerf ball, a Velcro dart board with Velcro balls, dominoes, blocks, and a small blackboard can be added to the other materials.

6

From Anxious Action to Mature Defenses

To take arms against a sea of troubles. . .

—William Shakespeare

In this chapter, I list and define the various defense mechanisms children use to manage anxiety and to maintain a sense of well-being. For heuristic purposes, the defenses are divided into two categories: primitive and mature. After defining the defenses, I present ways to encourage children to use the more mature defenses. These procedures include teaching them to play, to change their mood, and to develop mechanisms of restraint. The difference between uncovering repressed memories and structuring memory is featured as traumatized children misperceive and distort reality when under stress, particularly if traumatized before the development of speech.

When we experience something that makes us anxious, we tend to find ways to exclude the experience from conscious awareness should we experience it again. This process has been called selective inattention, dissociation, or repression. This mechanism helps us to avoid situations that could make us anxious. No one thinks clearly when anxious, and the discomfort anxiety causes is avoided whenever possible. Unfortunately, it is not possible to avoid many experiences, particularly inner experiences. We can't avoid our own unacceptable impulses. Consequently, we develop inner strategies to avoid anxiety stimulated both from within and from without. These strategies are called *defense mechanisms*.

Frequently, we hear one person say to another before a confrontation, "Now don't get defensive, but you hurt my feelings with that remark." When the offender simply says, "I feel bad, I really blew it making that tactless remark, I realize now that it hurt," he is not being defensive. He feels bad that he hurt his friend, but what is done is done. If he says, "That's not how I intended that remark; you misinterpreted what I said," he is being defensive; that he had not intended to hurt his friend is not relevant. His friend was hurt and he is *denying* that fact. If he says, "I didn't mean to hurt you, what I meant was. . . ," he is now trying to *minimize* his friend's pain. He could combine minimizing with *blaming* by suggesting to his friend that he is too sensitive, that others would not have been hurt by the remark. Or, he could claim that this is unlike anything he has ever done before. He is now using *negation* to avoid his anxious feelings. Suppose he takes every opportunity to compliment his friend during the rest of the evening. He is now trying to undo the effects of his tactless remark. The anxiety he feels is decreased by his *undoing* efforts. Or, he could explain to his friend that he recently became aware of his tactless behavior and that he is taking corrective action through a planned series of readings on proper etiquette. He is now using *intellectualization* as a defense. He controls his anxious feelings by thinking about them instead of experiencing them.

But suppose he felt nauseous all evening, could not eat, felt tired, or got a headache. Now he has used *somatization* as a defense. He has converted the painful affect into bodily sensations. He could also decide that his friendship with this individual is not that important. "So who cares if I hurt his feelings!" This defense is called *rationalization*. In the future, he could *avoid* being in situations where he would run into his friend and reexperience the embarrassment of his tactless remark. He could use a combination of defenses. Initially, he could minimize his remark and avoid his friend in the future.

All of us behave like the insulter on numerous occasions. But if we never admit to ourselves any wrongdoing, because we cannot tolerate the anxiety of being imperfect, we would be viewed as being very defensive and possibly as maladjusted. But if we had no defenses, and each time we got anxious we also became overwhelmed and could not function, we would also be maladjusted.

The well-adjusted person uses defenses sparingly when faced with low levels of anxiety. When faced with high anxiety, he will use them initially and then gradually drop their use as the anxiety state becomes more manageable. When a child dies, a parent's first reaction is denial.

Only with time does the parent accept the finality of the child's death, and even then the child's room may remain unchanged for a long period.

Most of us are defensive when our anxiety is high, but after the passage of time we reevaluate our behavior and give up our defensive posture. Later we admit our mistake to ourselves and resolve not to repeat it. *This fact is very important.* Rarely will an individual whose defenses are made clear to him during a counseling session give up his defenses at that time. Each time the counselor points out how the client has used a defense to avoid experiencing a feeling, the client will resist accepting this fact. He most likely will increase the use of the defense for a time because his anxiety has increased following the interpretation.

Only with time and repeated revelations will the client begin to accept that he makes use of certain defenses to contain his anxiety. Counselors call this gradual process of acceptance *working through.* The client comes to accept certain truths about how he deals with anxiety, truths that he has resisted accepting; after a time, he will also learn the reasons why he became so anxious in the first place. Sometimes unacknowledged wishes that one part of ourselves finds unacceptable cause anxiety, and other times anxiety results from repressed traumatic experiences. In addition, the client needs time to replace these maladaptive defenses with more appropriate ones. Should the tactless person become a counseling client, he might want to know why he was so anxious when he made a mistake or why he made so many tactless remarks to his friends.

I need to emphasize that defenses are adaptive responses to anxiety. We all need defenses to keep anxiety from overwhelming us and disrupting our functioning. At times it is helpful to deny anxiety. A mother's initial denial of her newborn's diagnosed disability helps her to maintain the maternal behavior necessary to insure bonding to her child. But if she continues to deny her child's disability and pushes him to excel beyond his ability, then her denial is maladaptive. Similarly, the mother who, six months after her child's death, still hopes that her child will return to his unchanged room is now pathologically denying her child's death.

But what about a child who denies the reality of his rejecting parent's behavior? Is this denial pathological? I think not. This child has to deny reality, otherwise he will be overcome with fears for his own safety. He has to deny to survive! I will now turn to a detailed presentation of the various defenses with specific reference to children.

The Most Primitive Defenses

Introjection: When a child is made anxious by his mother's departure, he creates an inner image of her in his mind to soothe himself; he *introjects* parts of her as a defense against anxiety. His sense of well-being and security depends upon his utilizing this mechanism of defense. The sum total of a child's introjections contributes to his identification with adult caretakers. A child's identifications can be witnessed in his immature behavior and play; when he feeds his doll he is identifying with his mother's caring behaviors. When he spanks his doll he is identifying with her punishing behavior.

Denial: Denial is directed against acknowledgment of frightening or objectionable impulses, feelings, or preoccupations. It is a common defense of young children. "I didn't do it." "I'm not afraid." "I'm not angry." Denial is not lying. The child firmly believes that what he is asserting is true. But after mulling things over and reaffirming his self-worth, as well as getting some distance from the situation, often he can begin to accept that the action he denied did, in fact, really happen. Constant denial is a sign of immaturity. The child can deny in words or in acts, or he can deny in fantasy. A child's defense structure sometimes is revealed in his fantasies and stories.

CHILD (3½): The little rabbit went into the lady's garden to eat her lettuce. He didn't go into her garden to eat it. He goes into the woods to eat it. He chews the lettuce all up. He doesn't eat any more lettuce at all. He goes home to bed. He sleeps. He goes out to play.

CHILD (4): Once the bear had a fire. And he got burned in the fire and had to go to the hospital. And he got better and had a new house. There was no flames in it. There was no burner burning. There were no stoves working. There was no heat coming out of the radiator. There were no rats in the basement. The end.

In the first story, the child attempts to deny the basic oral needs of the rabbit, while in the second, the child denies the initially frightening image of damage by fire. The second story is even more revealing when you discover that the child has just learned about an upcoming move to a new home.

More sophisticated denial in fantasy appears when the child's fantasies are the complete reversal of the real situation. The child who is frightened of the lion becomes the lion tamer. The child also transforms anxiety-provoking objects into friendly beings who either protect or obey him. Sometimes the child's fantasy becomes a play action invested with immense meaning. He wears a Daniel Boone hat or a Rambo shirt and becomes extremely upset if he cannot wear this protective garment. The garment has the same effect as a daydream of omnipotence, except that reliance on the garment is a more primitive mechanism because its effectiveness depends upon its concrete presence.

Negation: When a two-year-old is embarrassed each time he soils his pants, he may deal with this unacceptable part of himself in denying his lack of toilet skill by making another child (or doll) the one who lacks this skill. "This is not like me." Many of us negate parts of ourself. The child may not only negate unacceptable parts of himself, he may split off these parts so that they are never integrated into his sense of self. This is called splitting.

Splitting: When a child feels the pressure to express a forbidden impulse, he can suppress its expression and perhaps eventually repress its awareness. It goes underground. In the course of such repression, the anxiety arousing aspects of what is repressed becomes "split-off" from the child's conscious image of himself. Splitting serves the purpose of alienating from his self-image those parts of his feelings that are anxiety ridden. But when repression fails and anxiety is generated, the child's feeling is not that "I feel this emotion," but "Something alien to me operates within me!" "The bad me made me do it."

Splitting, then is a form of negation: "This is not me." Negation also applies to the play actions the child displays. Children often display rather marked breakdowns in this defense. For example, if a child, in his magic omnipotence, accidentally hits another child too hard and sees that he has inflicted pain, his negation quickly disappears and he either displays wildly aggressive behavior or the opposite, instant lameness.

Splitting during play is a normal phenomenon. The play figure who kills or messes is not the child himself; as a result, the child is free from guilt or shame since he does not feel responsible for the action of the play figures. Overreliance on splitting to overcome anxiety, however, is pathological. A child can split off so many unacceptable parts of himself ("This is not me," "That is not me," etc.) that he has difficulty functioning without confusion. He appears fragmented.

Early in development a child splits his image of his caretakers. The same adults can be viewed one time as all good and another time as all bad. When they are givers, they are good, and when deniers, they are bad. Eventually the developing child learns to fuse the two images of the same person so that the person is no longer seen as all good or all bad—the person is seen independent of his function as a need satisfier. Yet, we never truly outgrow the tendency to split. Romantic love also involves a similar process. Many lovers only see certain parts of each other. Others see each lover more objectively and often wonder what the lovers see in each other.

Externalization: When the child negates his split-off parts, he is externalizing them. Someone else becomes the bad parts the child denies and splits off from his sense of self. I will talk more about this defense in chapter 7, because many children externalize their unacceptable parts onto the counselor. He becomes the stupid one, the retard, and the counselor finds himself bombarded with insults.

Projections: A child is projecting when he attributes to another person the wishes or impulses he feels but which create anxiety in response to his internalized parental standards. The child, therefore, blames another for possessing these impulses. Often the child fears the counselor because he has projected his own unacceptable anger onto the counselor. He also fears his own parent for the same reason. The child often sees his parents as more rejecting than they are because he projects his retaliating anger onto them.

> A small group of children are watching television. A commercial for women's bras comes on and Jim hits Phil for no apparent reason. Jim is asked why he did that and he replies, "Philip said a nasty thing." The adult seated with the children heard no such comment from Phil. The staff hypothesized that Jim was sexually stimulated by the bra commercial and projected these feelings to Phil whom he then punished for having them.

Psychologists use projective techniques, such as the *Rorschach Test* (the child tells what ink blots look like) or the *Thematic Apperception Test* (the child tells stories to pictures) to measure need states. The child projects his needs and feeling states into these relatively ambiguous stimuli. If he sees violent angry images or tells violent stories, he is felt to harbor violent and angry feelings. Projections also abound in children's fantasies. The king is the one with the angry bad impulses, not the good knight who slays him to free the people from tyranny.

Identification with the aggressor: In addition to incorporation of positive images of another, children also introject the threatening features of the parent. Being the threatener is less anxiety producing than being the person threatened. In the beginning, the child tends to split these two images, but later he fuses them into an identification with a prohibitive-protective figure as he learns that his parents' discipline is in his best interests. The child with a rejecting, critical parent will maintain this self-critical incorporation because it helps the child feel powerful. The incorporation is self-enhancing. At the same time, however, it is self-defeating because it makes the child feel worthless. Consequently, the child develops a method to handle this double-edged sword. He protects himself from external self-criticism by both *externalizing* his negative self-image and *projecting* his unacceptable impulses onto others. This process is called *identification with the aggressor.*

> A three-year-old came for a preplacement visit to a therapeutic preschool. In the playroom, the child immediately hit a baby doll with a drumstick, saying, "The baby is not going to bed, she needs a whipping." Then, dissatisfied with the drumstick, she asked the interviewer for his belt so she could beat the bad baby. Then she wanted to take the doll with her and bit the interviewer when he went to retrieve it from her.

Provocative behavior: When a child expresses his hostility against another by inducing the other to attack him first, his hostility appears as a self-defense. In this way he can express his hostility without internal conflict. The provocative behavior, however, may also occur as a defense against feeling guilty. By getting another to inflict punishment upon him the child can reduce or eliminate guilt feelings without becoming conscious of their nature.

Displacement: Expressing an emotion towards a substitute object is displacement. The child attacks Sally when he is really been angered by Bill (who is larger). The child who is angry at his mother becomes easily annoyed by his teacher's instructions. Displacement abounds in children's fantasies. The wicked witch stands for mother, the evil king for father, the wolf for himself. Fairy tales play on children's tendency to displace feelings. In chapter 5, I talked about *masking symbols*. Fairy tales are full of such symbols. When the child denies his fears in reality by making himself the lion tamer, the lion he tames is not always a lion; often it is the masked symbol for his father.

Regression: When a child reverts to earlier, less-mature patterns of behavior when overcome by anxiety, he is regressing in an effort to use previously successful coping strategies. Two of the most popular foods in hospitals are milktoast and oatmeal, foods many of us ate as children. Under the stress of hospitalization, earlier satisfactions help to ease our fears. Under stress, children will revert to more disruptive behavior, baby talk, thumb sucking, soiling, tantrums, and inability to understand schoolwork they knew earlier (cognitive regression). They revert to methods of need satisfaction they found successful in the past, and to the use of less mature defenses. Witness the following story:

CHILD (age 9): He wanted to play the violin but he didn't know how. He asked his mother to teach him. She was too busy. He asked for her help, but she couldn't help, so he got out his silly putty and made snakes.

Regression occurs in counseling when the child wants to mess the finger paints, to be pushed in a wagon, curls up on the counselor's chair, or sucks his thumb. With aggressive, macho children, such behavior may signal progress in developing trust. They have stopped inhibiting their needs for affection.

Oscillating behavior: Very often, both the defense and the direct expression of the unacceptable impulse occur simultaneously. A child may be excessively concerned about keeping his dresser drawers neat and orderly, and yet leave his clothes all over the floor. The child presents a picture of extreme disorder and extreme order, oscillating between defiant messiness and an anxious, self-righteous perfectionism. An article of clothing out of order in the drawer causes panic while the same article is discarded on the floor after it is worn.

Many children referred to counseling utilize exclusively the defense mechanisms just reviewed. The children deny their shortcomings, fail to take responsibility for their feelings, split off and attribute their faults and wishes to others, and retreat to less mature behavior under stress. As a result, they have almost no energy to meet developmental challenges. They cannot move to the stage of initiative where a relatively calm, impulse-free state is needed to initiate and complete the tasks required to become the industrious children of the next stage.

The More Mature Defenses

When I speak of more mature defenses, I speak of those defenses whose use results in less resistance to socialization and educational practices. Their use is more adaptive. For example, the child who converts his anxious feelings into stomachaches may feel physically stressed and could develop an ulcerated condition. Nevertheless, he will elicit more caring feelings from adults than he would if he consistently used projection and displacement.

Somatization: When a child converts anxious feelings into bodily symptoms, it is called *somatization* or *inversion*. Somatization is a widely used defense against anxiety. Anywhere from 20 to 30 percent of adults who visit a medical doctor develop physical symptoms resulting from stress rather than from physical causes.

Avoidance: The child can avoid talking about painful feelings or facing painful situations. If afraid of the dark, he may act up at bedtime, trying to avoid sleeping alone. Avoidance can be subdivided into *inhibitions, restrictions, and distancing.* The child inhibits the expression of forbidden impulses and thereby constricts his functioning. In restriction, he limits his activities to ones he predicts will cause no anxiety. In inhibition, the child is avoiding painful feelings from within, while in restriction he is avoiding painful feelings stimulated by outside sources. Most aggressive children are avoiders, fearing failure, confusion, punishment, censure, etc. They also inhibit their affectionate feelings because these wishes also cause anxiety. Children who distance from anxiety are those who make use of masking symbols to put what is feared in faraway places. Angry parents turn into angry monsters who dwell on distant planets.

Reversal: When the child attempts to mask anxious feelings by displaying behaviors seemingly incompatible with anxiety, he is using *reversal* as a defense. He may laugh or joke when hurt or punished. He may profess love when he feels hate.

Turning feelings against one's self: Instead of expressing anger or hatred against another, the hatred is turned against the self in the form of self-hate and self-accusation. Similarly, the feeling of love for another can be withdrawn and turned into self-love. Many aggressive children display marked self-love, often called self-centeredness or narcissism.

Undoing: When a child attempts to recant or undo the possible effects of an anxiety-producing thought or act the defense is called *undoing.* This defense is most often employed when the child feels both anger and affection for the same person. It can also be used when the child both hates and fears the same person. The child who angers his mother and then offers to make amends by running errands could be employing undoing to handle his anxiety. The child has a hostile wish toward his baby sister and then continually checks the child to see if she is all right. He is "undoing" the possible effects of his hostile wishes. A child's removal of stones from a playground could be his effort to undo the hostility he feels in seeing them as dangerous objects. A child who destroys parental figures in his play and then rescues them in an ambulance is displaying undoing in his play. Childhood and superstition are full of undoing games. "Step on a crack, break your mother's back." The dreaded consequence of spilling salt is annulled by throwing a pinch over the left shoulder. Magical expiation has been used in religion since recorded history.

Overcompensation: The child makes use of an acceptable attitude to cover up an unacceptable one. Pity may cover up unconscious cruelty, shyness can serve as a defense against exhibitionism, or boastful conceit against feelings of inferiority. The conscious attitude is the polar opposite of the repressed unacceptable tendency.

Reaction formation: The child substitutes an acceptable feeling for an unacceptable one. He represses his angry jealous feelings toward his baby sister and instead substitutes solicitous behavior in its place. Children who were once fascinated with bodily functions and talked endlessly about "poopies, snot, and pee-pee" now vehemently profess disgust with such talk. Reaction formation helps guarantee against expression of an unacceptable impulse by reinforcement of the opposite trend.

Rationalization: The child made anxious by failing to accomplish a task or to please another person now reinterprets the situation to excuse his behavior.

CHILD (age 5): A cowboy rode a bucking horse and the horse ate the saddle. So the boy gave his horse to some Indians because Indians ride bareback.

Sublimation: In sublimation, the unacceptable impulse attains a certain amount of direct expression in a socially acceptable manner. The girl who desires to show off her body finds an outlet for these needs in dance or drama. The sexually curious child reads about sex instead of touching the opposite sex.

Anticipation: Very successful adults anticipate what will make them anxious and plan accordingly. It is the one defense that is consciously employed. Most disturbed children are excellent anticipators, but instead of planning an appropriate action to handle the anxiety, they avoid the feared situation. Public speaking, competition, or new social situations make us all anxious, so some of us take planful actions to handle the situations. Others of us simply avoid them and thereby restrict our opportunities for growth. Disturbed children do not know how to develop a plan or to carry the plan through to completion.

The Development of More Mature Defenses

I have organized defenses into the two chief categories of primitive and mature defenses. A summary list appears below:

Primitive	*Mature*
Incorporation	Somatization
Denial	Avoidance
Minimizing	Inhibition
Blaming	Restriction
Negation	Distancing
Splitting	Reversal
Externalization	Turning anger against
Projection	one's self
Identification with	Undoing
aggressor	Overcompensation
Provocative behavior	Reaction formation
Displacement	Sublimation
Regression	Anticipation

This organization of defenses suggests that the maladjusted child would progress if he made more use of the defenses in the "mature" category. Their use does not mean that the children are not free from problems. Quite the contrary, a school-phobic child or a child with ulcers can be quite disturbed. But he is typically more socialized.

The word *mature* is also used because some of these defenses help move the child from early stages of impulse expression into the period of development often characterized by a period of latency. These defenses help convert the child's behavior from the undifferentiated, massive drive discharge typical of regressed behavior (often referred to as anal-sadistic) into the controlled child who can profit from learning experiences. Charles Sarnoff labels this group of defenses that modify aggressive behavior into states of calm assertiveness as the *mechanisms of restraint*. Among this group are the defenses of sublimation, undoing, reaction formation and repression. Also utilized are obsessive-compulsive activities and symbol and fantasy formation. It is the activation of these mechanisms that produce the psychological state of calm, pliability, and educability that characterizes latency and allows the child to adapt to a world that requires social compliance and knowledge acquisition.

Building Defenses

The disturbed child needs to make more effective use of the defenses he employs and to develop more mature defenses. A disruptive child immediately attempts to mess up the toys in the counselor's office, accompanying his efforts with the following chatter:

CHILD: I'm playing a game called "wreck everything." I'll wreck everything, then I'll be even stronger. It will make me even stronger, lifting weights makes me feel strong, too. I like doing things that are dangerous. If I fall, that wouldn't hurt me. I'm wrecking the "house." Bare naked, eee, eee, ha ha ha, make me angry (baby talk); me wreck it, hee, hee.

The child proceeds to tell "playground jokes" about urination, defecation, and sexuality. The child's play (crashing cars together, dropping dolls off cliffs, burning down houses with people trapped inside) is chaotic and continually interrupted by his own thoughts and by flights into action or new play. Other than the most primitive defenses of "fight or flight," he appears to have no well-developed defenses against the expression of forbidden impulses.

In addition to exercising limit setting communications, counseling needs to include efforts to help the child build a defensive structure. Efforts to build *displacement* would include encouraging expression of anger towards toy objects. The counselor can model hand puppets talking angrily to one another or miniature figures in sociodramatic situations. The counselor can draw soldiers fighting (stick figures for poor drawers). Forts can be built from blocks and toy soldiers employed to defend them. Toilet play can be modeled with miniature dolls bathing and toileting.

Efforts to teach *undoing* can include using a toy ambulance to rescue injured victims of the child's displaced aggression. Toy fire engines can rescue the people from the child's pretend fires. Army medical corps men or Red Cross dolls can rush injured soldiers to medical stations. Injured dolls can be fixed by the doctor kit, hugged, and given tender loving care.

Distancing is encouraged by labeling the male dolls as kings, witches, sorcerers, or robots and the destroying child as the barbarian warrior or knight who slays the sorcerer. By encouraging the child to displace and distance his anger from actions into play actions, we are also encouraging splitting. By verbalizing that the "lion has a right to be angry because the tiger attacked him," the child can split in his play and feel less overwhelmed by anxiety.

If the child begins to split adults into good or bad, or begins to split a preferred adult (sometimes the counselor), oscillating between clinging independence and angry defiance, this should be viewed as progress. Nevertheless, the extremely jealous, demanding child can be more difficult to manage than the indifferent, distrustful child and many children are "lost" during this stage of treatment.

With children who display some defenses (variable controls), the counseling effort is directed at reinforcing defenses used and introducing new ones for possible use.

CHILD: Once there was a witch who killed everyone in town and a burglar came and killed the witch. And a policeman came and killed the burglar. Then another burglar took the policeman to jail. Then one man, the chief of police, that was me, I killed them all. And I ate them all—meat and blood and guts. (Child leaves play area to run around the room)

Here the child attempts to use both distancing and undoing, but they both break down. The policeman is not strong enough to overcome the burglars, and the child, identified with both the burglars and the police, becomes himself, and is made anxious by his own oral-aggressive fantasies.

ADULT: It must be real scary to live in this town where all the good people are killed. Let's give the police chief some more deputies and together the chief and his deputies can round up all the burglars and witches and put them in jail.

A child is playing air raid. The child is the pilot and the counselor controls the airport. The child says:

CHILD: I am the pilot loaded with bombs and I am coming to bomb you.
ADULT: Airport to pilot. You're about to bomb a friendly airport. Please divert mission and drop bombs into the sea.
CHILD: (Ignores airport controller and bombs town anyway)
ADULT: Attention, airport medical corps needed. Alert antiaircraft guns not to fire, repeat, do not fire. Pilot temporarily confused and mistakenly bombed airport as a result of angry confusion. Repeat, pilot is not an enemy.

Alongside of modeling defenses, the counselor helps the child to feel good about his achievements and to reaffirm the child's present and past positive relationships. Often aggressive children hold sustaining fictions about themselves. These are beliefs about themselves or their past that are not true but maintain their sense of well-being. The counselor should acknowledge and reinforce these fictions.

It is especially important to save all the drawings and artworks the child produces, as well as the counselor's process notes about each session. Periodically referring to these materials helps the child to develop a continuity of self and a past he can relate to his present. Progress can be concretely demonstrated. Each child's works should be kept in a locked file or file box used for just this purpose.

Verbalizing Alternative Defenses

The counselor can verbalize defenses he used as a child.

ADULT: When I got upset because I didn't get an award, you know what I did?
CHILD: What?
ADULT: I decided "who needs that stupid old ribbon anyway!"

. . .

ADULT: When another child hit me and hurt me, instead of hitting him back, you know what I did?
CHILD: What?
ADULT: I pretended that he hadn't hurt me a bit. By not hitting him back I was showing him that his blow didn't bother me at all, otherwise he might hit me again.

. . .

ADULT: When my mom paid more attention to my sister and made me jealous of my sister and angry at my mom, instead of hitting my sister, I used to pretend that the doll in my room was her and I would make believe that all kinds of awful things happened to her. I also used to pretend that I really liked her and I would do nice things for her when my mom was around so Mom would notice me being good and praise me for it.

Distinguish between Feeling and Action

When a child experiences angry feelings, a purely reflective response is one in which the counselor attempts to reflect the feeling beneath the anger. "It is upsetting to be treated unfairly." If the child experiences guilt over his angry feelings, a supportive response can be added. "It's all right to feel angry, everyone gets angry when someone is mean to them, but it's hard to be angry at someone you also love and need to take care of you." With the aggressive, undefended child, the painful feeling can be reflected and the angry reactive feelings legitimized, but the angry *retaliatory behavior must be met with disapproval.*

Many adults fail to appreciate this difference and reprimand the child for his behavior without acknowledging his feelings. Below the counselor responds appropriately:

ADULT: I can understand your feeling of being unfairly treated and your feeling angry in response, but hitting Billy is not acceptable. If you want to tell Billy or me how angry Billy made you feel, that's fine. But often when you do that you get even more angry in the telling and you want to leave me and hit Billy. I will deal with Billy after I hear your side of the story, but I won't be able to listen to you if you continue to try and leave me to seek revenge on Billy. Hitting Billy is not an acceptable way to handle your anger.

In the Milieu

One role of the counselor is to help others to accept the child's defenses as the most adaptive defenses he can use at the time. Educational staff and parents should be advised not to confront the child's defenses since such tactics typically result in escalation of behavior into fight or flight, the most primitive responses to anxiety.

When a child angrily throws his schoolwork down and accuses the teacher of giving him work that is too hard (blaming denial), he should not be challenged.

ADULT: Maybe I did give you the wrong work. Come on up here and we will look through my lessons and pick the right one for you.
CHILD: I'm staying in my seat.
ADULT: Okay, I'll bring you several and you can choose one.
CHILD: I ain't doing no more work. You gave me the wrong lesson the first time so that's that. (Child's refusal now less desperate, more calm)
ADULT: Okay, so why don't I give you some Magic Markers and you can draw until you feel like working? But don't draw for too long because you get upset when you lose the opportunity to earn points for your schoolwork.
CHILD: I don't care about your lousy points.

ADULT: I can understand your feeling like that right now, but when I hand out points to the others, I feel bad when I can't give you any.

CHILD: That's your problem.

ADULT: Okay.

Some educators think that such tactics feed the child's sense of omnipotence and reinforces his use of his maladaptive defenses. Quite the contrary. When a child's defenses are continually confronted by adults, he typically increases their use. He becomes so busy defending himself and anticipating confrontation that he never develops more mature defenses. When adults sidestep or ignore a child's defenses, he has less need to bolster their use. Think about your own defensive behavior. Think about what you do when confronted. You're so busy handling the confrontations that your anxiety and your defensiveness increases. Children are no different. Attack them and they will attack back. As I will illustrate in later chapters, the counselor, either directly as the "ignorant interrogator," or indirectly as the "inquisitive wizard," can gently confront and interpret the child's defenses during counseling sessions. Others should be encouraged to avoid confrontations.

Incorporating Positive Images

The most difficult defense to modify is the child's identification with the aggressor. Only when the child has incorporated the more benign and supportive images of the counselor and other nonpunitive and protective adults can he begin to give up the threatening and hostile behavior he incorporated from his family members. Remember that the child also has incorporated a self-critical, self-punitive self-image, which he externalizes and projects onto others. He cannot give up directing his anger outwardly because he would become aware of his self-hate and marked depression would follow. Only when he has incorporated others' benign qualities and *self-forgiving traits* will he become less self-condemning.

The counselor staying calm in the face of the child's onslaughts contributes to the child's incorporation of calm in the face of his storms. Remember, too, that the child will resist efforts to incorporate the benign caring qualities of others because his self-criticism also serves to guard him against the overwhelming feeling that his parents reject him. The child will actively attempt to make the counselor, and other caring persons, act like the child's incorporated images of authority figures. He does so to reduce the tension resulting from changes in his incorporated images. The child projects his highly critical conscience onto neutral figures.

Change is easier for the child when his parents have been helped to be more supportive and have made progress with their own self-hate, which is aggravated by the child's noncompliant behavior. Elsewhere I have outlined basic principles to follow when working with parents of aggressive children (see references).

Support Is Not Siding with the Child

Supporting the use of a defense is not siding with the child so that the defense is intensified. Siding with the child will diminish the child's awareness of the part he plays in provoking others. For example:

CHILD: My classmates all ganged up on me today and it wasn't my fault, I didn't start anything.
ADULT: I would get angry too—why can't they just leave you alone?
CHILD: That's right—they're all nothing but a bunch of bullies.

Here the counselor is not supporting the defense of denial, he is identifying with the child's plight and encouraging denial. His use of denial is a well established defense and now that the child is no longer actively engaged with his peers and not in danger of regression, the defense can be gently confronted by the ignorant interrogative approach.

ADULT: I wonder why the whole class ganged up on you like that? That must have made you very upset.
CHILD: They had no right to pick on me.
ADULT: So some of the kids who you thought were your friends turned on you?
CHILD: None of them are my friends.
ADULT: That's sad, having no friends.
CHILD: I don't care.

ADULT: There you go again—giving up on yourself and thinking you'll never make any friends. It gets pretty discouraging, huh?

CHILD: (Silence)

ADULT: While sometimes you make trouble, you're not that awful a guy that kids should dislike you for no reason. I wonder if you didn't do something, maybe even accidentally, that upset the kids in your class, some of whom liked you last week.

Reward Mature Coping Efforts

When you notice a child using more mature defenses, actively comment on this improvement. Children with a long history of aggressive behavior get extremely pessimistic about their ability to change. They need reassurance when you see change. They need hope. Improvements come in steps so small that neither the child nor other adults notice them. Often a child's improvement is viewed as regression rather than progress. For example, when the pseudoautonomous child experiments with abandoning this behavior and giving in to his unfulfilled dependency needs, he often becomes a clinging child who talks baby talk, and who, at times, seems confused and disoriented.

ADULT: I wonder if you ever thought about what it would be like to be a baby again and to be taken care of. Lots of guys had to be tough to survive but they never got the hugs and love they needed. I think you've made a lot of gains now that you can allow yourself to think about "soft" things rather than being your old, angry tough guy self. But it's confusing and scary to feel such things. Real growth is hard— I'm proud of you.

A child who continually made demands on the counselor to give him things and who would respond to the counselor's refusal with angry, limit-testing behavior gradually replaces his angry behavior with requests to play a game. The child is displaying more mature behavior. Such behavior should be praised.

ADULT: Did you know when I used to deny your requests to take things from the room you would get angry and play roughly with the dolls? Now, when I deny your request you ask to play a game. That really shows me how grown-up you can be.

Often a counselor confuses the development of a defense with resistance to counseling. A child who used to get very anxious, agitated, and disruptive every time the counselor would explore his relationship with his mother now states, "I don't want to talk about it." He has now initiated avoidance to handle his anxiety. That's actually progress rather than resistance.

ADULT: You feel real nervous talking about your mother right now.
CHILD: I just don't want to!
ADULT: So not talking, pulling back helps you not to feel so anxious. Is there anything else you are doing right now to prevent you from feeling anxious?

Developing Displacement and Distancing: Teaching the Child to Play

Let's look more closely at the child's use of symbols to assist in maintaining the state of calmness that characterizes normal latency. A child's latency state can be overwhelmed or subjected to trauma if overstimulated. The child who has developed symbolization quells the humiliation of trauma and the excitement of overstimulation, and the latent fantasies they stir up, by actually reorganizing and resynthesizing these experiences into highly symbolized and displaced stories. By reliving the events couched in the symbols and stories of latency play, the child finds an outlet for his heightened drives.

The child without adequate symbolization skill acts out his conflicts. In addition to the reasons we reviewed in the last chapter, Jo Ann Fineman's observations of mother-infant interactions suggest that some children do not play because their mothers exert an inhibiting influence on their imaginative play. Children who constantly feel threatened by the loss of mother's approval and affection express this fear by being unable to relinquish what cannot be handled or touched. They simply play with the objects in ways dictated by the objects themselves; they do not make use of objects to represent or animate a fantasy.

Unlike such mothers, the counselor not only encourages fantasy play but actively models and rewards the child for playful behavior. Hopefully, the child will learn to play and his play will reveal some of the child's preverbal and presymbolization expressions that produce disturbing impulses and activities.

Changing Mood

Some years ago, I administered the Thematic Apperception Test to a very anxious, disruptive child and found that almost all of the stories he told to the pictures were of violent, hostile interchanges between the figures depicted. In an effort to tap other feelings, I asked him to tell me new stories to each of the cards, but the "new rule" was that he could not tell me any violent or aggressive ones. To my surprise, he proceeded to do so. At the end of the day, his special class teacher asked me what I had done to him during testing because he came back calm and worked better than he had all week.

Pondering over what had taken place, I concluded that his telling of nonviolent stories must have changed his mood. He had to look into his memory and find images to project into the cards that were not violent ones. The process of searching for and finding these images calmed him. Perhaps the images were of positive times he had spent with caretakers, and thereby served to strengthen his positive feelings about himself, or perhaps the images distracted him from the violent images that excited him. Whatever the reason, this serendipitous finding altered my approach to working with aggressive children. I began to teach them strategies to change their mood and to calm themselves.

I was encouraged in this effort by Jerome Singer's research. In contrast to the prevailing view that expression of aggression in fantasy helps reduce aggressive behavior (catharsis theory), Singer found that individuals who are practiced daydreamers handle aggressive feelings by daydreaming of pleasant and enjoyable states. They obtain relief from negative affect following frustrating experiences by emoting fantasies that change their mood. Singer also discovered that individuals who rarely daydreamed tended to remain aggressive when frustrated. The calming strategy I taught children who became overly upset when frustrated was to remember those activities they enjoyed and to perform these activities when upset and angry. For some children, it is thinking about going to a ball game with a relative. For others, it is coloring with brightly colored crayons. Each child is helped to find and to utilize his own calming, mood-changing procedures. For some, it is images, for others, it is actions. For those for whom it is actions, an effort is made to find a symbolic equivalent. The child who is calmed only by eating is encouraged to draw foods and to color his drawings.

This effort to help the child to learn how to change his mood when angered is not incompatible with the effort to get the child who harbors specific, retaliating aggressive fantasies to relate them to you in detail. The first effort is used when the child is upset and the goal is to help the child develop calming skills. The second effort is employed when the child is calm and is designed to generate guilt or anxiety that will result in the inhibition of direct aggression. It is not hard to tell if the second effort is working. If the child delights in relating his specific hostile fantasies and regularly repeats them unchanged with vengeful relish, the effort has failed.

Getting at Preverbal Concepts

There are two chief reasons to teach the child to play. First, the limited nature of the young child's experience leads him to group together events, feelings, and sensations that have occurred together in his real experience at different times and that have the same quality. They may or may not "belong" together in the way an adult would group them. These concepts are aggregations of sensations, emotions, and images grouped together in highly individual configurations long before the child developed speech. They resulted from the child's needs to make sense of, to introduce order into, his own experiences. Once these concepts are formed, the child acts as if they are true when in actual fact they may be false. For healthy later development, the child must have an opportunity to externalize these concepts in play. Lacking such an opportunity, the concepts become "stuck" and become the source of later pathology. For example, the child who has been force-fed as an infant may group together in his mind a spoon with other "painful" objects because of his strong nonverbal associations to a spoon. Similarly, the child does not realize why he is particularly anxious around adults who want him to eat all the food on his plate. The child never gets to test his highly personalized symbols against reality because his anxiety levels bring into play defenses that retard further cognitive growth.

Structuring Memory

The second reason for teaching play is the fact that trauma disrupts even the verbal child's organizational abilities. A child exposed repeatedly to traumatic experiences fails to perceive and to register these experiences adequately. Even mild anxiety restricts and distorts perception. Such experiences, when repressed, are registered in the unconscious as poorly structured images, such as somatic memories or cognitive distortions, or, as has been repeatedly stated, the need to act or to be acted upon (repetition compulsions).

Traumatic experiences are imbued with painful feelings and are, therefore, different from normal memory traces. Jonathan Cohen uses the term *deviant mental organization* to describe one's response to trauma. The disorganization trauma causes results not only in the formation of defensive wishes (wishes to avoid the trauma's repetition or wishes to control the experience by fantasies of active mastery), but also in the failure to develop normal wishes.

The child who plays out his traumas can be helped to understand his play as *forms of memory* and *defensive wishes* and to transform the feelings connected with them into forms that can be verbally expressed. The counseling task with many conflicted children is to uncover memories and wishes that were structured to begin with. With the repeatedly traumatized child, the task is *to construct memories.* The former task is an uncovering process while the latter is a structuring one.

> ADULT: You want to hit me with the spoon because the spoon makes you anxious. You also get anxious around mealtimes, particularly with adults who want you to eat everything on your plate. (Child has repeatedly force-fed dolls in the counseling room.)

To the counselor's task of interpreting active defenses against the expression of unacceptable wishes is added the task of transforming pathological forms of memory into normal memories. In chapter 3, Betty's preoccupation with claws in her drawings and her nightmares were traced to her mother's abuse of her as an infant.

The child resists efforts at transformation, partly because the feelings associated with the traumas are experienced as overwhelming and "crazy." The child actively avoids reexperiencing the frightening physical sensations that accompanied his trauma. He, therefore, resists understanding the fantasy elaborations that accompany his effort to master the traumatic experience. These elaborations become part of the deviant mental organization and makes it hard for the child to distinguish fantasy from reality. The counselor needs to help the child to make such distinctions.

ADULT: The monster in your nightmares can't really hurt you anymore. You are too big for the daddy–people to smother you with a pillow like they did when you were little. You can run and call for help. Besides the daddy–people couldn't stand your screaming when you were little—you don't scream like that any more. Only babies scream like that. Now your dad hits you when you talk back and it hurts, but he has never hit you hard enough to kill you. Your big brother is still alive and I'll bet Dad hit him a lot.

Keep in mind that a child remembers by playing. When we introduce toys that stimulate his memory, and when we help him to elaborate on his play and thereby stimulate associations to the memory, we are helping the child to transform traumatic registrations into normal memories. Much of counseling involves modeling a different way to play with the materials selected. All normal latency aged children, because they cannot express drives directly, act them out in fantasy. Consequently, we are helping the child to develop the symbolization he needs to construct need-fulfilling distant fantasies.

ADULT: Let's make the little boy into Superman so he can capture his enemies and put them in jail. Here, put this little cape on the boy doll and fly him around.

. . .

ADULT: The little boy can pretend to be a lion and he can growl ferociously at his enemy.

When a child can verbalize a feeling he is encouraged to do so, but when he cannot, he is encouraged to draw the feeling on paper, mold it in clay, or re-create it in a miniature world.

Charles Sarnoff presents an example of a child who felt compelled to look at smokestacks through binoculars. When asked to draw a picture of smokestacks, he indicated that there was something behind the smokestacks that he wished to see. Sarnoff then suggested that the child make clay figures of the smokestack. He made one with a hole in the base. The boy said that snakes went into the hole and he needed to watch them. He said that if his brother could see the stack he would say it looked like a penis. Two years earlier, the child had penile surgery for the correction of a congenital deformity. Whatever residual memory he had of his response to the injury was now part of his fear fantasy involving smokestacks. Working with clay, the child could be helped to deal more effectively with the feelings associated with this traumatic experience.

With younger children, the situation is more difficult. Typically, they cannot draw nor can they work in clay. Dollhouse equipment and miniature-world toys need to be utilized to help the very young child.

A three-year-old girl was referred for nighttime terrors of seeing "monsters with different-colored hair." When encouraged to play with the dollhouse people, it became apparent that the "monsters" were all the different men her mother had been entertaining in her house, the majority of whom yelled at her or put her angrily in her room. The child was then asked what she would like to do with these "daddy–people" who kept visiting her. She proceeded to bury them in the sandbox. She was also asked what she would like to do with the "mommy–people." She treated the one mommy she selected similarly, angrily burying her in the sand and telling her to "go to her room and stay there." Mother was also instructed to be more discreet with her boyfriends or to take the child to her grandmother when she entertained.

Developing Mechanisms of Restraint

A large portion of counseling time is spent in helping the child to develop those defenses that Sarnoff groups under the heading of mechanisms of restraint. These defenses not only calm the child but help him to get some distance from himself so he can participate with the counselor in observing his behavior.

A lot of material in traditional play-therapy rooms stimulates regressive, immature behavior. Sandbox tables, finger paints, and clay are examples. With impulse-ridden children, the counselor should not keep a sandbox table in his room and finger paint and clay should be stored in a locked cabinet where small amounts can be obtained when needed. Miniature-world sand play can be introduced later when the child has gained some control over his impulses.

A portion of counseling can include encouragement of obsessive-compulsive activities that serve as calming behaviors. The child can be encouraged to collect rocks, baseball cards, coins, stamps, etc., and to play repetitive meaningless games like organizing dominoes so that they fall down in sequence. Children can collect lollypop sticks to glue onto cardboard, pictures of athletic figures, etc. Any elementary art teacher can give you ideas to employ. The child can draw and color geometric forms, with all the forms of one shape colored black, those of another shape colored red, etc. If the child is in a special education or day-treatment center, the art teacher will usually help the child to develop these skills, freeing the counselor from this task. If the child is removed from class for disruptive behavior, he can calm himself by doing one of these tasks.

Children can be encouraged to sublimate their unacceptable impulses through study of special topics or participation in activities that are symbolic equivalents of their wishes. Aggressive children can study about wars and instruments of war, the purpose being to develop intellectualization as a defense. "The more I know about war and defense the less anxious I will feel about my vulnerability." If the special education teacher cannot teach the child about such topics, the counselor can. Collecting war pictures and making war scrapbooks can be encouraged.

Games also can be used to develop mechanisms of restraint. The games should be simple repetitive ones like Candy Land, Chutes and Ladders, and occasionally, checkers. The value of games lies primarily in inculcating a sense of organization and adherence to regulations in a manner that can be pleasurable. They allow the child to engage in a calming activity while the counselor is helping the child to verbalize feelings aroused during problematic situations that have occurred during the week. The child plays while the adult talks.

Even better than games are the partially absorbing miniature "puzzles" that many children play, such as getting all the little balls in the holes on those plastic-enclosed frames. Pick-up Sticks and other "nonsense" games engage the child just enough to give him distance from the counselor's interpretative monologues about his feelings and behavior, the subject of the next chapter.

7

From Defensive Behavior to Insight: The Role of Interpretation

> But what am I?
> An infant crying in the night:
> An infant crying for the light,
> And with no language but a cry.
>
> —Alfred, Lord Tennyson

A great confusion surrounds the term *interpretation* and its role in child counseling. Many experienced counselors fail to appreciate the delayed and hidden influence of a well-timed interpretation, while others are not sure how to interpret, when to interpret, or even what to interpret.

Historically, the concept of interpretation came from psychoanalysis where the task was to unmask the unconscious motives of the client: in short, to make the client aware of how his symptomatic behavior was influenced by unconscious determinants. The client already knew that all his conscious efforts to change had failed, and that he could not will himself healthy.

But simply discovering the unconscious motivations and verbalizing them was not enough. First, the analyst had to create a special kind of relationship with the client. For interpretation to work, the client needed to reexperience his earlier conflicts within this therapeutic relationship.

I have described how the child speaks through fantasy and play, how he makes use of illusion, analogy, displacement, condensation and symbolic representation in place of conveying meaning directly. I have described how he uses defense mechanisms to avoid perception. "I must not know what I know." "I must not feel what I feel." The child defends against perception to manage the overwhelming anxiety that the undeveloped self can experience. The child's purpose is to keep his perceptions both from himself and from threatening adults. The counselor's job is to "explain the child to himself." To make the child more emotionally aware that his behavior, possibly adaptive at one time, now keeps him from meeting his real needs.

Interpretations are not made simply to help a child gain insight. In working towards the ultimate goal of changing the child's habitual ways of responding, interpretations have various intermediate aims. They include: fostering the therapeutic alliance, overcoming resistance, clarifying the child's relationship with the counselor or with others, facilitating remembering, and creating dynamic shifts in functioning.

I have subdivided interpretations into two major categories. Those that any empathetic adult can employ to help a child to understand his feelings better, which I have called *Empathetic Interpretations,* and those that only trained counselors should employ and which I have called *Dynamic Interpretations.*

Interpretations

Empathetic	*Dynamic*
Any concerned adult:	Trained counselors only:
1. Of universal feelings	1. Of defenses (contents of fantasies)
2. Of individual feelings	2. Of transference and displacement
3. Of individual conflicts	3. Of drives or wishes (contents of dreams, fantasies, and bodily sensations)
4. Of others' behavior	

Empathetic Interpretations

A counselor interprets behavior when he tries to anticipate the feelings that a child or a parent might have upon starting counseling. When he says to a quiet, somewhat fearful looking child that, "Often children are upset when they first come to a new place and don't know what to expect," he is making an empathetic interpretation. In chapter

3, many of the communications addressed to children to illustrate the principles of communication were examples of empathetic interpretations. I have classified empathetic interpretations into four categories: of universal feelings, of individual feelings, of individual conflicts, of other's behavior.

Interpretations of universal feelings are those in which the adult attempts to normalize the feelings a child might have about a situation. To make universal interpretations requires knowledge of how children feel who experience particular stresses. For example, children often blame themselves for many happenings over which they have no control. Interpretations of universal feelings are efforts to help the child realize that many children have similar feelings, to facilitate discussion of how things really are, and to correct the child's self-defeating misconceptions:

> ADULT: Lots of kids spend lots of time trying to figure out how to get their parents back together again. It keeps them from concentrating on their schoolwork. Does this ever happen to you?

Interpretation of individual feelings are similar to interpretations of universal feelings because many children experience stresses similarly. An interpretation of an individual feeling follows:

> ADULT: I guess you're very disappointed at not winning student of the week. I knew you were trying very hard and when you try hard and don't make it, it sure can feel bad.

Interpretation of individual conflicts would be:

> ADULT: I wonder if you're not torn between your two friends who are fighting and looking for your support. You feel you have to choose one over the other even though you don't want to.

> OR

> ADULT: You'd like to tell your friend that he hurt your feelings but you're afraid he'll get even more angry at you.

OR

ADULT: It's hard to get angry at your mother when you visit home because you're afraid she won't want you to visit anymore.

OR

ADULT: Part of you would like to say you're sorry but another part insists that it was his fault.

Interpretations of other's behavior are simply explanations of how another might feel in response to the child's behavior or to the behavior of an important figure in the child's life.

ADULT: Did you ever think that your teacher might feel bad when you rip up the work she prepared for you?

OR

ADULT: Did you ever wonder how Mom might feel having to be so responsible for you while Dad gets to take you fun places each weekend? Might she not feel like the bad parent while Dad gets to be the good guy?

OR

ADULT: Did you ever think how awkward Dad must feel only being able to see you every other weekend? He plans an activity and it doesn't work out, or you get angry at him; he doesn't get to set it right for another two weeks.

Empathetic interpretations help the child to understand and to accept himself and to understand the feeling world (aims 4 and 5 discussed in chapter 2).

Dynamic Interpretations

Dynamic interpretations refer exclusively to unconscious material, such as defensive operations, repressed drives, distorted memories, or the hidden meanings of behavior patterns and their unconscious connections. Dynamic interpretations transcend the clinical data and are preceded by a prolonged preparatory process where the child's misconceptions have been clarified through empathetic interpretations. Conflict always blurs reality and anxiety distorts it. Clarifying comments change the nature of the child's play as the child integrates his new knowledge. The play becomes more elaborate, less disguised, and more interpretable.

Dynamic interpretations should be made only in a therapeutic relationship with a trained counselor. More importantly, they are made in a planned and supportive manner, and only when the child's relationship with the counselor will support him through the anxiety he will experience each time an interpretation is made.

Confrontation versus Interpretation

Unfortunately, many adults use dynamic interpretations when they are annoyed by a child's behavior.

ADULT: Everytime you feel defeated you storm off the field and refuse to play. Grow up and accept defeat like a man.

This admonishment is actually an interpretation of a defense. The child was disappointed, perhaps because he expected to hit the ball and win admiration. He defended against this disappointment, and the self-disparagement following it, by getting angry and leaving the game. Such comments (interpretations) *are never helpful.* If the child knew how to handle his disappointment better, he would not behave in this fashion. Pointing out his behavior is adding insult to injury. Never take away a child's defense until he has a better one.

If our "strike-out boy" was handled empathetically, the adult would have responded as follows.

ADULT: Bill, I'm sorry you didn't get a hit. I know you wanted to hit one bad. You're swinging well; maybe next time you'll hit one. When you calm down you can rejoin us.
CHILD: F—— you, I'm not coming back.
ADULT: That's how you feel now. If you change your mind, let us know. We'd like to have you back.

If Bill were referred for counseling, the counselor will ask himself a number of questions before he even considers interpreting Bill's behavior to him. Why does Bill get so disappointed by his failure? Who is he identified with? What are his self-perceptions? Whose admiration is he trying to win? What are his standards, and where did they come from? He will leave the child's defenses alone until some progress is made in answering these questions.

Dynamic interpretations have been subdivided into interpretations of defenses, of transferences and displacements, and of drives or wishes. The material interpreted appears in behavior displayed, play and fantasy, bodily sensations, and dreams. The material relates to defenses used, wishes held, transferences experienced (feelings about the counselor that are actually feelings about parents) and displacements made (misdirected anger).

Interpretation of Defenses

Beginning counselors often interpret the wrong things at the wrong time and with the wrong words. Often they interpret the child's wishes before they interpret the child's defense against the wishes expressed.

CHILD: (Playing aggressively with clay, mixing clay with water to make mud pies)

ADULT: You're so angry with me today that you'd like to throw mud pies at me.

. . .

CHILD: (Playing in sexual fashion with mother doll)

ADULT: Lots of children have sexual feelings toward their moms. Sometimes they even wish to marry their mom. Have you ever felt that way?

In the first example, the child is liable to become frightened by the counselor's knowledge of her angry feelings and will either run from counseling because she fears retaliation or throw the "mudpies" in order to strike the first blow. Such comments often are seen as "permission" to act out the impulses the child now "feels" more strongly. Before the counselor can interpret the child's angry wishes he needs to help the child to learn how she defends against expressing her wishes. If the child is unaware that she is angry at the counselor, she first needs to learn the mechanisms she uses to avoid perceiving her anger and how to express it more directly. In addition, making mud pies is an acceptable way for a child to handle anger. If consumed with making mud pies and never appropriately expressing anger, then an interpretation may be in order.

> ADULT: I notice that whenever I have been late or have missed a session with you, you make mud pies instead of expressing your disappointment or anger at me for my letting you down. Have you noticed that?
>
> CHILD: (More attention to counselor, less absorbed in play)
>
> ADULT: Most kids would be angry at me for missing a session or being late. Maybe making mudpies is safer than being angry at me. You think I'll get angry back?

The child may have to "hear" such communications for some time before she will give up her defense of making mudpies, and the unspoken fantasies that accompany their making, and directly express her annoyance at the counselor. Only after the child acknowledges both her anger at the counselor and her manner of suppressing its awareness and its expression can she be guided to see that she does this with other adults in her life.

The second example illustrates an additional error. Not only was the wish interpreted before the defense against its expression, but the counselor violated *Communication Principle 5: Feelings communicated in counseling are most often feelings held toward the counselor and created by the counseling situation.* The child's sexualized play with the mother doll may be stimulated by the interpersonal closeness with the counselor, regardless of the counselor's sex. This interpretation about sexual feelings towards Mom is an example of "wild analysis" and is more often the fantasies of the counselor who is familiar with psychoanalytic concepts of development but not with their application in a helping relationship.

The child who reveals his sexual curiosity or sexual interests in doll play should be encouraged to further develop and elaborate on such play before any comments are made about it. In fact, if the child becomes increasingly agitated by his own play, the counselor should introduce another topic (i.e., "Here, play with these trucks").

To illustrate the choices that face a counselor, I will present a case of a nine-year-old girl in a children's home who wanted to take with her some drawing she and the therapist had made together and that she had been content to keep in her special closet in the counseling room. The counselor knew that she was scheduled for a weekend visit home with her mother and her mother's latest boyfriend, a visit that caused noticeable agitation, but that she had not admitted worried her.

The counselor could make any of the following responses: He could draw her attention to her behavior, "I wonder why you might want these drawings now?" He could reflect the feeling that, while she was home, she wanted something to remind her of positive times she had with the counselor. He could make a more direct statement, such as, "I wonder if you don't want these drawings now because their presence will help you handle your upcoming trip home." This interpretation of her defense, however, might force the girl to face abruptly her anxiety without the counselor's support. He could make a more powerful interpretation of her wish for the counselor's protection, but such a move might leave her feeling stripped and defenseless, and violates the rule that defenses are interpreted before wishes. He could link this wish with her reactions in other similar situations in which she had become anxious (reduction statement), but this could not be done without the previous steps. He could make a connection for the girl between this coming event and earlier events in her life. This interpretation would be of no value, because the girl did not have a clear idea of her feelings about this coming event. He could say nothing at all, and let her have the drawings. This last "response" could be viewed as supporting the child's use of this defense (utilizing a soothing, transitional-type object), a topic that I discussed in the last chapter.

Perhaps the best course of action would be to make a comment that would temporarily buttress the child, and offer support at the same time that both the defense and the fear were acknowledged. "How nice it will be to take something home with you that you feel good about, especially if you are worried about the visit." The counselor might decide to include an aspect of the transference, but in a supportive way. "I think you would like to have something that's partially mine with you on this visit," he might say, and allow the girl to take the drawings and reserve for a later date further exploration of the act. "When you come back, we can talk more about how you feel when you visit home."

Preparatory Statements

When a counselor interprets a defense, however, he rarely does so without preparatory work. Such preparation involves the use of *attention statements, reductive statements,* and *situational statements.*

Attention statements: The aim of an attention statement is to direct the child's attention to the facts that his actions or verbalizations reveal. Attention statements are preliminary clarifications. While attention statements may be directed to coincidences the child seems not to have registered or to paradoxes revealed, often attention statements are made simply to highlight what the child is doing. The most elementary attention statements are running comments about the child's silent play.

> ADULT: The house is on fire. . . . The man and woman escape to the roof . . . The fire engines come . . . The house collapses.

Such comments serve two purposes: First, children have difficulty reflecting on their actions. If their actions are impulse driven, reflection is even more difficult. One way children gain greater consciousness of themselves is by describing their own actions in words. Many children cannot put their actions into words. The counselor's running comments assist them in this process. Secondly, children are receptive to expanding upon their play if they see similarity between what the counselor is doing or verbalizing and what they themselves have already been doing.

When making running comments, focus on the result of the child's actions, not on the child's efforts. For example:

> CHILD: (Engaged in making mounds of sand)
> ADULT: The sand is getting fatter.

The adult should not comment that the child is "making mountains" simply because that is how they look to the adult, nor should he comment, "look how fat you're making it," because the child could interpret the comment as a criticism. Simply comment on the result. Often such comments help the child to shift his focus from small details to larger issues (to decenter).

At other times the counselor may offer a verbal or action counterpart to the action or feeling the child portrays to clarify what the play might mean.

ADULT: Let's bring an ambulance to the fire so we can rush the victims to the hospital.
CHILD: No, no ambulance, they all die.

A child repeatedly plays a scene where a car full of family members gets stuck in the mud, and can go no farther. The parents and siblings get out of the car and sink over their heads into the mud. The counselor comments:

ADULT: The boy is left all alone in the car, unable to rescue his family.
CHILD: He didn't try hard enough.

Melvin Lewis presents an example of an attention statement directed at the conspicuous absence of something from a child's play. He describes an eight-year-old school-phobic who repeatedly enacted a war scene in which the general was attacked and almost killed. Many fantasies were revealed in the play but one prominent feature was the absence of any female. After attention was drawn to this "fact," the child recognized his anger at his mother, his fear of her, his resentment that his father offered him no protection, and his displacement of his anger towards his mother onto his father, the safer target.

Reductive statements: Reductive statements are made to reduce apparently disparate behavioral patterns to a common form that the child has never noticed about himself. A child may display similar forms of behavior whenever he is upset and be unaware of this fact. For example, every Monday on her return to a children's home after a home visit, an eleven-year-old girl would mock, insult, and degrade the counselor during her sessions. She was unable to respond to comments and questions about her anger. The counselor verbalized that she only seemed to get angry at him following a home visit. This reductive statement was accepted by the child. It was then followed by an interpretation of content: "Perhaps part of you hated coming back to the home and that I am the safest person towards whom you can express your anger." The child intensified these insults but subsequently verbalized that her parents are only able to care for her on short visits and never allow her to be angry at them.

An example of a more dramatic reductive statement is provided by Edith Buxbaum. She describes an eight-year-old boy who stole, was truant, set fires, and who was admitted to an institution. There he behaved in a provocative manner, making it difficult for child care workers to avoid manhandling him. When the workers did not respond to his provocations, the children did. This gave him justification for hitting and hurting them. The counselor repeatedly pointed out to him how his provocations led to punishments. Later, the child-care staff reported that after being beaten by a boy, the child would attempt to engage the same boy in sex play. When the counselor pointed out to the boy this sequence of behavior, he recognized that he needed help to stop it. The next step would be to examine the "reasons" for his engaging in this behavior.

Situational statements: These statements naturally follow from those previously described. For example, when the child is aware that he is angry, he can be shown the situations that give rise to his anger and how he contributes to situations that create the anger.

> ADULT: Everytime you ask me for something that you know I can't give you, you can get angry at me for denying you.

When the child recognizes this pattern, *then and only then,* can the counselor attempt to show the child how he employs this same tactic to make another adult rejecting—his parent or teacher. When he recognizes that he employs this tactic with many adults in his life, *then and only then,* can the counselor help the child to look at how long he has been doing this and how it contributed to the development of problems with caretakers.

Step by Step Progression

Rudolph Lowenstein has outlined the steps in making an interpretation to an adult:

1. Show the client that certain common elements exist in a series of events (attention statements).

2. Point out the similar behavior of the client in each of these situations (reductive statements).

3. Demonstrate that such behavior was manifested in circumstances

that all involved, for example, competitive elements and where rivalry might have been expected (situational statements).

4. Point out that rivalry does exist unconsciously, but is replaced by another behavior, such as avoiding competition (interpretation of the defense).

5. Show how the defense, for example, avoiding competition, results in avoidance of perceived humiliation and loss of self-love.

6. Show how this behavior originates in certain initial events in the client's life and encompasses reactions and tendencies that could be grouped under the heading, for example, of rivalry with father.

In all the stages just outlined, interpretation of the client's defense is emphasized rather than interpretation of content. Later, the counselor may help the client to deal with the wishes that were defended against. In the example given, the rivalry with Dad was not just created by the father, who may have ridiculed his child's immature rivalrous behavior but was also initiated by the child. What was the wish that lay behind the desire to win out over Dad? With children, many of these steps take place through use of metaphoric communications.

Interpretation within the Metaphor

I have illustrated the use of attention, reduction, and situational statements directed at the child's behavior. Many children will need intermediate steps, such as making these statements indirectly through some other hypothetical child or within the context of their play. Many dynamic interpretations are first made within the context of the play or fantasy the child expresses, called "interpretation within the metaphor." When a child is playing that a doll named Betty is attacked by a lion, the counselor can initially reflect that "lions are frightening." When the child elaborates that other dangerous creatures surround the doll, the counselor can respond with "Betty sure lives in a dangerous world." Both of these comments may set up reverberations that bring out the child's concealed perceptions of her real world, but they are comfortably contained within the fantasy. If the child responds with "Betty is brave," or even with "I am brave," she has maintained the distance from reality required. Questions put to the child to clarify issues also are asked within the metaphor. Why was the lion so mean? Who let the lion escape from the circus? Was the lion always so mean? No matter how transparent a child's fantasy appears (remember Tad and the plastic dummy) children are often still some distance from being able to acknowledge directly even small parts of it.

Whenever a counselor violates the framework of the fantasy or the play and reaches into reality for the meaning of the symbols (e.g., "You must be scared of some grown-ups"), the child will terminate her fantasy and withdraw from the counselor. Dorothy Block, a well-known child and adult psychoanalyst, relays a report from a colleague that dramatically illustrates the error in "describing the unconscious to the patient." When this analyst asked his client if he understood the meaning of the characters in his murderous fantasy, the client's immediate reply was, "If I understood what they meant, I'd kill myself."

A disturbed child is constantly engaged in defending himself, whether in fantasy, play, or verbal communication, from experiencing forbidden and painful thoughts. Always remember that when the child's fantasy is of pleasant experiences, it is expressed unmodified. When the fantasy thought leads to fear of harm to self or others it must be distorted, modified, and masked. The child is only willing to examine his pain in very small doses and only in the presence of a supporting, trusting adult. The child's defensive efforts must be respected. Interpretations are not for the counselor's benefit.

Each time the child achieves increased understanding of his fantasies, he can elaborate upon them in such a way that new fantasies appear and the counselor is assigned new roles. Those children that involve the counselor in their play will often cue in the counselor and give him his lines. The counselor elaborates on the directions only when a feeling the child requires can be expanded upon. As long as the child indicates a particular response from a counselor, in most cases this response should be provided. When it has served its purpose—to stengthen the child's self—the child typically abandons it and moves on to something else.

Wording the Interpretation

Considerable tact is required when interpreting a child's defense, even if the interpretation is made within the metaphor. Direct attempts to analyze defenses are experienced by the child as an attack on his personality. Even sympathetic exploration is often taken as implied criticism. In addition, disturbed children have great difficulty tolerating ambivalence, and find it difficult to accept that they have hostile wishes or fantasies. Placing the anger in a fuller context may help ("It is very hard to be angry at someone you love"), but often it does not. Remember that interpretative statements should always be put tentatively, and in the form of a question that leaves room for doubt. The interpretation should always carry the implication that it is all right to have the feeling that is interpreted. This requires careful wording to convey this implication. None of the following interpretative statements accomplish this goal.

ADULT: I think you're feeling angry at me and your silence is your cover.

OR

ADULT: Behind your silence is lots of anger.

OR

ADULT: I think you're really very angry at me.

There is a subtle difference between the above three statements and the following three:

ADULT: I get the feeling that you're angry but feel you're not supposed to be.

OR

ADULT: I wonder if you're staying silent because you feel you had better not say anything if what you're feeling is anger.

OR

ADULT: I find that sometimes when I have nothing to say, after a while I realize it's because I'm angry.

The last three statements do not emphasize hiding or denying feelings, but rather that the child fears expressing his anger and that the fear might be unnecessary. Skillful wording of an interpretation can bring forth a favorable response, even in aggressive children with brittle defenses.

> ADULT: Your anger at me for not being available to you over the weekend when you were feeling alone is understandable because you've had such feelings many times before, particularly when your mom was not around when you needed her.

This interpretation conveys an empathetic understanding of the child's insatiable wish by focusing on the wish per se. Such interpretations result in the child's reexperiencing himself in relation to others. They strengthen the child's feelings that his emotions are understandable, that there are reasons for his feelings, and that this reason occurred from past deprivations.

In contrast, the counselor remarks:

> ADULT: You are angry at me and perceive me as cold and uncaring because I was not available to you over the weekend when you were feeling needy. You would like me to be available at all times and in all places.

Such a comment emphasizes that the child has insatiable needs that cannot be realistically gratified. This is not an interpretation, it is a confrontation. A child will experience it as a reprimand and respond accordingly. Similarly, when the child displays hurtful or hostile behavior towards the counselor, limit setting can be accompanied by:

> ADULT: I think you want to hurt me today because somebody hurt you today. Who did something mean to you today?

> OR

> ADULT: You need to treat me this way because you think I might do this to you today.

> OR

> ADULT: I wonder if you don't worry that I might do things to you in here like others have done to you?

OR

ADULT: You show me by your behavior how hard it is for you to control your excited, angry feelings. Sometimes, even when you talk to me, these feelings come out.

Contrast these supportive interpretations with the confrontive ones below:

ADULT: Your effort to get me angry is an excuse for you to express your anger at me.

OR

ADULT: Do you do things elsewhere to get people angry so you can be angry back?

OR

ADULT: Whenever you get angry about something, your increased anger gets others more angry at you.

Poorly worded interpretations can convey to the child that he has negative self-attributes. They communicate what he is like rather than what he can be. For example:

ADULT: You seem to have difficulty talking.

Contrast this remark with the following one:

ADULT: Sometimes you talk more easily than at other times.

The second comment contributes to delineating who the child talks to and why he has difficulty. Also remember that all of us are better off facing difficult issues when we feel stronger than when we are fearfully hiding. Yet is is usually when the client is down that we call attention to such matters. Sometimes we should wait until the client is very expressive and comment:

ADULT: You are being quite expressive right now. I wonder why you can do this at this time?

Stages in the Acceptance of an Interpretation of a Defense

There are seven stages in a child's acceptance and integration of an interpretation of a defense. Often the process is not observed until after the interpretation has been verbalized on many different occasions. These stages are:

1. The child presents the material that prompts the interpretation.
2. The child assimilates the contents of the interpretation:
   a. The child perceives and registers the interpretation on a preconscious or unconscious level.
   b. The interpretation threatens the child's sense of well-being and he becomes anxious.
   c. The child represses contents of the interpretation and, therefore, the anxiety evoked by it diminishes.
3. The child emulates the power he perceives the counselor has in understanding his behavior. (He turns the passive into the active.)
4. The child denies in subsequent fantasies the painful aspects of the contents of the interpretation.
5. The child represses aggressive retaliatory impulses towards the counselor.
6. The child's successive symbolic representation in fantasy and play of the wish to give up the denial and to come to terms with reality reveals his considerable ambivalence about resolving this conflict. The child's play oscillates between accurate and distorted representations of reality.
7. Insight, but without conscious awareness.

These stages will be illustrated by examining clinical data from the therapy sessions of an aggressive latency-aged boy. This youngster had responded favorably to limits set by the counselor and looked forward to counseling sessions. He identified with superhero figures and his play behavior revealed his preoccupation with violence. The counselor had interpreted his aggressive behavior as a counterreaction to his fears of being destroyed and vulnerable. Such interpretations had been conveyed both through the metaphor and directly. How the boy responded to these interpretations will be illustrated by looking at material from four sessions of his two-year stay in counseling.

Session 23: Interpretation and Response

CHILD: (Goes immediately to building blocks and makes a moat surrounding a castle. A knight tries to cross the drawbridge to invade the castle, but sometimes the drawbridge is pulled up and the knight falls in the moat, to be eaten by crocodiles. On other occasions, he just makes it into the castle and defeats those inside.)

This scene and similar ones have been repeated in a number of prior counseling sessions.

ADULT: (Interpretation within the metaphor) Maybe the knight needed to attack this fort before his enemies inside attacked him. Maybe he needs to strike the first blow to feel safe.

CHILD: But sometimes he falls into the moat.

ADULT: (Elaboration) Yes, but that's the price he has to pay for the fighting that makes him feel safe. He falls into the moat because of his fighting—his fighting causes him lots of troubles.

CHILD: (Continues)

ADULT: (Direct interpretation) I wonder if sometimes you don't feel a little like the knight, that you fight to feel safe and you get into trouble like the knight falling into the moat?

CHILD: (Leaves blocks, gets out puzzle and proceeds to put pieces together) When I'm done, it will turn out to be a lion.

In session 23, a major interpretation was made. The knight, like the child, attacked the castle because of fear. The first interpretation was within the metaphor, and because the child actively listened to this interpretation, the counselor related his interpretation directly to the child's problem. The child's aggressive behavior was his attempt to protect himself from helpless feelings that were a greater fear than the trouble his misbehavior got him into. The counselor had made similar interpretations before, but no noticeable changes had followed their communication. The counselor also chose not to interpret the child's play in relation to the counselor ("You need to be strong to avoid some injury I might cause you"—a transference interpretation), but instead interpreted what he felt was the child's characteristic way of feeling and behaving.

Outwardly, the child seemingly ignored the interpretation by abandoning his play and initiating an unrelated activity. He assembled a puzzle (this behavior is not unlike the child who hears his mother's scoldings for not cleaning his room and yet goes outside to ride his bicycle). We know, however, that anxiety disrupts play. The child withdrew abruptly to a more remote and less disturbing activity. In addition, he exchanged a passive attitude of a child's listening to an adult with one where he was active and the counselor passive. The activity was one where he would be successful because he knew the outcome in advance. He bragged about this upcoming accomplishment to elevate his self-image.

The contents of the interpretation exposed the child's inadequacy and elevated his anxiety. In response, he chose a new task where he would be completely adequate. His successful feelings helped him to repress his anxiety. From this behavior, the counselor can infer that the child unconsciously, at least, understood the message.

Of interest is the fact that the child chose to complete a puzzle to help dampen his anxiety. The puzzle pieces may be considered as the manifest phenomena and the lion as the hidden Gestalt. Assembling the puzzle results in making manifest a latent content. The child turns from passively experiencing the interpretation to duplicating the feat of the counselor and making an "interpretation" of his own. This feat spares him from humiliation and allows him to "impress" the counselor. The child's active mastery reduces the anxiety stimulated by the interpretation and thereby facilitates its assimilation.

Sessions 24 and 25: Working Through

CHILD: (Sets up the blocks, but this time he gives the knight wings that enable him to fly over the moat and successfully vanquish his foes. Following this play, he uncharacteristically puts away the blocks by himself without prompting by the counselor or without asking for the counselor's help. He then asks to play a game with the counselor.)

· · ·

CHILD: (Again plays knight with wings vanquishing foes)

ADULT: Now the knight has wings and doesn't have to worry that he will fall in the moat. He can attack his enemies and not get into trouble. It sounds like you'd like to have wings also, so you won't get hurt when you fight with classmates.

CHILD: Merwin, the magician gave him them.

ADULT: Wouldn't it be nice if you also could find magic so you could fight and yet stay out of trouble? Do you make believe you are the winged knight in class and that no child can hurt you?

CHILD: I don't daydream. The teachers are a pain in the ass.

ADULT: What do you think about in class that keeps you from doing your work so that no note goes home telling your mother how much you learned during the week?

CHILD: Lots of things, being a stunt-car driver. I have to do what's best for me!

The child attempts to deny the impact of the interpretation by intensifying the fantasy in session 24. He gives the knight wings. The knight can now slay his enemies without fear of harm. He does not want to acknowledge his weakness and vulnerability. Nevertheless, his alteration of the fantasy signals that his fantasy life is negotiable, that if he wishes he can bring it into a closer adaptation to reality.

Following this play, he picks up his constructions. While he gave the knight wings, he eliminated the threat to his affectionate feelings for the counselor (the winged knight could destroy the counselor) by cleaning up to safeguard his relationship. He becomes a "good" client and picks up after himself. In session 25, the wings sometimes fall and the knight has to struggle without his magical powers.

Session 26: Insight

CHILD: (Again he plays the winged knight, but occasionally the wings fall and the knight falls into the moat. Nevertheless, he laughs at the knight's flapping efforts to remain aloft. He also reported that he had gotten into a fight in school, and while he had started it, he accepted his punishment. He then began to draw a cartoon of a dog who lived in the desert in a cactus. This dog was alone in the desert one day and he met a zebra whom he befriended. The zebra and he went camping. The dog taught the zebra how to start fires from sticks, put up a tent, and hunt for food. The dog wanted to play with the zebra, but they didn't know what to play, so they went to sleep.)

The child talks about his functioning in school and admits for the first time that he started a fight. He then makes a cartoon of a lonely dog who tries to befriend a zebra, a theme suggesting that he wants to make friends, but the two do not know what to play so they simply sleep. The child showed that the interpretation was effective by both admitting to starting fights and by developing a new fantasy, a less distant one, where friendships are sought.

During the process of working through, the child maintained his sense of well-being, a sense threatened by the interpretation, by fantasizing a state where he cannot accept or reject the reality situation revealed by the interpretation. The knight can fly or walk and can be in or out of the moat. Total denial can be maintained alongside of an accurate representation of reality.

Generalization, Externalization, and Projective Identification

When counseling children, particularly defiant children, three phenomena are important to keep in mind. These are: *generalization, the defensive use of externalization,* and *projective identification.*

Generalization occurs when a child, becoming aware of his wishes towards an adult, naturally assumes that the adult has similar wishes towards him (people in love often make similar assumptions). When angry at the counselor, he assumes the counselor is angry at him. Children arrested at this cognitive level of development need the counselor to serve as an auxiliary self. The child needs to realize that he cannot know others' thoughts and feelings unless they are communicated to him, and they cannot know his. Many people wrongly believe that they are not loved unless their partner can intuitively recognize their unspoken needs. The disturbed child feels similarly. He also needs to learn that others are not like himself and have thoughts and feelings different from his own. This topic was discussed in chapter 2.

The term *externalization* subsumes those processes that lead to the *subjective allocation of inner phenomena to the outer world.* Externalization is the opposite of internalization (introjection, incorporation, identification). Externalization is a way of dealing with unacceptable parts of oneself.

When a child attempts to integrate the various parts of his emerging self, he has the most difficulty with the dissonant, unacceptable parts. As a transitory phenomenon, externalization is a normal defensive process. It's prolonged use results in a restricted personality with important aspects of the self permanently split-off and unavailable for integration. It is a defense not primarily directed against drives or wishes, nor against love-linked anxieties. Its aim is to avoid the pain consequent upon accepting devalued aspects of the self.

The child who says the counselor is a stupid, dumb, ugly person is clearly denying the reality of the counselor and simply using him to discard undesirable aspects of himself. The child who externalizes will also project his anger onto the counselor. When the child attributes hostile intent to the counselor there is often a degree of fit between the projection and reality. The child may hang the projection on some real event, such as a canceled session. But what if the child calls the counselor a messy person? Is it the messy, unacceptable aspect of the self-representation that is being externalized, or a drive derivative, such as the wish to mess upon the counselor? The counselor should note whether the child's statement leads to relief or to anxiety. If the child is projecting and, therefore, experiencing himself as an object of the counselor's wish to mess, the child will wish to flee from the situation. If an externalization, the child will perceive the externalization as unrelated to himself and as something to be ignored, derided, or treated with contempt. Often, however, it is difficult to make this distinction because the child may be displaying his *projective identification* with the counselor. He both externalizes the unacceptable parts of himself and projects his unacceptable wishes onto the counselor and then identifies with this "unreal" image of the counselor. As a result, he may fear the counselor because he has made him into an undesirable autocratic tyrant.

If the differentiation can be made, it follows that interpretation of externalizations must focus on the need to defend against damaged self-love, whereas interpretations of projection must focus on the need to defend against the anxiety related to drive expression. Let's see how the two mechanisms occur in the same child:

Gloria was a thirteen-year-old girl in a special education class, who rarely talked, kept her head bowed, and elicited much ridicule from male classmates whom she then would taunt and tease in retaliation. She continually belittled her female counselor. She included "stupid" and "ugly" among her various insults. Gloria's behaviors could be considered a direct expression of aggression or an attempt to ward off anticipated insults from the counselor. Gloria's affect and subsequent material clearly indicated that Gloria identified with her powerful, arrogant father who felt humiliated by his daughter's special class placement and clearly made her aware of his disappointment in her. In response, Gloria externalized the "little Gloria" who was laughed at, criticized, and often ignored.

The counselor consistently responded to Gloria's outpourings of criticisms by verbalizing how she was being viewed by Gloria, how she was being seen and treated as a stupid little girl, and how it feels to be treated in this manner.

ADULT: You talk to me this way because you have been called stupid and ugly, and it's very painful to be called these things. Sometimes I think you even believe these insults. It's hard being in a special class and not thinking you're dumb. Just because you take longer to learn things doesn't mean you're not a worthwhile, loveable person. I enjoy you when you're not insulting me.

Because Gloria frequently experienced insulting attacks from her father, she expected such attacks from her counselor. Following the principle of turning what is passively experienced into what is actively managed, she directed insults onto others. Frequently, the counselor was the target of displaced anger. She was also the target of projected anger. Her anxiety about the counselor's "anger" was revealed in her nonverbal behavior. She would refuse to come to counseling sessions, walking way ahead or way behind the counselor. If she did come to counseling, she would sit far away from the counselor. She also shouted angry insults at her from a distance when she met the counselor between sessions.

Gloria would accuse the counselor of disliking her when her requests were denied or when sessions were canceled. The counselor did not deny Gloria's view of these events, accepting them as possible, but suggested that what was feared more than the counselor's dislike or inconsiderateness was her fear that the counselor may actually wish to harm her in retaliation for all her earlier insults. In some sense,

Gloria externalized her harsh and severe conscience onto the counselor, as well as projected her own anger. When Gloria eventually admitted to this fear, the counselor then attempted to show her that it was her wish to harm the counselor, who stood for all adults who had hurt her, that was projected onto the counselor. "Simply because you wish to harm me doesn't mean that I wish to harm you. Often you think that your wishes will come true, but wishes are just wishes. I know that you are angry at me and I'll never harm you, even if I am angry."

Often a child incorporates the externalizations of a parent. A child who views himself as a damaged unacceptable person may have accepted a parent's externalization of this self-image. His acceptance of the parent's externalization lies in his realization, at some level, that the parent needs such a devalued child and that failure to comply with this need would result in his abandonment. Treatment of such children is difficult because the externalizing parent becomes disorganized in response to the child's improvement. Not only does the child feel guilty about depriving the parent of a needed vehicle for externalization, but as the parent struggles to find a new target, the child can feel rejected. Similarly, a child can be the victim of a parent's projections. The parent who harbors long-standing hostility may feel that her child harbors similar feelings towards her. The child is viewed as a "monster to be feared" when the murderous impulse actually resides within the parent herself.

Many of the children being referred for counseling make extensive use of externalization and projection. The counselor will be confronted with a child who greets his helper with hostility. Understanding the dynamics behind this aggression will help the counselor to keep some distance from this hostility and to maintain objectivity.

Transference Interpretations

Sigmund Freud initially felt that the strong feelings of love or hate that invariably developed towards the analyst was a hindrance to progress in treatment. Later, he learned that these feelings were those transferred from the client's childhood relationships within the family to the therapeutic relationship. Frued discovered that clients not only remembered earlier situations of conflict and anxiety from their childhood, but always transferred them to the current analytic situation where they *reexperienced and relived them*. He then discovered that improvement only occurred when this happened and when the analyst helped the client to understand the transferred feelings. This necessarily involved a lengthy "working through" of childhood conflicts and feelings towards the analyst, becoming fully aware of them and their origins, and gradually finding new solutions to these old conflicts.

Melanie Klein verified that children also transfer feelings for their parents onto the counselor. The child transfers and projects his unconscious images of his parents or aspects of his parents, images created by a fusion of his own impulses and feelings, his own fantasies, and external experience.

The child needs to learn that many of the feelings he has for the counselor are directed toward a fantasy person and not a real one. He needs help to contrast his fantasy of the counselor with the reality of the counselor. To achieve this task, the counselor must continually ask himself, "What is the child doing to me at the moment? What is he feeling in relation to me now?" The counselor should follow these questions with, "Whom is the child trying to make me like? How is the child viewing me? Am I the angry, hostile father or the dominating, intrusive mother? Does the child have an image of me that is like himself; a 'narcissistic transference,' where he views me as he views himself? Am I being made a past or a present person in his life?"

For example, a child initiates a session by drawing a picture of a monster devouring a small animal. Is he the monster who can destroy his enemies? Is he the animal about to be devoured? He probably identifies with both creatures. He becomes the monster that he fears. But why does he draw this now? Does he feel himself to be the helpless animal confronted by the counselor? While the counselor can reflect this fear, until he knows who the monster really is, or was, he cannot show the child what role from the past and from his own inner experience he has transferred to him. When the fear is reflected and no attack from the therapist is forthcoming, the child's anxiety will decrease, and in his play he will feel safer to become the more complete monster and threaten to devour the counselor. These attacks will be followed by increased anxiety, no retaliation from the counselor, more play, and so on. Eventually, it may become clear who the monster really is.

Many counselors feel a need to make a conscious effort to link the child's transferred feelings towards them with the child's past or present feelings toward his parents. Such efforts are rarely successful when tried directly. When a child is in counseling, his parents and his home are not in his immediate experience. Thinking about them in a detached and intellectual manner is difficult for most children. The more important task is for the counselor to stress in his interpretations the current anxieties and conflicts the child has with the therapist, with the link to the past being implicit in the counselor's wordings. "You treat me as the mother you want all to yourself." "You treat me like the father you want to eliminate." "You are angry with me now, just as you were angry as a young girl with your mother when she wouldn't take you with her when she went out."

Transference Distinguished from Other Phenomena

The child's relationship to the counselor is a complicated mixture of a real relationship, a wished-for relationship, habitual ways of relating, an extension into counseling of current relationships, and a repetition or revival of past relationships. It can be difficult teasing out children's transference manifestations from among these other phenomena. Examining behavior outside of the counseling setting sometimes helps to make this distinction. The child who is displacing anger onto the counselor typically improves outside of sessions while transferred anger rarely results in improvement. Only when such anger is interpreted and worked through will improvement be noted outside of sessions. When an entirely new behavior resulting from repressed infantile conflicts emerges in counseling, symptoms may diminish elsewhere. Here, the transferred feelings can result in improved behavior. For example, the child who lets himself be babied by the counselor and who "messes" on the counselor often improves outside of sessions.

On other occasions, a child's behavior will deteriorate outside of the session as a direct consequence of feelings aroused by the counseling experience and by an effort to resist the expression of these transferred feelings in the session. For example, a child with incest fantasies transfers these incestual feelings onto the counselor, and then defends against their expression by becoming sexually involved with schoolmates.

Alex Holder describes his treatment of a thirteen-year-old who always drew the curtains in the counseling room before beginning his sessions. The child never commented on this behavior, but from later material, it was uncovered that the behavior occurred in response to the screen memories of witnessing the sexual activities of his parents. It contained the communication that he could only hear and not see because of the darkness. Holter labeled this behavior as "acting within the transference" because it was stimulated by the intimate relationship with the counselor within a confined space.

Interpretation of Wishes

After the child understands the defenses he uses to ward off the anxiety aroused by unacceptable or forbidden needs and desires, the counselor can begin to interpret the wishes that caused the child to become anxious. Some of the transference interpretations cited earlier included referring to the child's wish. "You treat me as the mother you want all to yourself." Examples of interpretations of wishes follow:

ADULT: Sometimes you wish you could have Mommy all to yourself and that Brother (Father) were gone.

. . .

ADULT: Beneath that rough, tough part of yourself is a part that would like to be taken care of. But that part becomes afraid of Mom's rejection if it shows Mom loving feelings.

. . .

ADULT: Sometimes you wish your dad was dead, but that thought makes you very anxious because part of you loves him.

With very angry children, the counselor needs to help the child handle his unacceptable wishes towards parent figures. He needs to help the child to realize that while his wishes are understandable, they will not come true and that some should not come true. A part of the angry child does not want to kill his parents. The child needs to be protected from such actions; to understand that wishes are only wishes and need not come true.

Children typically show their positive response to an interpretation of a wish in how they modify future play or fantasy behavior. Henry

Coppolillo's description of his treatment of a child with impulse-control problems beautifully illustrates the gradual changes in a child's play in response to interpretation of wishes. The child would regularly leave the counselor's office and taunt the counselor to chase him and bring him back.

ADULT: It appears that you like to be caught and held but would like it to be all my idea.

CHILD: (Child giggles and takes counselor's hand, begins tugging and pulling it as if he had been caught and heads back toward the office. When back, Child plays with boy and girl dolls. He makes them hug and kiss and chase each other around.)

ADULT: Why are they chasing each other?

CHILD: They did lots of wrong things and that one chased the other to hold it so it would not do wrong.

ADULT: Ah, now I understand, you want to be chased and to be held close, but you feel ashamed of this because it makes you feel like a little boy. So you play the pretend game of being naughty and having to be held.

CHILD: Will you come to my house and play lots?

At the beginning of the next session, the counselor announced that he could no longer be the child's policeman. The child would have to be his own policeman and do those things he knew were good for him and avoid those things that were not. The child ran out of the office.

ADULT: I will not stop you or chase you anymore.

Five sessions later, the child brought a fifteen-foot length of cord with him to the session. He tied the cord to the counselor and then said that he was going to run away. He said he was pretending that the counselor would still like to chase him and hold him but could not because he was tied. He then tied one end of the cord to his waist and gave the other end to the counselor to hold. He then left the room and went as far as the rope permitted him to go. He called out, "Pull me back," to which the counselor responded, "You want me to be your policeman because your own policeman inside your head is too mean." He gleefully returned and repeated the game several times.

In the next session, the child reported that he had learned two new poems. He told about Jack and Jill and Humpty-Dumpty. He gave a confused account of Jack only having broken his crown while Humpty-Dumpty broke "his whole self." He then added, "And that mean policeman inside his head got out." He sadly added that a king put Humpty together again because you need a policeman inside your head to be a good boy.

In Conclusion

When a child responds to the interpretations of the counselor, he repeats and relives conflicts in the counseling relationship rather than merely remembering them as matters from the past. Remembrances of the past that result in changes in present feelings are called *insight*. But in child counseling, the goal is rarely insight into the roots of a conflict, rather "insight" is revealed as a shift in the child's attitude of mind, a lessening of the need to project feelings and anxieties, which eventually leads to the increased capacity for self-understanding, and which results from the internalization of an insightful or insight-seeking counselor. In essence, what the child requires is what Bertrand Russell calls "knowledge by experience," as opposed to "knowledge by description."

8

From Action to Verbalization

If you'll be my bodyguard
I can be your long lost pal

—Paul Simon

"You must be very patient," replied the fox. "First you will sit down at a little distance from me . . . I shall look at you out of the corner of my eye, and you will say nothing. Words are the source of misunderstandings. But you will get a little closer to me every day."

—Antoine de Saint-Exupéry*

There are children brought for counseling who, like the fox, need to be tamed. These children also lack the ties that the fox suggests the little prince needs to tame him. In the last two chapters, I emphasized that the counselor's task is not just to resolve these children's conflicts, but more importantly, to build a sense of self that includes mature ways to defend against anxiety. In this chapter the focus will be on techniques that combine confrontational and educative efforts with efforts to support more mature defenses.

The chief tasks are to: (1) block disruptive interactions, often referred to as "limit setting"; (2) shift feelings acted out to verbal expression and verbal discussion; (3) change the child's negative self-image ("I'm not a monster").

---

*From Antoine de Saint-Exupéry's *The Little Prince*, K. Woods, trans. (New York: Harcourt, Brace & Jovanovich, 1943). I am indebted to Carolyn Gruber, MSW, for familiarizing me with this quotation.

Block Destructive Interactions

In all children, but particularly in those with severely arrested development, counseling is a *corrective emotional experience*. The child is provided in the here and now with a different reaction from his previous experiences, one that does not perpetuate the malignant interactions to which the child has become accustomed. With most children, reflections, clarifications, and correction of misconceptions create an environment quite different from the scoldings, lectures, and admonishments they get elsewhere. But the aggressive child's goal is to create familiarity. He will initiate his relationship with thinly veiled anger.

The taming process begins with blocking the child's aggressive behavior. It also includes verbalizing what the child feels when his actions are limited. "I want to help you to control yourself, and I also realize that you feel helpless and weak when I won't let you do something." Any attempt at self-control is acknowledged and praised.

To improve the child's reality testing, the counselor needs to verbalize continually what could happen following the child's dangerous or reckless behavior. "I know you climb on that cabinet to show me how strong you are, but the cabinet's not stable and I can't let you hurt yourself should it fall." He also needs to verbalize the difference between reality and fantasy. "Wishing won't make it so."

With limits the child will initially escalate his aggressive behavior. If the counselor withdraws under the child's provocations, the child intuitively reacts to this withdrawal with new provocations, which can increase the counselor's withdrawal. The child interprets this withdrawal as either a lack of interest in him or moral condemnation. This is a *guaranteed reaction*. The counselor who fails to anticipate that he will lose his temper with such children is headed for trouble. When the child angrily destroys drawings displayed by another child or spits in your face, you will get angry. Your feelings have to be continually verbalized.

ADULT: If you continue to do that, I am going to get angry. I'm not angry yet, just annoyed, but you need to stop that. Dolls are for playing with, not for breaking.

CHILD: And what will you do to me?

ADULT: I will have to take it from you.

CHILD: (Runs around the room, breaking legs off the doll) See, you can't catch me!

ADULT: Next time I will remove those toys from the room until I learn to trust that you will use them properly.

Under no circumstances should a child be allowed to destroy objects in a playroom or use materials in a random destructive manner. These children are master limit testers. When you limit their behavior in the macrosphere, they will switch to the microsphere. Do not let them take clothes off dolls where the clothes are supposed to be permanent. Do not let them mix up all the finger paints. Do not let them continue to pour water into the sandbox until the sand is soaking wet. Do not let them continually ask for more paper when obtaining paper is more important than drawing on it. In many cases, do not see such children in a playroom but in an office without objects that can be damaged. Equip the office with minimal toys (Magic Markers and paper, clay, human and animal puppets, and a cloth punching bag kept behind a puppet stage).

If you conceive of these children as infants, limit setting becomes immediately understandable. No good mother of an eighteen-month-old would let her children do any of the above inappropriate actions; neither should a counselor. I recently read a published case where the counselor suggested using natural consequence as a limit setter:

ADULT: You can break the crayons but you will have to use the broken crayons for drawing.

Absolutely not! Would a mother of a two-year-old respond in such a fashion? No! She would say:

ADULT: I am taking these crayons from you before you break them all. When you can play with them correctly I will give you one or two to use. If I let you break them now you'll be upset that there are none to play with later.

The limit tester is breaking them to see what you will do. To allow him to break the crayons is bad enough. It not only frightens the child that the adult allows him to be disruptive (or can be so easily manipulated to let rules slip) but broken crayons have become a way of life for him—"So what's different about this place?"

If the child is breaking the crayons because his drawing is "imperfect" and his self-hate is displaced onto the crayons, the response is similar:

ADULT: (Quietly rescues remaining crayons) I can't let you break the crayons because you're not happy with your drawing. Part of you sure gets angry at another part when that part can't do something right. Can I talk to the angry part, the part that says to you, "That drawing stinks"?

CHILD: No.

ADULT: Well, someday maybe I can speak to the critical part. I will call him "Mr. Critical."

CHILD: Shut up.

ADULT: Okay. When you silence me you also silence Mr. Critical. I guess he's a pretty powerful guy. I sure would like Ralph, who's a pretty good drawer, to be able to stand up to Mr. Critical more.

CHILD: Talk, talk, talk, that's all you counselors do!

The corrective emotional experience is created by the counselor's constant noncritical objectivity and by his not responding in kind to the child's intense anxiety and hostility. The counselor needs to be seen as a powerful person who will use his power for the child's benefit and not to hurt him or to support his regressed behavior. This power is felt by the child when he faces the counselor's steadfast commitment to his task:

CHILD: What does it take to get you angry?

ADULT: You've made me angry often.

CHILD: No, you just raise your voice.

ADULT: You mean what will it take to see me lose control and act wildly and run around like a crazy man, screaming and yelling?

CHILD: Yeah.

ADULT: I may yell at you someday and I will restrain you, but I will never punch you in the face, call you awful names, or deliberately deceive you.

CHILD: (Silence)

ADULT: I can understand how you feel since you don't trust anyone who tries to stop you from doing something you want to

do. My job is to help you explore why you feel and act as
you do. While I won't try and put anything over on you,
I'm sure you will do so to me since that's a serious problem
of yours.

CHILD: What do you mean?

ADULT: You will try and get me to do things for you that you can do
for yourself and you will try and get me upset to prove that
I neglect you and don't do things for you.

CHILD: I want to leave now. You can't make me stay here.

ADULT: (Counselor places himself at the door) I will stay here until
the time is up. I could let you go and be unconcerned
about you but this is not what I'm going to do. I will help
you not to run from your problems all your life.

CHILD: I've got no problems.

ADULT: But lots of adults and kids have problems with you. Your
mother reports she can't get you up for school in the
morning, that you're not working in class, that you hit
other children. It would seem to me that you're not very
happy.

CHILD: Well, that's what you think.

In order for the counselor to be effective with such children, he
needs to fuse two seemingly disparate images of himself. First, he has
to display a strong, firm attitude. While this attitude will help the child
to feel protected against feared deeper emotions, the attitude also
arouses rebellious attitudes in response to feared loss of control and
self-respect. Second, the counselor has to display a comradely parental attitude with which the child can identify. The child hopes to be
as strong as the counselor so he can conquer the emotions he fears.
The counselor also has to be seen as kind but not weak. Kindness is
linked with distrustful contempt. This link must be broken before
much progress can be made in helping the child to curb his impulses.
And, we know that the child will resist such efforts because he is
thrown into an identity crisis when he starts to give up his identification with the aggressor.

In chapter 2, I talked about the therapeutic alliance. All counselor
actions early in the counseling of the aggressive child need to be
directed at building this alliance. The child needs to develop a positive
tie with the counselor. The child cannot be interpreted out of his
anger any more than he can be talked out of it. The counselor's goal is

to create feelings in the client that will tame his anger. All children, no matter how tough, are looking for a redeeming relationship. There is a chink in their armor and that chink is the need for love—the need to fill that "vast empty space," for which their "hunger" is a substitute, with feelings of self-worth.

The goal of initial sessions is to make a connection. To focus on the child's anger can impede that task. The child cannot understand his rage, nor the reasons for it, until he has built up a reservoir of positive images of the counselor and of himself. Helping the child to build an alliance with you is identical with the first aim of counseling: *strengthen relationships with caretakers*. You are a potential caretaker and the aim applies to you as well. The goal is to support the child's control of impulses—he has a long history of ventilating them.

> ADULT: I realize how upset you are with me. And I'm pleased that you have kept control of yourself and your feelings. Can you draw a picture of how you feel?

Shifting Feelings Acted out to Feelings Verbalized

There are three major approaches to this task. The first is to *continually bring reality into the counseling sessions*. Misbehavior displayed outside of the sessions needs to be discussed within the session, particularly when the child produces no feeling material within the session. The second is to *encourage, model, or teach play* in an effort to develop defense mechanisms. The third is an effort to get the child to *communicate the violent diffuse fantasies* he keeps hidden in his head.

Bringing In Reality

When the child remains "defensively silent" (by silent, I mean unrevealing—solitary play, endless drawing, model building or game playing) in order to avoid revealing himself, information obtained from parents or teachers must be used to confront the defenses of denial and isolation. Richard Gardner uses the term *ignorant interrogator* to refer to the style of questioning put to the child. With younger children I often use a wizard puppet to ask questions, and on some occasions I will be a TV news reporter interviewing the child.

Every antisocial act that the child displays needs to be explored both in terms of its appropriateness and the ideas in the child's head that produced these actions. Because you do not punish or scold the child for these disclosures, he learns that disclosure is not traumatic. Introducing confrontations in the role of the ignorant interrogator usually provokes the child to tell his side of the story.

Sometimes parents, and even teachers, are unwilling to share information about a child's behaviors. If the teacher is reluctant to let you observe the child, see the child with a peer for several extra sessions and you will easily see his difficulties.

The counselor needs to "think out loud" in the presence of the "silent" child. The counselor talks about various problems currently troubling his parents or teachers and postulates the past and present reasons for their occurrence.

ADULT: I understand that you hit your favorite teacher today. You must feel bad.

CHILD: No, I didn't—I don't feel anything.

ADULT: No, it's not true that you don't feel anything. You just don't feel bad or guilty, perhaps you feel defiant—a defiant feeling—"I don't care!" Maybe you feel righteous—she deserved it because you feel she treated you unfairly. Maybe you feel indifferent—numbed.

Because the child initially responded with a "feeling" instead of an excuse, the counselor took the opportunity to help the child to label his possible feelings. Labeling is an educational approach often used with aggressive children who feel that anger is the only response to frustration. They cannot label feelings of disgust, embarrassment, discouragement, shame, jealousy, worry, etc. Helping them to do so also helps them to realize that there are other ways to deal with feelings than simply striking out.

When reality is brought into sessions, habitually aggressive children are masters at excusing their behavior, avoiding effort, playing the victim, refusing to accept obligations, and refusing to acknowledge fear. They feel entitled to display unrealistic expectations and false pride, fail to plan ahead, and make irresponsible decisions. All these behaviors are part of the child's power tactics, as well as his defenses. They are efforts to overcome others in struggles and to avoid shame and helplessness. They will use them with you! Yet they are also *manipulative.* I use this word with caution because so much of children's anxious and symptomatic behavior is described by parents and educators as manipulative. I use the word here to mean the child's efforts to discredit you as trustworthy. If you "believe" his stories you are weak and not worth identifying with. Moreover, you cannot really like the child because you do not really know who he is. A person strong enough to resist the child's manipulations provides the child with the security he needs.

At the same time, one part of the child believes his own stories (assumptive realities). Confrontations, put in the form of gentle puzzlement, are required to chip away at the child's "reasons" for his inappropriate behavior.

ADULT: Did you bring your point sheet to show me?
CHILD: I forgot.
ADULT: Gee, last week you remembered that I said I'd help you build a model. Suppose I forgot to bring the model?

· · ·

CHILD: I'm taking this car from the room.
ADULT: You still expect that I will give you things you know you can't have? You want to see if I value things more than I value you, and you think that I won't give you things because I value possessions more.

· · ·

CHILD: My mom's going to give me that race-car set.
ADULT: I think Mom is too upset with you to give you that, particularly since you order her to buy it like you order me to give you things. You're going to be disappointed.

· · ·

CHILD: (Knocks checkers on floor)
ADULT: A guy can feel mad about losing a game but it's more grown up to say so than to scatter checkers all over the room.

· · ·

CHILD: You don't trust me.
ADULT: That's true, you have betrayed my trust on several occa-

sions. Once when you promised me that if I let you go you wouldn't hit Jim, and when I did, you ran over and hit him.

. . .

CHILD: I can't do that.

ADULT: Lots of times you didn't feel like doing something you're capable of doing, particularly when you know an adult wants you to do it—you hate feeling controlled by an adult. Sometimes just to do your schoolwork makes you feel like the grown-up held you down and sat on you—that's what "feeling controlled" can feel like to you.

. . .

CHILD: I'm too tired to do that.

ADULT: Gee, you have lots of energy for those things you want to do.

. . .

CHILD: It was all Bill's fault that we didn't go to the park.

ADULT: Sometimes things don't always work out the way we want. I'll bet Bill feels bad too.

. . .

ADULT: Sometimes I wonder if you need the teacher to pay attention to you because you feel lonely when no one notices you.

. . .

ADULT: You get others upset so you're not alone in your own upsetness.

. . .

CHILD: I did not make a mistake, you did.

ADULT: If I did, I'm sorry. But mistakes are things to learn from so we can do better next time. But some children think they'll never do better. You think like that a lot.

. . .

CHILD: I'm not afraid.

ADULT: Every time I go near the edge of a cliff I fear I'll fall so my fear keeps me away from the edge and keeps me from ever falling. But you—you'd walk near the edge to convince yourself you're not afraid, and you might fall.

. . .

CHILD: Bob always teases me.

ADULT: Even when you complain about Bob teasing you, it also sounds as if you have some other feelings about Bob's behavior towards you!

Many people are angered by the aggressive child's chronic lying in his attempt to avoid responsibility for his actions. Do not confuse lying with denial or feelings of entitlement. These children, not unlike other children whose "facts" become truths, quickly believe their own lies, a quick fix for their inability to tolerate shame or guilt. They are masters at distorting situations and the lie is part of this distortion. Direct confrontation of the lie is useless. They also feel entitled:

A child care worker heard a noise in the kitchen, went downstairs, and turned on the lights. The room was empty, but when he opened the door to the small pantry, a nine-year-old with cookie crumbs on his face immediately cried out, "I didn't take the cookies!" When this incident was discussed in the next counseling session, the child insisted that he felt entitled to the cookies because he felt he had been unfairly deprived of his dessert at the evening meal.

Let me reiterate that these confrontations of the child with his behavior are not done in the manner of a child in the principal's office. The child usually is engaged in an activity with the counselor. Sometimes the counselor is making something or doing something for the child, timing symbolic giving with his "taking away."

Encourage, Model, and Teach Play

Many angry children will not draw or play out their feelings. Nevertheless, the goal is to convert action into fantasy. Often the progression is first from action to action fantasy. For example, the counselor uses a cylindrical cloth punching bag on which drawings can be made in chalk to encourage play action. The child can be given a Nerf ball and told to throw it at a fantasy target on the wall. The child can be asked who the target is, why he is mad at the target, etc. These outlets are initially used to block destructive interaction and to encourage movement towards symbolic and verbalized aggression. Getting the child to talk while he is engaged in play action is adhering to *Communication Principle 3: Encourage the child to talk about anything.* Talking about his anger is a step toward delaying its direct expression.

Much time will be devoted by the counselor to both helping the child who does not play to learn to play (much like the mother who plays with her two-year-old) and to divert his feelings into play. The counselor models make-believe play and helps elaborate on the primitive play themes the child does display. The counselor helps the child who simply bangs trucks together to make the trucks deliver something, contain people, etc.

An important point to remember is that *fantasy unfolds in response to the play materials.* The fantasy is not in the child's head in a planful fashion and the toys are merely used to express it. Rather, the toys create the expression of thoughts that are there but are not consciously organized. Teaching the child to play and providing the "right toys" for the child brings the child's concerns to the suface. A toy wheelchair can help a child express feelings about his mother's or his own illness; a toy ambulance can help a child bring out feelings about bodily harm. The counselor can help the child expand upon the ambulance play so that it becomes more elaborate and thematic.

Sometimes the young child becomes frightened by his own projections. The child who picks up the scissors and then flees saying, "You're going to hurt me," reveals his confusion between attacker and victim.

The child who wants to make swords will quickly want to duel. He is closer to tearing the room apart than is the child who draws swords or spins fantasies about sword-wielding warriors. Encouraging fantasy development sometimes alternates with discouraging grandiose fantasies that feed omnipotence.

CHILD: (Picks up a large piece of paper and says it's a sword)
ADULT: You wish it were a sword.
CHILD: I once had a sword.
ADULT: It was not a real one.
CHILD: It was plastic but it had a real pearl handle.

ADULT: It could not have been real pearl. When you make up such stories it's because you're worried about something. What's troubling you so much that you need a sword to defend yourself with?

On some occasions, the counselor will have to interrupt an ongoing play activity that leads to excitement. When the child's talk or play relates to sexual concerns the feelings expressed can lead to dancing around, undressing, and attempts at touching.

ADULT: We can talk about genitals but we cannot show them.

Remember *Interview Goal 6: Be alert to the possibility that the child may be reexperiencing some critical moment from his recent or distant past.* The counselor can forget that the action-oriented child can also use his actions to communicate. If he "hurts" himself during counseling sessions, or repeatedly hurts himself outside of sessions, he may be experimenting with hurting himself as a reaction to his having been hurt or witnessing the hurt of another child with whom he identifies.

Encouraging Communication of Violent Fantasies

The counselor needs to encourage the child to reveal his violent primitive fantasies. Some years ago, John Leon of the Violence Clinic in Baltimore found that when he encouraged clients to express in detail the fantasies of their anticipated violent behavior, it reduced their acting out. The development of the fantasy seemed to produce anxiety, and this anxiety inhibited action.

Not only the beginning counselor, but all of us want to deny the existence of hostile fantasies. We believe the child incapable of such thoughts. However, when they trust their counselor, who is not shocked by their angry fantasies, sometimes they will reveal them. Maxwell Gitelson presents the case of a young adult who had the following fantasies throughout his life, sometimes when he masturbated and other times during daydreaming:

He is commanding a powerful air fleet which is executing a bombing mission. He is in an underground country where people cannibalize each other, especially eating each other's genitals, which preferably are torn from the living person. He is a ten-year-old boy and an older girl is about to do this to him. Another boy kills the girl by stabbing her in the rectum or vagina.

Leon Shenken presents the case of a sixteen-year-old who killed his six- and three-year-old sisters as part of a plan to kill his father. After the child turned himself over to the police, a large volume of prose and poetry was discovered in his room. Many of his stories involved multiple murders, mutilation, and dismemberment. The culprits were always apprehended and given the death penalty.

There was a story in which he visualized his own death, and there were many others liberally illustrated with drawings of men being hanged or lying dismembered, and one drawing in particular was captioned with his own name as "preacher and gunman."

Although the boy had idle thoughts about killing his father, his literary efforts were never at any stage concerned with interfamily violence. The characters—killers and victims—were strangers. If he was depicted, he was the victim. Evidently, the child lost the distance from his murderous feelings that these fantasies provided him and could no longer contain his murderous feelings. When these feelings were discharged in the acts against the sisters, the child's sense of reality returned and he turned himself over to the authorities. He killed his sisters painlessly because he reasoned that they would have no one to care for them after he killed his father and mother—and he killed his mother because she would be lonely without a husband.

An example of a confrontation that led to a discussion of fantasy appears below:

ADULT: Your mother tells me you can't get to sleep at night.
CHILD: I like staying up.
ADULT: And you and your mother argue endlessly about your bedtime.
CHILD: So.
ADULT: I wonder if you're actually unwilling to fall asleep because you think you might die in your sleep.
CHILD: (Silence)
ADULT: Or maybe you have bad dreams. Children who are angry a

lot usually dream of scary things—monsters, evil men, or vicious criminals.

CHILD: Sometimes.

ADULT: I could help you to stop having these dreams.

CHILD: How?

ADULT: By helping you to understand why you're always so angry at everybody. But first you need to tell me about your daydreams and what you think about each time you get angry at someone.

CHILD: What do you mean?

ADULT: Like when your dad hits you and sends you to your room. How do you plan to get even with him?

When you explore these fantasies in detail or when the child presents a violent dream, the idea is not to trace their origins to anger at parents but to keep the boundaries between fantasy and reality clear. The task is not to bury the hostility but it is also not to deal with the feelings explicitly. The goal is to strengthen the child's feeling that his emotions are manageable and that he will not run wild.

ADULT: Lots of kids who are upset have some of the feelings you reveal in your dream. But remember it was only a dream. Your mother didn't really die in that accident. Part of you must have felt frightened by your dream.

This statement helps the child to avoid the repressive process that results in explosive behavior and supports control over the underlying feelings. Even when death wishes towards parents are barely concealed in an aggressive child's dreams or play, the need for connectedness far outweighs the need for awareness. Only when the child gains control over his anger can he begin to examine its sources. If the child is openly hostile at his parents the response becomes:

ADULT: Often kids get angry at their parents and this anger stirs up all kinds of confusing feelings. We will be talking about these feelings often in counseling.

Sometimes the child will experience his anger as "voices telling him what to do." These voices not only frighten him but also others whom he talks to about these voices. "Only crazy people hear voices."

ADULT: The voice telling you to do things is really the anger you feel that you often hate feeling. If it comes from outside you, you can own it. Remember when we talked about "Mr. Angry"? Now Mr. Angry has become so strong that you've put him outside of yourself and have him actually talking to you. I'll bet that's really scary.

When helping a child develop play actions or when exploring his primitive fantasy, the counselor is always walking a thin line. Talking about feelings or developing action fantasy can lead to action. It's no easy task to help the action-oriented child develop delay mechanisms.

Changing Negative Self-Image: Conveying its Nonreality

Many of the parents of aggressive children refer to them as monsters, viewing their child's aggressive reactions to their frustrations as willful assaults. In addition, these parents both externalize and project their own unacceptable behaviors onto the child who accepts them to avoid rejection.

During the first stage of counseling the child typically intensifies the manifestation of his nonhuman identity. He puts himself in the same role with the counselor as he experienced with his parents, repeating his maladaptive but familiar experience.

The counselor needs to bring the negative self-image out into the open so it can be clarified as a meaningful fantasy rather than as the reality both the child and his parents believe it to be. The counselor also shows the child how he uses this behavior to arouse anxiety in others and to maintain distance from them.

One day, eleven-year-old Valeria, a streetwise, pseudosophisticated girl, made clay cookies, put them on a plate, and put the plate on the floor. She then got down on her hands and knees, crawled around on the floor, growled like a dog, and started to eat the clay. The counselor took the plate from the floor, saying, "You're not a dog, but you're trying to show me how sometimes you feel like one."

Lora Heims Tessman and Irving Kaufman present the case of a nine-year-old girl who often thought of herself as a pig. She would say, "At home I'm always a pig. People don't invite pigs into their houses, they let them stand in the street." This child was seen at the same clinic six years earlier, at which time she endlessly dipped toilet paper into the toilet bowl and retrieved it. Her first complete sentence was about toilet activity. She seemed identified with feces, suggesting that the self-image can change its literal form but retain its dynamic meaning—from feces to pig. Her mother was simultaneously attracted and repelled by the idea of smearing. She unconsciously needed the child to portray her concrete symbolism of this messy component of her self. Thus, the girl's self-image was a reflection of her mother's unconscious view of her.

The counselor conveys that he is trying to understand and is not frightened by the child's communication of angry feelings, and that the child's images of destruction and of himself as both the destroyed and the destroyer have symbolic meaning. Gerald (from Tessman and Kaufman) reveals how a child's angry behaviors are often communications about his self-image rather than communications about facts.

> Five-year-old Gerald was seen in a hospital where he had been sent after attempting to cut his sister's arm off with a saw. He was destructive to himself and to others, seemingly unaware of the consequences of his behavior. Early in counseling he filled a glass with red paint, yelled that it was blood, and started to throw it. The counselor stopped him, telling him that no blood would be spilled here, that in here he would keep him safe. He then showed her a scratch on his finger. She replied that he must have lots of hurts. He replied, "They used to kick the football bloody." In later sessions, he conveyed his concept of himself as the football between his parents, who had both used him in some perverse sexual practices. Still later, Gerald tried to break the limbs of a baby doll, saying, "I'll break it so I can use it for a ball." The counselor stopped him, saying she knew how he felt like a broken baby, but that he was a real boy.

Rudolph Ekstein talks of forming a working alliance with the monstrous self-image. The counselor points out that the child's monsters seem to serve a positive function despite their cruel sadistic methods. "He wonders if they cannot be helped to become more rational so that they can give reasons for what they do." When appropriate, the counselor directs his remarks to the monsters. Each monster becomes someone with whom the child and the counselor can negotiate. Through this process each monster becomes more reasonable. The child becomes able to influence the monsters to help him be less punitive, less destructive, and more adaptive. Eventually the monsters fuse, become more benevolent, and recede into the background as the real child emerges.

A Concluding Remark

Salvador Minuchin and his colleagues, formerly on the staff of the Pleasantville Cottage Schools in New York, believe that the powerful sense of entitlement aggressive children display comes from internalizing their parents' feelings that whatever they gave to their children was never enough. Consequently, the children come to expect more. I think the feelings are more basic than that—I think they come from the feeling that they were actually cheated in life and that they deserve more. In the long run, these children need help to forgive a world that basically wasn't very good to them.

ADULT: It really stinks having to be in the middle of fights between Mom and Dad.

. . .

ADULT: It really hurts that your parents never come to see you play in the ball games.

The child also needs to learn that some of his behavior was, and perhaps still is, in response to inconsistent and erratic parental behavior.

ADULT: I don't know what made your mother so mad. Either you never know where you stand, or sometimes something you do will be naughty and another time it won't.

. . .

ADULT: Because your parents' rules seem unfair, the only rule you follow is to do what you think is best for you.

. . .

CHILD: I don't need any help.

ADULT: You need to reject my help because you learned to do things for yourself when no one helped you when you were little. You couldn't count on anybody but yourself.

9

The Process:
Stages of Counseling

Recovery is not an isolated event that suddenly appears; rather, it is a process that expresses itself in a wide range of subtle changes that occur during treatment.

—Hilde Baruch

Counseling proceeds in stages. It begins by acquiring as much background material about the referred child as possible. This material can include observations of the child in his natural settings. Erik Erickson, perhaps the "father" of play-therapy, always had dinner in the child's home prior to initiating treatment. Counselors in schools can observe the child in the classroom, during recess, and at gym. He can observe how the child interacts with his family when he holds an initial "planning conference." The goal of this information gathering is to arrive at a developmental picture of the child. If the assessment reveals a child with severe developmental arrest, then counseling will unfold differently than it will with a child whose development is more advanced.

In many instances, however, the counselor does not have reliable informants and will have to depend upon his sessions with the child to arrive at a developmental picture. Arriving at this picture is part of the first stage of counseling: *to obtain an understanding and an analysis of the child's problem.* In this stage the child is helped to realize that counseling is a process where he will learn about both his strengths and his weaknesses, and why he has the worries that he does, a process he will resist.

Getting the Child to Come

In chapter 4, I provided illustrations of a counselor setting the stage for the counseling process, anticipating the concerns of both the child and his parents, and reflecting the feelings behind these concerns. These efforts are important because you cannot counsel a child who does not come for counseling. Stage 1 includes obtaining and maintaining a commitment from all parties that the child will come regularly for counseling sessions.

Parents are often faced with their child's refusal to come. If the parents feel ambivalence about their child's coming, then they will have difficulty getting him to each session scheduled. If the parents are united in their resolve, the child typically makes little fuss about coming and begins to look forward to sessions. Parents who experience difficulty setting limits on their child will also experience similar difficulty enforcing the "rule" that counseling sessions are attended. Children of indecisive parents have learned that their parents will back down if they make a big fuss, so they fuss about counseling.

The older child usually understands why he has been brought to counseling. Typically, he has for some time displayed behaviors that disturb others. When his parents finally decide that something should be done, they find themselves helplessly unable to do so, and their defensive anger escalates. In response to these belated efforts, the child often becomes more angry and defiant, and new difficulties are added to the old ones. The child wants no part of counseling as he views it as a further effort to change the behavior he so desperately feels a need to hold on to. Often the parents see the child as getting worse and this destroys the little resolve they had to get the child to come.

The counselor should always explain to parents in an information sharing interview how the child is liable to behave when referred for counseling. He may temporarily improve, or he may escalate his troublesome behaviors and refuse to come. While refusal to come sometimes occurs initially, it recurs later when the child realizes that he will be examining his worries or when he resists the confusion that changes in his feelings bring about. A printed handout that explains the possible "side effects" of counseling is often helpful to parents. If a child misses a session, the family should be called and asked if the child's behavior contributed to this decision. If so, the parents need gentle reminding that they were "warned" about such behavior and encouragement to bring in the child for another appointment.

ADULT: Mrs. Brown, thank you for being truthful with me about how hard it is to get Joseph to come for his sessions. It must make you feel like an ogre to drag him to the car. I'll bet he even says you don't love him or he doesn't love you. But part of you knows that he needs to come and I'd like to acknowledge you for your efforts. I'm sure you'll have him here for his next session. Should I call your husband and ask him to help?

Initiating Counseling in Schools

Sometimes a parent asks for counseling to be part of a child's educational plan, but more often the parent simply complies with the recommendations of school authorities. Some parents fear that their child will reveal family secrets to the counselor that will reflect poorly upon them or involve them with child protective services. The child is aware of his parents' fears and he often verbalizes them to the counselor. "I ain't telling you my worries 'cause it's none of your business." "My mom said I don't have to talk to you if I don't want to."

Often children referred for in-school counseling go through periods where they refuse to come to sessions. Externalizers will verbally harass the counselor when he comes to get them, calling the counselor stupid, retarded, and other things the child has been called. Such behavior puts the child in a powerful position. He conveys his distaste in front of the teacher and classmates when the counselor comes to get him. If the child is given a pass to the counselor's office, he will refuse the pass and will tell his teacher he is not going. Adding insult to injury, children in the same class who see the counselor can band together and resist counseling.

The teacher needs to inform the child that it is his time for counseling, that she expects him to go, that she has nothing planned for him in class, and ask him to leave. She should not threaten him with loss of field trips or special activities. If he refuses, then the crisis worker should be called to escort him to counseling. "You have a choice, you either leave for your counseling or I will have you escorted." If the child chooses to leave and then wanders the hallway, then school rules about such behavior should be enforced.

The First Stage:
Establishing the Working Relationship

In chapter 4, I gave an example of an initial session with a mother and child. Often such sessions are preferred because the child immediately learns that the counselor does not join his parent in an expected scolding for his misbehavior, but simply asks his view of the situation and gives him equal time. Below is an interview with just the child present.

ADULT: Your parents brought you to see me today because they are concerned about your temper. They say you start fights with younger children and they're afraid you'll hurt one of these kids badly. They also say that you have no friends and seem to be very sad and unhappy. What do you think about your parents' concerns?

CHILD: I have friends.

ADULT: So you don't agree with your parents that you're friendless and unhappy?

CHILD: (Silence; nervous, fidgety)

ADULT: You can move around if you want to. We can talk without having to sit.

CHILD: I don't want to talk.

ADULT: Talking about worries and troubles is hard for some children to do. But talk helps us to keep the worries inside us from busting out in behavior towards others, like your parents and teachers don't like.

CHILD: I don't have any worries.

ADULT: Right now I think you're worried about what will happen here. Most kids are nervous about coming to a new place to meet a new person, particularly when they're coming about troubles.

CHILD: (Wanders over to the shelves in the office and asks if we could play checkers)

ADULT: We can play checkers while we talk.

CHILD: I like to play checkers.
ADULT: And who do you play with?
CHILD: My mom, once in a while.

The counselor could have asked the child if he played checkers with friends and perhaps gotten the child to admit that he had no friends to play with. But counseling is not a trial, it is not a place to get the child to confirm his parents' views or to confess his shortcomings. It is a place to start a process, to fulfill the aims of counseling presented in chapter 2. The counselor looks upon this last statement as an opportunity to achieve *Aim 1: Strengthen the child's relationship with caretakers.* Consequently, he proceeds as follows:

ADULT: Did your mom teach you how to play checkers?
CHILD: Yes.
ADULT: And these were good times? I'll bet you wish you could play with her more often. Maybe after you see me a while she'll play with you more, but I can't promise you that.

The counselor adheres to both the second part of *Interview Goal 1,* that the interviewer can enable the child, and to *Interview Goal 8,* that there is hope for better relationships with others.

ADULT: Why do you suppose Mommy played with you more before?
CHILD: (Silent, continues playing and then is distracted by his thoughts and seems uninterested in the game)
ADULT: Seems like my last question took your mind off the game.
CHILD: (No response)
ADULT: I have some drawing paper and marking pencils. Why don't you make a picture?

Initial counseling sessions should not be interrogative. The counselor should respect that the child is not yet ready to explore his feelings about his mother, at least not verbally. The counselor does not change the subject, he just changes the medium of expression.

CHILD: What shall I draw?
ADULT: Why don't you draw your family doing something?
CHILD: I'll draw a car.

The child's drawings were not particularly revealing. Drawings a child makes early in counseling are often understood in retrospect, e.g., a child's hero might be a race-car driver, he could have witnessed an auto accident, his family might have bought a new car, etc.

In the next session, the child again played checkers. As the counselor won more of his pieces, the child began to cheat, whereupon he accused the counselor of cheating, knocked the checkers on the floor, called the counselor ugly, and tried to leave the room.

ADULT: I know how hard it is for some kids to lose a game. They feel awful, but now I think I understand why Mom stopped playing checkers with you. Lots of grown-ups don't know how to play checkers with kids who feel awful when they lose. They want their child to be grown up before they are ready. Maybe your mom was disappointed that you felt so bad losing.

CHILD: She called me a "sore loser."

ADULT: Here, let's play again and I'll start with one less row of checkers than you because I'm older and should play better.

I do not deliberately lose to a child. If I cannot adapt the game so that it is competitive, I discourage its use and introduce a game that can be adapted or a game of chance. In adapting the game, three purposes are achieved. First, a model is presented of a way he and his mother might play in the future so that the odds are even. Second, if the game is modified to the degree that it is obvious the child will win, the intellectual awareness that "losing" is a problem looms so large that it becomes humorous. Third, when the game is modified to the point where the child cannot lose, the counselor can attempt to translate the game situation into a battleground on which deadly enemies are pitted against each other, each seeking the other's destruction. Since he cannot lose, the child may revel in his new powers, and in the context of the new definition of the game, reveal new feelings. This last tactic was not necessary in this present case.

ADULT: I kind of get the feeling that you love to win. Look how you gloat each time you beat me even when you know I start out with less checkers. I'll bet other kids don't like playing with you, just like your mother doesn't.

CHILD: They don't, they don't like me.

ADULT: And some of them call you ugly and it makes you feel bad and mad at the same time.

CHILD: I don't care; I don't like them, either.

ADULT: (Very softly, in a sad tone) You can't fool me, every boy I know who doesn't have friends feels lonely—but he thinks he needs to be brave and not admit it even to himself—the hardest person to admit it to because then loneliness replaces the anger. Often you've tried to start all over again, but you get in your own way. My job is to help you to find out why you can't make friends, and we've already discovered one of the reasons.

CHILD: What's that?

ADULT: Always having to win and making games more than just a game.

In these two initial sessions the counselor and, more importantly, the child obtained an initial understanding of the child's problem. In a tactful and supportive manner, the counselor and the child agreed that the child's behavior not only was troublesome to others, but was troublesome to him. It lost him some loving attention from his mother and it cost him friendships. He also felt poorly about himself, believing himself to be ugly. The counselor then gave the child the message that counseling will address these issues and help the child to do something about them.

The First Stage with Aggressive Children

With aggressive, impulse-ridden children, the first stage of counseling may take a long time, sometimes over a year. While the counselor understands the problem, the child resists understanding or gives lip service to the counselor's explanations of his difficulties. Often, under stress, the child will admit to feeling worthless and hopeless, only to revert back to denial of problems when the stress dissipates and his defenses are remobilized. When unconscious concerns burst out of the child and are "caught" by the counselor and understood, there is no continuity because the child immediately seals up.

After a time, the child begins to realize that the counselor is not like his perception of his parents; he is not contradictory, angry or placatory, but reliable and trustworthy, and a change begins to come over the child. His anxiety diminishes, he tests limits less often, and he begins to play. The activities he performed in a mechanical, robotlike way he now takes some pleasure in performing. The emotional atmosphere changes. This change is fostered by the counselor periodically assisting the child with everyday problems, such as helping him with schoolwork or intervening in conflicts with authority figures. It also is fostered by the counselor passing the child's many tests to see what the counselor is made of and if he is genuinely interested in him. These tests include: memory tests, such as telling you names of friends and enemies and expecting you to remember them weeks later; revealing weaknesses, such as making mistakes and awaiting your comments and judgments; tests of love, do you remember my special achievements or my birthday?; tests of fairness ("I had to wait five minutes for you, now I get five minutes extra at the end. I'm not leaving—you owe me five"); and tests of confidence—do you tell others about my misbehavior in counseling sessions?

Tests of confidence sometimes require the counselor to set limits. For example, the child shows you a pocketknife his father gave him and asks if you are going to tell on him because possession of a knife in school is against the rules.

ADULT: I guess you're proud that your dad gave you a knife and maybe you think you need it to defend yourself from other kids here. But I'm afraid that I'll have to keep it and return it to you after school. I hope you won't bring it tomorrow.

CHILD: That's mine, give it back!

ADULT: At the end of the day. I'll keep it safely here in my pocket. I know that you feel I betrayed you—you showed it to me and now I take it from you. That doesn't seem fair.

CHILD: You bitch.

ADULT: I wonder if you didn't show me the knife so you'd have a reason to get angry and reject me?

When the child begins to develop a trusting relationship with the counselor, he usually intensifies the manifestations of his "monstrous" self-image, thereby repeating his pathological but familiar experience. Remember that repeating and reliving conflicts in the counseling relationship is what produces change. Merely remembering them as matters of the past is of little value.

The Second Stage:
Analysis of the Problem and Its Cause

Earlier I described the child who admitted both to having no friends and to problems with his mother. The "cause" established during these initial sessions was the child's difficulty in losing at games. The next step would be to help the child peel away another layer. He needs to learn about his unrealistically high standards and how they are maintained by fantasies of grandiosity. He needs to learn that his illusions are temporarily shattered by losing. Self-criticism occurs and the anxiety that criticism generates is defended against by reestablishing his grandiosity. Then he needs to learn how he got these standards. If his parents are not overly critical, he may move through this process smoothly. His high standards may be misguided efforts to win parental approval that can be won more easily. They may be a defensive reaction to being learning disabled and being in a special class. In this instance, the child was struggling with the view that if he lives up to certain standards, his parents will stop fighting over him, more harmonious family life will occur, and his parents will not get divorced and abandon him.

ADULT: Do you ever think you have to be a perfect kid to keep your mom and dad from fighting and perhaps breaking up? And when you can't be, you get so angry with yourself that you create more problems—like when you lose at checkers.

CHILD: If my dad likes me, why did he go away and leave me with my mom who's always picking on me?

ADULT: Like you sometimes feel your teacher also does—pick on you? If Dad was back, everything would be better?

With relatively well-functioning children, following the analysis of the problem and its cause, the counselor moves to the third stage where he explains the problem to the child and *helps the child to establish and implement a formula for change.*

ADULT: You seem to have a lot of feelings about your parents' divorce. Maybe it's easier to be mad at yourself, and sometimes at your mom, than to be mad at your dad for leaving. Perhaps you feel that if you got angry at him he would see you even less. I think if we talk more about your feelings about the divorce, then some of the anger that gets you into trouble with your mom and your teachers just might go away.

The Second Stage with Aggressive Children

The major task of the first stage is forming a relationship, allaying anxiety and defining the nature of counseling. The major task of the second stage for the aggressive child is to encourage the child's entry into latency-age functioning and to aid his progress with the developmental tasks of latency. While the counselor has been able to define the problem and its cause, explaining the problem to the child is the major task of the second stage of therapy. Constant interpretation of the child's feelings, including those of low self-worth, and of the defenses he uses to avoid these feelings is the "explanation of the problem." At the same time, the counselor has implemented the formula for change by employing strategies to promote the child's development.

During the second stage, the child will experience considerable conflict about his identity. Counseling will progress only if the child begins to relinquish the pathological identity that he believes he needs in order to survive and to maintain his relationship with his parents. The child actively struggles with the feelings generated by the conflict between his old identity and the new identity that is evolving in his relationship to his counselor—and perhaps to other helpers in his environment.

By introjecting some of the empathetic qualities of the counselor, the aggressive child gets in touch with his passive longings and denied dependency needs. The urge to be taken care of, even babied, becomes strong. The stage is set for the emergence of these conflicts when the child begins to ask questions about the permanence of the counselor: "How long will you be my counselor?" "Will I change counselors when I change classes next year?" "Can I stay longer?" "Can I have more sessions?" The child wants to give things to the counselor or do things for him. The child might report that "I beat up other children because they said mean things about my mom (dad)," thinly disguised efforts to befriend the counselor. One child with a female counselor remarked that "I don't hate little girls or women, only girls my age who are pesty and bother me." The counselor who experiences such behavior should be forewarned that an affective storm is coming, and brace for it.

Some children immediately respond to dependency needs with massive denial. They continue to come to counseling but complain about how "dumb and boring" the sessions are. They are usually children who use "thrill seeking" to avoid depression. Escape from intimacy is a prime motivator. As their massive denial of intimacy needs wanes in the face of the empathetic adult, they often refuse to come to counseling, and there is very little the counselor can do about it. The child who actively struggles with this conflict is a healthier child. He is less disturbed, but more disturbing! The child willing to struggle often becomes interested in baby books or may wrap up in blankets. Many begin to talk "baby talk." Others want to wear the articles of clothing belonging to the counselor. One eleven-year-old, a streetwise, inner city girl, who came into counseling looking like a "little hooker," used to suck on a baby bottle and threatened to kill me if I ever told anybody. During this period, she also drew pictures of pregnant-looking women, with giant suction-cup stomachs that sucked in and spewed out babies. Because the fear of passive dependency increased, she temporarily resolved this conflict by killing the "babies within her."

These children initially defend against the expression of their passive longings by increasing their negativism. They also negate these feelings—"This is not me." They typically refuse to come, fighting against their dependent needs, and when they do come, they refuse to leave. As the intensity of the need to be taken care of grows stronger, the child experiences this as a loss of his own identity as a tough guy and of his willpower. Remember how it felt when you first fell in love—it was as if you lost your will. And remember, too, when you lose a loved one, you feel like you have lost your reason to be. The child experiences both of these feelings in his struggle. But even more powerful for some children is their unconscious feeling that change will result in the loss of the little parental love available to them. Part of the child "knows" that he is an externalization of his parents' negative self-images. By accepting them, he keeps his parents healthy and insures his place in the family.

When the child finally gives in to his dependency longings, he both overidealizes the counselor and increases his demands upon him. The child will then feel betrayed. When the counselor cannot meet the child's insatiable demands, the child temporarily reverts back to his old ways. "Since I can't get enough, what's the use in trying?" In addition, the counselor's empathetic caring arrives with a lost quality that precipitates depressed and angry feelings. "How come my mother never treated me like this?"

This problem can be confounded by sexual feelings associated with passivity. The child with the same-sexed counselor may experience homosexual panic, while the child with an opposite-sexed counselor may become seductive. A boy may often do things for the female counselor that are symbolic preludes to sexual invasion. He will show her things from his pockets, offer to clean out her desk drawer, or organize things in her purse. This will be followed by snatching her purse and rifling through it. He will want the counselor to show her new clothes to his father. He will want to draw marks on both his hands and the counselor's hands. He will save his marks and look to see if the counselor saved hers over the week.

All these factors, passive longings, identity confusion, loyalty conflicts, survival fear, betrayal feelings, and sexual stirrings combine to create a period of resistance to change. The counselor needs to convey steadfastly to the child that she recognizes the existence of these struggles in the tactful manner described in the last chapter, a task made difficult by the counselor's being constantly bombarded with hostility. The task is particularly difficult in school settings because the child's conflicts with the counselor spill over into the larger school environment and subject the counselor to unjust criticism by educational staff.

The counselor needs to remember that the child is reliving his old conflicts (his feelings of passive helplessness in response to angry parents). It is the successful resolution of these conflicts within the counseling situation that changes the child. Insight for a child is a shift in the child's attitude, a lessening of a need to project feelings and anxieties. It is tough to remember this goal when the child is tormenting you. The counselor needs to communicate to the child that his emotions are manageable and need not run wild. He also distinguishes his dependency needs upon the counselor, from which he rebels, from necessary dependency upon others. The passive-active conflict needs active verbalization.

CHILD: I'm not leaving.

ADULT: Sometimes it's hard to separate from someone you're beginning to like.

CHILD: Not me.

ADULT: And at other times you refuse to come. The need to be close to me really bothers you. You think I'll reject you.

CHILD: Don't be stupid.

ADULT: I wonder if there isn't a part of you that likes coming here and another part that doesn't. The part that likes it is the part that needs to be taken care of like all of us need. The other part is the tough guy that feels he needs nobody and can take care of himself.

CHILD: Counselors sure are screwy!

ADULT: And the tough guy part fights with the other part. Just because you sometimes fight this inner battle doesn't mean being taken care of a little makes you a helpless baby. You can't allow yourself to feel soft feelings because soft means weak and weak means girlish or faggish or whatever you say to yourself about soft feelings. I'll bet you've never seen men hug before, and when your mother hugs you, you squirm.

CHILD: My mom doesn't hug me.

ADULT: Did she ever hug you?

CHILD: I can't remember.

ADULT: Can you remember anyone ever hugging you? How about when you were a baby?

CHILD: I don't remember.

ADULT: Do you ever give your mother a hug?

CHILD: Ugh!

ADULT: That's sad that you've never been hugged—no wonder we're having such a struggle. Don't worry, I won't hug you, but someday maybe you and your mother will hug one another again.

The female counselor may have to address any sexual issues confounding this conflict.

ADULT: One way to avoid having to experience soft or warm and tender feelings is to make me into a girlfriend instead of an adult, then you don't have to deal with these feelings.

CHILD: You have a dirty mind.

ADULT: I think of you as a counseling student, not as a boyfriend, but the way you treat me tells me that this "dirty mind" you speak about is your own sexual feelings. But sexual thoughts are not dirty. All people have them—they're normal. But you confuse tenderness with these thoughts and that is a problem we need to work on even though it will make you very uncomfortable.

All these comments are typically made as the child stands in front of the door, turns the lights on and off, and insults the counselor. As the child works these feelings through, they continue to be discussed, but in a more calm and relaxed manner while the child engages in play or games. Often, the child has to be challenged to make progress at this stage.

ADULT: You only know how to hit or kick or yell at me, you don't seem to know how to talk to me. When you decide to talk, I'll be here for you, but right now if you can't talk, I'll have to have you escorted back to class. I'm proud that you found a way to accept your dependency feelings today, and I'll also be proud when you learn to leave and can give up feeling good temporarily.

The Struggle with Losing Parental Ties

The counselor needs to help the child to realize that the images of "good" and "bad" that he has projected onto the therapist and his family are not reality. His parents do possess some positive qualities but because he is often locked in power struggles with them, just as he is with the counselor, these positive qualities are unavailable to him. The child needs to know that his parents are also getting some help, when this is the case. It often occurs that when very disturbed children get better that their parents develop symptoms. The child needs to know that his parents can seek help just like he has. His improvement is not harming them; they have problems like he had and need help for themselves.

The Second Stage as a Talking–Playing Stage

During this phase of counseling, the child brings up issues with which he is struggling and the counselor attempts to relate them to the earlier or ongoing explanations of his problems and to the formula outlined for change. Topics like peer relationships, school functioning, or future plans are discussed alongside of play actions or playacting. Interpretations within the metaphor are made at the same time others are made directly. When the aggressive child develops real autonomy, his surface behavior can seem worse. The child will move into expressing conflicts of the next stages. He may become more competitive or exhibitionistic, or increase his sexual misbehavior outside of treatment. It is helpful to periodically reassess the child to determine if his new symptoms are signs of "higher-level" conflicts.

Some General Principles of Change

When a child first enters counseling, the counselor's empathetic focusing results in predictable gradual changes. The initial feelings the child expresses are diffuse and undifferentiated. They are global responses to anxiety. The child has lost contact with the experiences and the wants that aroused his negative feelings. His anxieties have become pervasive and are no longer tied to the reality situations that produced them. As these pervasive feelings are accepted, the child will himself begin to focus on the specific sources of his negative feelings. The depressed, withdrawn child will become more aggressive while the aggressive child will concentrate less on breaking everything and more on pounding the baby doll, etc. As these more specific feelings are accepted, some positive feelings are expressed and ambivalence is recognized. Feelings become more related to reality situations of the moment.

By discovering both the specific reasons for his anxiety and his suppressed needs, the child recaptures those phases of his earlier development that he had been unable to assimilate fully. The child's increasing activities in counseling are manifestations of the different stages of his development that were poorly assimilated. When he has moved to where his pressing concerns have lost their compelling power, the child will begin to play and respond to the counselor's play. As Erikson remarks, the play will then offer an outline of the "inner maze in which he is caught." If the child is capable of play, his play will move from disorganized regressed play to more complex play. Remember that the child's play is shaped by the presence of the counselor. Typically, children about five avoid adult observation of their play, making play in counseling a unique experience for the child.

The progression from diffuse, undifferentiated expressions of anxiety to more focused anxiety is illustrated by the behavior of Carol, a seven-year-old who fell asleep in school, cried a lot, appeared sad, and played tricks on other children. Her mother admits to not caring enough, to being too tired to spend time with Carol, but says she is such "a good little girl" and loves her little brother.

> Session 1: Carol enters the playroom and says, "I never do anything fun, I'm not happy." She looked sad and scooped sand endlessly for no apparent purpose. She saw the stuffed bears and said, "The bear is unhappy, too." She named the bears "Winnie Gentle Pooh, Small Bear, Honey Bear" and called herself "Carol Sunshine" because she liked that name better than her own. She called the counselor "Bracelet Mouth" (the counselor wore braces) and "Mousie."
>
> She then gave Pooh Bear a spanking and said he should "Ssh, he was a naughty bear." She built a house out of the blocks and put Pooh Bear in a room with no way out, and said, "He had to stay there 'cause he said naughty words, the 'f' words. His parents could say them but he couldn't." She said she disliked Small Bear. Pooh Bear swore at Small Bear and got sent to bed.
>
> She then made a "tea party" and brought some friends— "There's only Raggedy Ann and Andy and me." "Pooh Bear, Pooh Bear, Pooh Bear. There is the quiet box. He's got to go in the quiet box. Pooh—you're too fat. Too much honey. You take the slide and squish him, squish him, squish him. Nobody can look in and he's not going to look. Pooh would be screaming if they came in and didn't let him out of there." She then stacked four big blocks to block Pooh Bear in there. "I don't care— somebody cares, but not me. I don't care."

In this first session, the child, almost parrotlike, reports that she is unhappy. We are not clear whether she identifies with Winnie Gentle Pooh or if she hopes that the counselor will be gentle. Then she punished Pooh for bad behavior and locked him in the quiet box.

Pooh Bear is too fat because he eats too much honey (too needy?) and needs to be squished (to be thinner?).

Is the bad behavior calling the counselor "bracelet mouth?" She told Pooh to "ssh" and gave him a spanking. Most likely, it is a mixture of punishment for present and past behavior, all blurred and confusing to her at this point.

Sessions 2 and 3: Carol shows curiosity about the large "bean" bags in the room. She opens zippers and keeps plunging her arms in and out of each bag. She loves the soft feel of the styrofoam inside. She then tells a story about a girl who touched her mother's glasses and broke them. The girl got caught. She never wanted to touch anything again. But then she got *this friend* who told her what to touch and what not to touch. Then she could touch things again.

She then says that Pooh Bear doesn't remember her. The counselor replies that "Pooh Bear doesn't forget his friends." Carol then remarks, "I like to do things that scare me—Pooh Bear is scared, but I don't like it if people scare me."

In this session, she expresses her need for affection and for a new friend (the counselor?) to help her. She admits to doing things that scare herself (playing tricks on others, is it a counterphobic behavior?) and that she doesn't like being scared.

Session 4: "I can be mean. I was mean to you last week. Maybe I'll be mean again. I locked my brother in the bedroom, and told him he'd better shut up. I'd like to, but I won't. I'd like to make a sand pile and go 'potty.' Then you'd have to clean it up. I'd like to, but I won't." She hugged Pooh Bear, and then jumped on him, slammed him on the floor, and made him sit in a corner. She then went to the easel and said, "I hope you had fun when you were away, and we went to the beach. I made you a present."

By session 4 she is beginning to express her aggressive feelings more openly. She is uncomfortable with doing so, however, because she feels understood and accepted by the counselor. To make up for her aggressive feelings (to undo them), she makes the counselor a gift. The counselor reflects these ambivalent feelings in subsequent sessions. "It's hard to be angry at people you like and you can feel guilty when you get angry, but sometimes we need to get angry at others instead of always being angry at ourselves."

In later sessions, she added two friends to the guests at her tea party and talked about her father. "My daddy doesn't know how to do things. He never went to school, he 'quitted'—it bothers him. I never could quit. If I could quit, I would quit right now." She then talked about a little girl she knew "whose Mom enrolled her in the wrong class. She was put in the first grade for the second time—no one talked to her at recess—not even second graders like her. This little girl hurts inside 'cause no one likes her." She then talked more directly about herself. "I think it's really funny that when you're out of school you play school and when school starts, you wish you could play something else." She also reported that, "I have to lay my head sideways to see correct numbers on the page, then I get sleepy. The teacher told my mother I needed more sleep."

The Child Assigns the Counselor a Role

Often the child will engage in play actions where he assigns roles for the counselor to play in order for him to relive and work through various developmental issues. Dorothy Block describes the process:

> During this period of her fantasy, like her, I remained vague and shadowy. I had no clearly defined form, but was merely there. I waited for cues, however, and as I picked up the first one and then another, the fantasy began to evolve, and with it, both our identities . . . Her fantasy was to progress through three different phases and a coda, each one representing an advance on the way back to health, and each requiring a different set of identities for both of us . . . As long as she indicated that she needed a particular response, I provided it. When it served its purpose—to strengthen her ego—she automatically abandoned it herself and through her own decision moved on to the next stage.

The counselor's task is to meet the child's emotional and maturational requirements during each phase of the child's fantasy until the real child emerges. The counselor fulfills those needs by taking direction from the child and praising, punishing, scolding, caring for, or loving the fantasized characters.

For example, Block describes a child who pretended to be a bad dog that bit the counselor or destroyed the furniture. The counselor had to make a show of beating her, muzzling her, putting her in a cage and starving her, shouting at her, and denouncing her wickedness. Sometimes she had to be "beaten" so hard that a doctor was called. In that role, the counselor was solicitous and tender, commiserated with her, and expressed the hope that she would change and make such punishment unnecessary. After several months, a gradual shift in the fantasy took place. The wicked behavior was reduced and the punishment expanded. The roles were reversed. From having been a bad dog with the good but necessarily punitive owner, she became the good dog with the wicked owner. The counselor now was directed to engage in erratic, irrational cruelty. A third character was introduced, one that evolved from the healing "doctor." The counselor was to play two owners, a wicked one and a good one. The child was so bad with the wicked owner that she was sold to the good owner under whose care she blossomed and became a wonderful dog.

Block also introduces specific play materials into sessions to assist her and the child in playing out different roles. For example, when treating a child who assumed the identity of Mighty Mouse, she introduced two appealing little woolly mice, one white and the other gray. The child immediately named the white one Mighty Mouse and ordered a tiny red cape for him, and the gray one he named after himself. The use of these mice and of other play materials reveals how themes gradually evolve in play that contribute to a child's recall of traumatic events. The child angrily banged together a mother and father doll, proclaiming their wickedness. He then picked up the boy doll and charged, "They don't love their son!" He then confided for the first time that he remembered that day Mighty Mouse arrived. It was a terrible day. The man was put in jail and finally died because they did not give him any food. "He was worse than a pirate." He added, "It was twenty years ago." Thus, in response to his discovery that mice, and he, could be lovable, he could recall the traumatic battle between his parents the night they separated, when he was three.

Termination

Deciding when to terminate counseling isn't always easy. With the aggressive child, counseling may continue for some time. Counseling ends when the child's behavior suggests that he is mastering age-appropriate challenges. He may still be symptomatic, but he is on the road to recovery.

Carolyn Gruber suggests evaluating a child's functioning in three areas when attempting to assess improvement. These areas are: control of drive activity, reality testing, and identification. The child who can accept substitutes for gratification, shows a longer time delay between frustration and aggressive behavior, uses words instead of actions, displays self-soothing behavior, and who reveals less disorganization in his thinking is said to have improved his control over his drive activity. Similarly, the child who looks and verbalizes before acting, verbalizes the difference between reality and fantasy (e.g., "this is only pretend"), and reveals the ability to verbalize anticipation of changes and feelings about them reveals improved reality testing. The child who has begun to identify with healthy individuals is one who displays concern for others' feelings, plays cooperatively with others instead of either imitating them or omnipotently controlling their play, and responds in the socially accepted manner for his or her age.

Beatrice Klein and I have developed a guide to help counselors evaluate change in five basic areas: main focus of satisfaction, relationships, socialization, nature and source of disturbances that interfere with adaptation and development, and ego development. A child who formerly showed pleasure in buttock flaunting, nose picking, making messes, and "dirty talk" and who now shows competitiveness, envy, exhibitionism, and sexual curiosity has moved from the pleasures of a two-year-old to those of a four-year-old. While the child's chronological age may be eight, these new pleasures, while still not age appropriate, may reveal that he is on the road to recovery and counseling may no longer be needed. Similarly, the child who moves from intense interest in a preferred adult to friendships with peers shows developmental advancement in his relationships. A formerly aggressive child who begins to show guilt when he transgresses, who shows less self-esteem when he does not live up to his ideals, and who has developed affectionate feelings for peers is a child who has improved in the area of socialization. Before counseling is terminated the counselor needs to be clear that the child is showing behaviors indicative of developmental advancement. Summarizing across these five areas and looking at overall signs of progress, the improved child will reveal the following:

1. Decreased power struggles with adults. He becomes more com-

pliant. He may be verbally defiant, but his actions are generally compliant ones.

2. He has fewer unrealistic expectations of others.

3. He can tolerate emotional conflict. While he rebels at the thought of tender feelings, he has made several friends.

4. He is playful. His fantasy play is no longer constrictive and stereotyped.

5. He begins to accomplish things at school and at home.

6. He demonstrates interests and hobbies.

7. He can see beyond his own needs and appreciates the needs of others as different from his own.

8. He can finish tasks he initiates.

9. He has positive expectations for his efforts.

The counselor should not be surprised, however, if regression occurs when he broaches the subject of termination with the child. Often the child has come to rely on the counselor and the anxiety he experiences at the thought of ending can cause temporary setbacks. The child should be informed that this is to be expected and that he will bounce back after he realizes that the improvements he has shown will remain with him following termination.

The Process of Termination

The termination process needs to incorporate some procedures to help the child to deal with separation and loss. The termination process also can be a growth experience. Termination from counseling allows a child the opportunity to rework in the present the unfinished business of past separations. For those who have been through a series of disrupted attachments, termination is of special significance because the painful memories of past losses is relived. Children will react to the loss of the counselor with depression, feelings of rejection, fear, anger, panic, and the return of the original symptoms.

Successful termination increases the child's chances of making meaningful future attachments. Because termination can be such an emotionally charged process that is difficult for both the child and the counselor, David Crenshaw and his colleagues at the Astor Home for Children have developed three specific techniques to help children work through the termination phase of counseling. These techniques are especially helpful with children who have experienced multiple disruptions and traumas in their early attachments. The degree of trust required to perform good counseling with the extremely defiant child is a long time in coming. Once such children do make the necessary attachments, it is often even more difficult for them to give them up.

The Talk Show Interview

The talk show interview is used to introduce the idea of termination approximately two months prior to the end of counseling. This particular activity asks the child to reflect on the counseling experience in a mostly cognitive rather than affective way. The text of the talk show, which is audiotaped, follows:

Talk Show: "Kids in Therapy"

Introduction: "Our guest today is *(child's name)* who has been seen weekly (or twice weekly) in counseling for the past year. Since there are lots of kids listening to our show who either have been in counseling or perhaps will be some day, this topic is of great interest."

Part I: (Counselor as talk show host, interviews child)
1. Who is your counselor?
2. What do you like most about going to counseling?
3. What don't you like (or what is the hardest) about going to counseling?
4. What changes, if any, do you see in yourself since going to counseling?

Part II: (Child, as talk show host, interviews counselor) (Note: children who are not good readers can be coached to learn the questions by repeating after the counselor)
1. Who did you see in counseling this year? (counselor gives *child's name*)
2. What did you like most about working with *(child's name)* this year?
3. Was there anything you found difficult about working with *(child's name)* in counseling?

4. Is there anything you wish had been different?
5. What changes do you see in *(child's name)* since starting counseling?

The "talk show" runs about ten to thirty minutes with about fifteen minutes as average.

The Yearbook

A second technique, "the yearbook," can be used throughout the termination phase of counseling. Each child is given a photograph album that contains 20 blank pages and is told that he and his counselor will put together a therapy yearbook to help remember their year together. Each page is covered with clear removable plastic, which holds the pictures or other materials in place. The child is asked to recall significant events in counseling, i.e., a favorite activity, a particular turning point in the therapeutic relationship, and then to take pictures that remind him of these things. The counselor's role is to help the child focus on such events. The child can also cut out pictures from magazines to supplement actual photographs. Captions are added to the pictures. The child is given the yearbook to keep at the end of counseling. The counselor needs to provide a moderate to high level of structure over several weeks for this activity to be maximally useful in eliciting the child's feelings about termination. The yearbook is intended to elicit both cognitive and affective experiences from the child.

Jose and Pete on the Mountain

A third termination technique is the story *Jose and Pete on the Mountain*. This story was written by Crenshaw and his colleagues as a metaphor for the experience of counseling. This technique is designed to help the child most directly face the affective experience of termination. Each difficulty encountered by the characters in the story, Jose and Pete, is intended to convey some of the emotional struggles in the process of counseling. For example, the child's development of trust in the counselor is symbolized by the experience of Jose and Pete facing a storm together.

The counselor reads the story out loud to the child. This takes about ten minutes. The child is then asked to complete the story by adding a new chapter. After the child completes this task the therapist finishes the story by reading either Ending A, for the child leaving counseling, or Ending B, for the child transferring to a new counselor. The text of the story and the two different endings are found in the Appendix to this book.

These three activities focus the attention of the child on the termination phase of counseling. They also encourage the child, with the assistance of the counselor, to draw on his own resources to face the challenge of ending this meaningful experience.

In Conclusion

Stages in counseling are very much like stages in growth. Jean Piaget describes growth as transitions from one stage to another, resulting from a "set" or attitude that comes from within. What is learned at any given point is determined by what has gone before, not merely by what the child has experienced, but more by the elements to which he has paid attention. "Every instruction from without presupposes a construction from within."

Appendix

Jose and Pete on the Mountain

Once there was a boy named Jose. He was scared about climbing mountains, yet he wanted to climb one special, very steep mountain. He was introduced to a guide named Pete. Pete had climbed many mountains before but had not climbed this one. That meant that they had to work together closely to get up the mountain. Jose had tried to climb the mountain before and had fallen and gotten hurt.

During the course of a year, Jose and his guide Pete made many attempts to scale the mountain. At first, the trail was not very steep. They found a waterfall and a swimming hole with some pretty flowers. Later, the trail became very steep and they encountered many obstacles.

In the fall of that year, Jose and Pete decided they would attempt an especially steep and tricky climb on the west side of the mountain. They were roped together and feeling very confident. Jose was starting to feel a little tired when suddenly his foot slipped on some loose rock. He fell about five feet and landed on a narrow ledge. He became very angry with Pete because he felt Peter had pushed too hard too fast.

"It's your fault that I'm hurt!" he yelled.

His ankle was twisted and so sore that he could hardly stand up. Pete reached down to him and with his hand tightly gripped around Jose's wrist, he pulled him gradually off the ledge to safe ground. Jose was very scared that Pete might be pulled down in the struggle and felt like crying when the two of them sat together and rested on the side of the mountain.

For a week or so after the fall, Jose didn't want to go near the mountain and he was still a little angry with Pete for pushing him so hard.

A week later, Pete asked, "How about it, Jose? Are you ready to climb again?" Although still scared and angry, Jose knew that he really wanted to do it, and besides, Peter wasn't going to let him give up so easily. So they started off again.

Pete and Jose were walking up the mountain and everything was going well. All of a sudden, they both spotted a group of dark storm clouds in the distance coming quickly towards them. Pete, trying calmly to alert Jose, stated matter-of-factly, "There is a big storm coming. When it gets here, we will have to find cover." Jose did not respond as they continued their journey up the mountain.

As the two walked up the mountain watching the clouds get closer and closer, Jose became scared. He wondered to himself if Pete had ever encountered a storm before. Also, Jose wondered if he would be able to handle the dangerous situation that was certain to reach them soon. Pete was also silent as they walked. Instead of being scared, he was thinking how Jose would react. Pete knew the storm was very scary. Pete also wondered if Jose would be able to let Pete help him. Pete knew that for the two of them to survive, Jose would need to let Pete lead him without any questions.

All of a sudden, quicker than either thought possible, the storm was upon them. The winds blew strongly, the rain fell hard. Without a moment's hesitation, Pete grabbed Jose by the arm and walked off the trail. As they headed for a cave that could be seen from the path, Pete picked up wood for a fire, telling Jose to do the same. Pete also gave Jose many orders on the way to the cave, as well as when they were inside. Although Jose was somewhat angry at Pete for being bossy, he did feel safe. Jose found himself making suggestions about what to do. Pete agreed with many of them. Jose did not feel as scared anymore.

The storm passed as quickly as it had come. When it was over, Pete and Jose said in unison, "I'm glad it's over!" They started walking. As they continued their journey up the mountain, they walked in silence. There was a new closeness between them, however, brought about by their experience of fighting the storm together.

One day, Jose and Pete were carefully working their way along a ledge. They were quite a way up the mountain when suddenly they heard a threatening growl from behind them.

"Wildcat!" yelled Pete. "I knew there were quite a few of them on this mountain but I'd hoped we could get further along our climbing before we ran into one."

The cat loomed above Jose on a ledge. It bared its fangs and tensed its muscles menacingly. Unfortunately, Jose, who did not have much experience taming wild animals, was on the ledge closest to the mountain lion. Pete was a distance away and could not get past him to take charge. Jose realized this all of a sudden and felt panicky. He felt very afraid and helpless in the face of the large and powerful animal.

Pete said quietly, "I can't get over to you, Jose, so you're gonna have to handle it. We don't have enough weapons and we're not strong enough to kill it and I don't think we want to, anyway. They're beautiful animals and there aren't enough of them as it is. We just want to be able to continue climbing higher up the mountain and not get hurt. So, the idea is to just be cool and slowly take some of the food we were carrying for dinner out of your knapsack. Lay it right where you're standing."

Jose did as Pete suggested.

"Now," Pete whispered, "just start inching away, higher and higher up the trail. Slowly . . . slowly . . ."

Jose inched along with his heart pounding in his chest. The cat seemed to grow quieter as Jose moved away and began eyeing the meat with interest. When Jose had moved about twenty feet away, Pete whispered, "Good job. Now, let's walk quietly." When they had walked away, Jose sighed with relief and said, "Whew! I'm glad that's over!"

Pete laughed heartily and replied, "Don't worry, you'll run into animals all the time as you go higher. But I think now you've got an idea about how to handle them better." Jose thought to himself that he'd think about that before he started up the mountain again. For now, he was just very glad that the mountain lion was gone.

Pete and Jose had gone through some difficult times together and were again starting to make progress up the mountain. Jose was feeling as if he could really trust Pete to help him. They climbed higher. Jose had learned a lot from Pete about mountain climbing. As Pete and Jose climbed higher, Jose began to notice that it was getting cloudy on the mountain. He couldn't see things as far away as before. He couldn't see other mountains or even the bottom of the mountain he was climbing. Suddenly, the clouds seemed real close.

"Hey, Pete—what's going on?" Jose said a little louder than he expected to.

"It's just one of those mountain fogs," Pete answered. "They happen all of a sudden. Sometimes they last a while and sometimes not."

Jose felt glad that Pete knew what it was and did not sound worried. They kept climbing higher but the fog got worse. Jose was thinking maybe they should go back, but he did not want Pete to know he was scared. He decided to ask sort of casually, "Should we keep going up in this fog?"

"Oh sure," replied Pete. "No problem."

Jose was watching his feet so he could climb carefully up the rocks. The next time Jose looked up, he could not see Pete. "Pete!" Pete didn't answer.

Jose saw fog on every side of him and nothing else. He was completely lost. He did not know which way to go and he was alone. There was an awful feeling in his stomach. He sat down. He could feel tears coming into his eyes. He was really scared when something dark came toward him. All of a sudden, it turned into Pete. Jose was so glad to see him!

"I got lost," he tried to say calmly. "I didn't know what to do." Jose did not sound so calm.

"I realized you weren't right behind me," Pete explained. "I called you but you didn't answer."

"Me too," Jose replied.

"Sound doesn't carry very far in the fog, so I guess we couldn't hear each other."

"Oh."

Pete looked at Jose. "Did you get a little worried?"

"Yeah," admitted Jose.

Pete and Jose decided to climb the mountain one last time before parting. They started off together and (*ask child to complete this part of the story*).

After the last climb, Pete said to Jose, "I am going to miss you but I have enjoyed teaching you to climb mountains."

Ending A: "I think you are now ready to climb the mountain yourself. You have learned a lot about mountain climbing in the past year. Don't be afraid to make use of what you have learned." Jose felt really sad saying good-bye to Pete. He had lots of different feelings as Pete walked away. He knew he was really going to miss Pete, but he also felt like he could climb new mountains.

Ending B: "I think you have learned a lot about climbing mountains this past year. Don't be afraid to use what you have learned. There is another mountain I think you would like to climb and I will introduce you to a new guide who will help you with the new mountain." Jose felt really sad saying good-bye to Pete. He had lots of different feelings as Pete walked away. He knew he was really going to miss Pete, but he felt like he could climb new mountains.

What is the moral of this story?

What do you think we can learn from it?

(Courtesy of David Crenshaw, Ph.D., The Astor Home for Children.)

References

Block, Dorothy. "The Use of Interpretation in the Psychoanalytic Treatment of Children." *The Use of Interpretation in Treatment*, ed. Emmanuel F. Hammer, pp. 300–320. New York: Grune & Stratton, 1968.

Cohen, Jonathan A. "Theories of Narcissism and Trauma." *American Journal of Psychotherapy*, vol. 35, 1981, pp. 93–100.

Coppolillo, Henry P. "A Technical Consideration in Child Analysis and Child Therapy." *Journal of the American Academy of Child Psychiatry*, vol. 8, 1969, pp. 411–35.

Crenshaw, David A. and colleagues. "Therapeutic Techniques to Facilitate Termination in Child Psychotherapy," Unpublished paper, The Astor Home for Children, Rhinebeck, NY.

Ekstein, Rudolf. *Children of Time and Space, of Action and Impulse*. New York: Appleton Century Crofts, 1966.

Elkin, David. *Children and Adolescents: Interpretative Essays of Jean Piaget*. New York: Oxford University Press, 1970.

Erickson, Erik H. *Childhood and Society*, Second edition, pp. 249, 253, 257, 260. New York: W. W. Norton, 1963.

Fineman, JoAnn. "Observations on the Development of Imaginative Play in Early Childhood." *Journal of the American Academy of Child Psychiatry*, vol. 1, 1962, pp. 167–181.

Freud, Sigmund. "Fragments of an Analysis of a Case of Hysteria." *Standard Edition*, vol. 7, 1905, pp. 31–122.

Gitelson, Maxwell. *Psychoanalysis: Science and Profession*, p. 267. New York: International Universities Press, 1973.

Gruber, Carolyn: "Repairing Ego Deficits in Children with Developmental Disorders." *Child and Adolescent Social Work*, vol. 4, 1987, pp. 50–63.

Holder, Max. "Conceptual Problems of Acting Out in Children." *Journal of Child Psychotherapy*, vol. 2, 1970, pp. 5–22.

Klein, Beatrice and John B. Mordock. "A Guide to Differentiated Developmental Diagnoses with a Case Demonstrating its Use." *Child Psychiatry and Human Development*, 1975, vol. 5, pp. 243–53.

Klein, Melanie. *The Psychoanalysis of Children*. London: Hogarth Press, 1932.

Lewis, Melvin. "Interpretation in Child Analysis: Developmental Considerations." *American Journal of Child Psychiatry*, vol. 13, 1974, pp. 32–53.

Lowenstein, Rudolph M. "The Problem of Interpretation." *Psychoanalytic Quarterly*, vol. 20, 1951, pp. 1–14.

Masterson, James F. "The Acting–out Adolescent: A Point of View." *American Journal of Psychotherapy*, vol. 28, 1974, pp. 343–51.

Moore, Terence. "Realism and Fantasy in Children's Play." *Journal of Child Psychology and Psychiatry*, vol. 5, 1964, pp. 15–36.

Mordock, John B. "Working with Parents of Aggressive Children." *The Pointer*, vol. 33, 1988, pp. 13–26.

Rosenthal, Kenneth. "Rituals of Undoing in Abused and Neglected Children." *Child and Adolescent Social Work*, vol. 4, 1987, pp. 226–37.

Sarnoff, Charles A. *Psychotherapeutic Strategies in the Latency Years.* Northvale, New Jersey: Aronson, 1987.

Shenken, Leon I. "The Implications of Ego Psychology for a Motiveless Murder." *Journal of the American Academy of Child Psychiatry*, vol. 3, 1964, pp. 741–51.

Silvern, Louise and Keersvang, Lynn. "The Traumatized Children of Violent Marriages." *Child Welfare*, vol. 68, 1989, pp. 421–36.

Singer, Jerome. *Day Dreaming: an Introduction to the Experimental Study of Inner Experience.* New York: Random House, 1966.

Terr, Lenore C. "Forbidden Games: Post-Traumatic Child's Play." *Journal of the American Academy of Child Psychiatry*, vol. 20, 1981, pp. 741–60.

Tessman, Lori H. and Irving Kaufman. "Treatment Techniques, the Primary Process, and Ego Development in Schizophrenic Children." *Journal of the American Academy of Child Psychiatry*, vol. 6, 1967, pp. 98–115.

List of Readings

Books on Child Psychotherapy:

Adams, P. L. *A Primer of Child Psychotherapy,* Second edition. Boston: Little, Brown and Co., 1982.

Aichorn, A. *Delinquency and Child Guidance: Selected Papers (1923–1948).* New York: International Universities Press, 1965.

Allen, F. H. *Psychotherapy with Children.* Reprint. Lincoln, Nebraska: University of Nebraska Press, 1940.

Axline, V. M. *Play Therapy.* Boston: Houghton Mifflin, 1947.

Axline, V. M. *Dibs: In Search of Self.* Boston: Houghton Mifflin, 1964.

Barker, P. *Clinical Interviews with Children and Adolescents.* New York: W. W. Norton, 1990.

Barten, H., ed. *Children and Their Parents in Brief Therapy.* New York: Behavioral Publications, 1973.

Baruch, D. W. *One Little Boy.* New York: Julian Press, 1952. (Delta edition, New York: Dell Publishing Co., 1964).

Bender, L. *Child Psychiatric Techniques.* Springfield, Illinois: Charles Thomas, 1952.

Bernard, M. E., et. al. *Rational-Emotive Therapy with Children and Adolescents.* New York: Wiley, 1984.

Boston, M., and R. Szar, eds. *Psychotherapy with Severely Deprived Children.* Boston: Routledge and Kegan Paul, 1983.

Bush, R. *A Parent's Guide to Child Therapy.* New York: Delacorte Press, 1980.

Carek, D. J. *Principles of Child Psychotherapy.* Springfield, Illinois: Charles C. Thomas, 1972.

Chetnik, M. *Techniques of Child Therapy: Psychodynamic Strategies.* New York: Guilford Publications, 1989.

Colm, H. *The Existential Approach to Psychotherapy with Adults and Children.* New York: Grune & Stratton, 1966.

Cooper, S., and L. Waterman. *A Casebook of Child Psychotherapy: Strategies and Technique.* New York: Brunner/Mazel, 1984.

Cooper, S., and L. Waterman. *Children in Treatment: A Primer for Beginning Psychotherapists.* New York: Brunner/Mazel, 1977.

Coppolillo, H. *Psychodynamic Psychotherapy of Children*. Madison, Connecticut: International Universities Press, 1987.

Dodds, J. B. *A Child Psychotherapy Primer: Suggestions for the Beginning Therapist*. New York: Human Science Press, Inc., 1985.

Donovan, D. M., and D. McIntyre. *Heal the Hurt Child: A Developmental-Contextual Approach*. New York: W. W. Norton, 1990.

Dreikurs, R. *Children, the Challenge*. New York: Hawthorne Books, 1964.

Ellis, A., and M. E. Bernard. *Rational-Emotive Approaches to the Problems of Childhood*. New York: Plenum, 1983.

Ekstein, R., ed. *In Search of Love and Competence*. Los Angeles: Reiss Davis Childhood Center, 1976. (Distributed by Brunner/Mazel, New York, New York).

Fine, M. J., ed. *Systematic Intervention with Disturbed Children*. New York: Spectrum, 1984.

Freud, A. *The Psychoanalytic Treatment of Children*. New York: Schocken Books, 1964. (Original Publication 1946)

Gardner, R. A. *Psychotherapeutic Approaches to the Resistant Child*. New York: Jason Aronson, 1975.

Gardner, R. A. *The Psychotherapeutic Techniques of Richard A. Gardner*. Cresskill, NJ: Creative Therapeutics, 1986.

Gardner, R. A. *Psychotherapy with Children of Divorce*. New York: Jason Aronson, 1976.

Gardner, R. A. *Therapeutic Communication with Children: The Mutual Storytelling Technique*. New York: Jason Aronson, 1971.

Geleerd, E. R. *The Child Analyst at Work*. New York: International Universities Press, 1967.

Ginott, H. G. *Group Psychotherapy with Children*. New York: McGraw Hill, 1961.

Glenn, J., ed. *Child Analysis and Therapy*. New York: Jason Aronson, 1978.

Gondor, E. I. *Art and Play Therapy*. New York: Doubleday and Company, 1954.

Graziano, A. *Behavior Therapy with Children*. Chicago: Adline, 1971.

Grumaer, J. *Counseling and Therapy for Children*. New York: Free Press, 1984.

Hamilton, G. *Psychotherapy in Child Guidance*. New York: Columbia University Press, 1947.

Hammer, M. *The Practice of Psychotherapy with Children*. Homewood, Illinois: Dorsey Press, 1967.

Hartman, D. P., and D. M. Gelfard. *Child Behavior Analysis and Therapy*. New York: Pergamon Press, 1984.

Haworth, M. R., ed. *Child Psychotherapy*. New York: Basic Books, 1964.

Howard, T. W. *How to Use Magic in Psychotherapy with Children*. Long Beach, Mississippi: Emerald Press, 1977.

James, B. *Treating Traumatized Children*. Lexington, Massachusetts: Lexington Books, 1989.

Jernberg, A. M. *Theraplay*. San Francisco, California: Jossey-Bass, 1979.

Johnson, J. H., W. C. Rasburg, and L. J. Siegel. *Approaches to Child Treatment.* New York: Pergamon Press, 1986.

Keller, P. K., and L. G. Ritt, eds. *Innovations in Clinical Practice: A Source Book,* vol. 4 and 5. Sarasota, Florida: Professional Resource Exchange, 1981–1986.

Kendall, P. C., and L. Braswell. *Cognitive-Behavioral Therapy for Impulsive Children.* New York: Guilford Press, 1985.

Klein, M. *Contributions to Psychoanalysis, 1921–1948.* London: Hogarth Press, 1948.

Landreth, G. L. *Play Therapy: Dynamics of the Process of Counseling with Children.* Springfield, Illinois: Charles Thomas, 1982.

Lord, J. P. *A Guide to Individual Psychotherapy with School Age Children and Adolescents.* Springfield, Illinois: Charles C. Thomas, 1985.

Mills, J. C., and R. J. Crowley. *Therapeutic Metaphors for Children and the Child Within.* New York: Brunner/Mazel, 1987.

Mishue, J. M. *Clinical Work with Children.* New York: Free Press, 1983.

Morris, R., ed. *The Practice of Child Therapy.* New York: Pergammon, 1983.

Moustakas, C. E. *Children in Play Therapy.* New York: McGraw Hill, 1953.

Moustakas, C. E. *Psychotherapy with Children.* New York: McGraw Hill, 1959.

Moustakas, C. E. *The Child's Discovery of Himself.* New York: Ballantine Books, 1972. (Former title: *Existential Child Therapy.*)

Myers, A. W., and Craighead, W. E., eds. *Cognitive Behavior Therapy with Children.* New York: Plenum, 1984.

Ollendick, T. H., and J. A. Cerny. *Clinical Behavior Therapy with Children.* New York: Plenum Press, 1981.

Parker, B. *My Language Is Me: Psychotherapy with a Disturbed Adolescent.* New York: Basic Books, 1962.

Reisman, J. *Principles of Psychotherapy with Children.* New York: Wiley, 1973.

Rubin, E. J. A. *Child Art Therapy: Understanding and Helping Children through Art.* New York: Van Norstrand-Reinhold, 1984.

Schaefer, C. E., ed. *Therapeutic Use of Child's Play.* New York: Jason Aronson, 1976.

Schaefer, C. E., ed. *Therapeutic Use of Childhood Games.* New York: Wiley, 1986.

Schaefer, C. E., and H. L. Millman, eds. *Therapies for Children: A Handbook of Effective Treatments for Problem Behaviors.* San Francisco, California: Jossey-Bass, 1977.

Schaefer, C. E., and H. L. Millman, eds. *Therapies for Psychosomatic Disorders in Children.* San Francisco, California: Jossey-Bass, 1979.

Schaefer, C. E., and K. J. O'Connor, eds. *Handbook of Play Therapy.* Boston: Houghton Mifflin, 1983.

Schiffer, M. *The Therapeutic Play Group.* New York: Grune & Stratton, 1969.

Shapiro, L. E. *The New Short-Term Therapies for Children.* Englewood Cliffs, New Jersey: Prentice-Hall, 1984.

Slavson, S. R. *Child Psychotherapy.* New York: Columbia University Press, 1952.

Swanson, F. *Psychotherapists and Children.* New York: Pittman, 1970.

Szurek, S. A., and I. N. Berlin. *Training in Therapeutic Work with Children.* Palo Alto, California: Science and Behavior Books. 1967.

Taft, J. J. *The Dynamics of Therapy in a Controlled Relationship.* New York: Dover Press, 1962. Reprint. New York: Macmillan, 1933.

Van Ornum, W., and J. B. Mordock. *Crisis Counseling of Children and Adolescents.* New York: Continuum, 1983.

Winicott, D. W. *Therapeutic Consultation in Child Psychiatry.* New York: Basic Books, 1971.

Witmer, H. L., ed. *Psychiatric Interviews with Children.* Cambridge, Massachusetts: Harvard University Press, 1946.

Wood, M. M., ed. *Developmental Therapy Sourcebook.* Baltimore: University Park Press, 1981.

Wolman, B. B., ed. *Handbook of Child Psychoanalysis: Research, Theory and Practice.* New York: Van Nostrand/Bernhold, 1972.

Other Helpful Books:

Burns, R. C., and S. H. Kaufman. *Actions, Styles, and Symbols in Kinetic Family Drawings (K-F-D).* New York: Bruner/Mazel, 1972.

Burns, R. C., and S. H. Kaufman. *Kinetic Family Drawings (K-F-D).* New York: Bruner/Mazel, 1978.

Child Study Association of America. *Insights: A Selection of Creative Literature about Childhood.* New York: Jason Aronson, 1973.

DiLeo, J. H. *Young Children and Their Drawings.* New York: Bruner/Mazel, 1970.

DiLeo, J. H. *Children's Drawings as Diagnostic Aids.* New York: Bruner/Mazel, 1973.

Eng, H. *The Psychology of Children's Drawings.* London: Rouledge and Kegan Paul, 1954.

Fassler, J. *Helping Children Cope: Mastering Stress Through Books and Stories,* New York: Free Press, 1978.

Fraiberg, S. *The Magic Years—Understanding and Handling the Problems of Early Childhood.* New York: Charles Scribner, 1959.

Freeman, L., and K. Kupfermann. *The Power of Fantasy.* New York: Continuum, 1988.

Freud, A. *Normality and Pathology in Childhood: Assessment of Development.* New York: International Universities Press, 1965.

Gardner, H. *Artful Scribbles—the Significance of Children's Drawings.* New York: Basic Books, 1980.

Goodnow, J. *Children Drawing.* Cambridge, Massachusetts: Harvard University Press, 1977.

Gould, R. *Child Studies Through Fantasy.* New York: Quadrangle Books, 1972.

Kellogg, R. *Analyzing Children's Art.* Palo Alto, California: Mayfield Publishing, 1970.

Koppitz, E. M. *Psychological Evaluation of Children's Human Figure Drawings.* New York: Grune & Stratton, 1968.

Lowenfeld, M. *Play in Childhood.* New York: Wiley Science, 1967.

Machover, K. *Personality Projection in the Drawing of the Human Figure: A Method of Personality Investigation.* Springfield, Illinois: Charles Thomas, 1965.

Mahler, M. *On Human Symbiosis and the Vicissitudes of Individuation.* New York: International Universities Press, 1969.

Montessori, M. *The Secret of Childhood.* Notre Dame, Indiana: Fides Publishers, 1966. (Dome edition, 1970).

Piaget, J. *Play, Dreams, and Imitation of Childhood.* New York: Dutton, 1951. Reprint. (Original publication 1945)

Werner, H. *The Comparative Psychology of Mental Development.* New York: International Universities Press, 1940.

_____Lucy Freeman and Kerstin Kupfermann
THE POWER OF FANTASY
Where Our Daydreams Come from, and How They Can Help or Harm Us
This is the first book to explain the role of both daydreams and unconscious fantasies in our lives, helping us to distinguish between those that can unleash our creativity and those that can emotionally cripple us. $16.95

_____John Gerdtz and Joel Bregman, MD
AUTISM
A Practical Guide for Those Who Help Others
An up-to-date and comprehensive guidebook for everyone who works with autistic children, adolescents, adults, and their families. Includes latest information on medications. $16.95

_____Marion Howard
HOW TO HELP YOUR TEENAGER
POSTPONE SEXUAL INVOLVEMENT
Based on a national educational program that works, this book advises parents, teachers, and counselors on how they can help their teens resist social and peer pressures regarding sex. $14.95

_____Marion Howard
SOMETIMES I WONDER ABOUT ME
Teenagers and Mental Health
Combines fictional narratives with sound, understandable professional advice to help teenagers recognize the difference between serious problems and normal problems of adjustment. $9.95

_____E. Clay Jorgensen
CHILD ABUSE
A Practical Guide for Those Who Help Others
Essential information and practical advice for caregivers
called upon to help both child and parent in child abuse.
$16.95

_____Eugene Kennedy
CRISIS COUNSELING
The Essential Guide for Nonprofessional Counselors
"An outstanding author of books on personal growth selects
types of personal crises that our present life-style has made
commonplace and suggests effective ways to deal with
them."—*Best Sellers* $11.95

_____Eugene Kennedy
SEXUAL COUNSELING
A Practical Guide for Those Who Help Others
Newly revised and up-to-date edition of an essential book on
counseling people with sexual problems, with a new chapter
on AIDS. $17.95

_____Eugene Kennedy and Sara C. Charles, M.D.
ON BECOMING A COUNSELOR
A Basic Guide for Nonprofessional Counselors
New expanded edition of an indispensable resource. A
patient-oriented, clinically directed field guide to
understanding and responding to troubled people.
$27.95 hardcover $15.95 paperback

——Bonnie Lester
WOMEN AND AIDS
A Practical Guide for Those Who Help Others
Provides positive ways for women to deal with their fears,
and to help others who react with fear to people who have
AIDS. $15.95

——Helen B. McDonald and Audrey I. Steinhorn
HOMOSEXUALITY
*A Practical Guide to Counseling Lesbians, Gay Men, and Their
Families*
A sensitive guide that will inspire the reader to reflect on the
great many situations in life wherein a greater sensitivity to
issues related to counseling gay men and their families
would be helpful. $17.95

——Janice N. McLean and Sheila A. Knights
PHOBICS AND OTHER PANIC VICTIMS
A Practical Guide for Those Who Help Them
"A must for the phobic, spouse and family, and for the
physician and support people who help them. It can spell
the difference between partial therapy with partial results
and comprehensive therapy and recovery."—Arthur B.
Hardy, M.D., Founder, TERRAP Phobia Program, and Past
President, Phobia Society of America $17.95

——Cherry Boone O'Neill
DEAR CHERRY
Questions and Answers on Eating Disorders
Practical and inspiring advice on eating disorders from the
best-selling author of *Starving for Attention.* $8.95

____Paul G. Quinnett
ON BECOMING A HEALTH
AND HUMAN SERVICES MANAGER
A Practical Guide for Clinicians and Counselors
A new and essential guide to management for everyone in
the helping professions—from mental health to nursing,
from social work to teaching. $19.95

____Paul G. Quinnett
SUICIDE: THE FOREVER DECISION
For Those Thinking About Suicide,
and for Those Who Know, Love, or Counsel Them
"A treasure—this book can help save lives. It will be
especially valuable not only to those who are thinking about
suicide but to such nonprofessional counselors as teachers,
clergy, doctors, nurses, and to experienced therapists."
—William Van Ornum, psychotherapist and author $18.95
hardcover $7.95 paperback

____Paul G. Quinnett
THE TROUBLED PEOPLE BOOK
A practical and positive guide to the world of psychotherapy
and psychotherapists. "Without a doubt one of the most
honest, reassuring, nonpaternalistic, and useful self-help
books ever to appear."—*Booklist* $9.95

____Judah L. Ronch
ALZHEIMER'S DISEASE
A Practical Guide for Those Who Help Others
Must reading for everyone—from family members to
professional caregivers—who must deal with the effects of
this tragic disease on a daily basis. Filled with illustrative
examples as well as facts, this book provides sensitive insights
into dealing with one's feelings as well as with such practical
advice as how to choose long-term care. $17.95

———Theodore Isaac Rubin, M.D.
ANTI-SEMITISM: A DISEASE OF THE MIND
"A most poignant and lucid psychological examination of a severe emotional disease. Dr. Rubin offers hope and understanding to the victim and to the bigot. A splendid job!"—Dr. Herbert S. Strean $14.95

———John R. Shack
COUPLES COUNSELING
A Practical Guide for Those Who Help Others
An esssential guide to dealing with the 20 percent of all counseling situations that involve the relationship of two people. $17.95

———Stuart Sutherland
THE INTERNATIONAL DICTIONARY OF PSYCHOLOGY
This new dictionary of psychology also covers a wide range of related disciplines, from anthropology to sociology. $49.95

———Joan Leslie Taylor
IN THE LIGHT OF DYING
The Journals of a Hospice Volunteer
A rare and beautiful book about death and dying that affirms life and will inspire an attitude of love. "Beautifully recounts the healing (our own) that results from service to others, and might well be considered as required reading for hospice volunteers."—Stephen Levine $17.95

———Montague Ullman, M.D. and Claire Limmer, M.S., eds.
THE VARIETY OF DREAM EXPERIENCE
Expanding Our Ways of Working with Dreams
"Lucidly describes the beneficial impact dream analysis can have in diverse fields and in society as a whole. An erudite, illuminating investigation."—*Booklist* $19.95 hardcover $11.95 paperback

_____William Van Ornum and John B. Mordock
CRISIS COUNSELING WITH CHILDREN AND
ADOLESCENTS
"It is the kind of book every parent should keep on the shelf
next to nutrition, medical, and Dr. Spock books."—*Marriage
& Family Living* $12.95

_____William Van Ornum and Mary W. Van Ornum
TALKING TO CHILDREN ABOUT NUCLEAR WAR
"A wise book. A needed book. An urgent book."
—Dr. Karl A. Menninger $15.95 hardcover $7.95 paperback

At your bookstore, or to order directly send your check or
money order (adding $2.00 extra per book for postage and
handling, up to $6.00 maximum) to: The Continuum
Publishing Company, 370 Lexington Avenue, New York, NY
10017. Prices are subject to change.